IMAGES
of America

HIGHLAND

On the Cover: One of the many Highland parades makes its way down Highway Avenue on a bright summer day in 1966. The car advertises a service called Welcome Wagon, which many towns like Highland utilized. Welcome Wagon representatives visited new residents with small gifts such as coupons for local businesses. Welcome Wagon International was founded in 1928. The organization no longer has representatives conducting home visits, as many services are performed online. (Highland Historical Society.)

IMAGES
of America

HIGHLAND

Dan Helpingstine and Jim Roumbos

ARCADIA
PUBLISHING

ISBN 978-1-4671-2770-7

Published by Arcadia Publishing
Charleston, South Carolina

Printed in the United States of America

Library of Congress Control Number: 2017945987

For all general information, please contact Arcadia Publishing:
Telephone 843-853-2070
Fax 843-853-0044
E-mail sales@arcadiapublishing.com
For customer service and orders:
Toll-Free 1-888-313-2665

Visit us on the Internet at www.arcadiapublishing.com

Dedicated with love to Delia Helpingstine, daughter Leah, Diane Barr Roumbos, and daughter Alison.

Contents

Acknowledgments

In pursuing a project like this, any writer will need assistance from experts and people who have historical knowledge and a keen insight.

First and foremost, we want to give special recognition and thanks to the Highland Historical Society (HHS), which provided almost all of the photographs for this book. Unless otherwise noted, all images in this book appear courtesy of HHS.

Additionally, we would like to recognize Sue Douthett, the president of HHS. She is extremely knowledgeable about Highland, and we found her expertise invaluable.

One fascinating person we interviewed was Paul Doherty, who served ably as a town councilman and then as Highland's clerk-treasurer for 11 years. He spoke about growth in Highland and recognized that growth also presented new problems and challenges. Doherty passed away just months before this book was published.

George Van Til was a force in Lake County politics until recently. Like Paul Doherty, he also sat on the Highland Town Council, first attaining his seat in the early 1970s. It was interesting listening to Van Til talk about Highland in political terms.

Mark Hines has owned and operated the Town Club Restaurant since 1997. The Town Club has been a Highland fixture since 1947. He spoke to us about the challenges facing a local businessman.

Highland Fire Department chief William "Bill" Timmer spoke of his department with real pride. He noted that the department has changed and modernized but is still manned by citizen-volunteers.

Alex Brown, superintendent of the Highland Recreation and Parks Department, spoke of the changes in his department. Brown takes pride in the fact that the Lincoln Center is economically self-sustaining.

Andy Finick, a lifelong Highland resident, provided several photographs for this book. He also provided insight about how the town has physically changed over the years.

Highland Police Department chief Peter Hojnicki took time to give a historical perspective about a department that was a volunteer force until 1955. The Highland Police Department still has 30 volunteers but now also has a complement of 42 full-time officers.

Theresa Pecsek supplied some of her Highland photographs, and her work provides solid images of life in the town.

Rebecca Grochowski, who works at Print Pro in neighboring Crown Point, was instrumental in upgrading the book's photographs to print quality, and we are grateful for her assistance.

We also would like to acknowledge our editor at Arcadia, Caitrin Cunningham. She was always professional and pleasant, and we are grateful to her for her guidance.

INTRODUCTION

"Indiana No-Place" was the condescending insult lobbed at Highland and the whole state of Indiana by crabby *Chicago Tribune* columnist Mike Royko. In a piece he wrote in the early 1980s, Royko defended his home state of Illinois and hometown of Chicago by denigrating everything connected with Indiana. The "Indiana No-Place" slur was aimed directly at Indianapolis, Indiana's capital and largest city

Chicago is known for its many ethnic neighborhoods, and its southern rim is less than 20 miles from Highland. Some Highland residents work there, and most cheer for and identify with the city's major-league sports teams. Despite this, most people in the town do not identify with Chicago, even with its local economic and cultural influences. Conversely, Chicagoans regard Highland and northwest Indiana as a distant and isolated place.

Highland is an isolated place in some ways. With its location in the upper northwest corner of the state, Highland and surrounding communities can seem detached from Indianapolis and the rest of Indiana. Highland is in a different time zone than Indianapolis and other parts of the state. Hoosiers outside the area think the northwest corner of Indiana has a stronger connection to Chicago than Indiana.

Highland, along with its closest-bordering communities, has another biased image or perception to overcome. The town is almost smack dab in the center of what is labeled "the Region." Residents of the Region are stereotyped in some ways. The authors have run into Hoosiers who mark the Region as a hub for gangsters. The proximity of Chicago encouraged this train of thought. Additionally, Region residents are viewed as being rougher, blue-collar types. The once-sprawling presence of the steel mills on Lake Michigan adds to this image partly because it is a contrast to some of the more scenic and rural spots in Indiana.

At first glance, Highland may not jump out at people. Lake Michigan is nearby but does not border the town. Wide open spaces have been replaced by residential districts and business developments. The town has something of an urban flavor but does not have the characteristic architecture of a large city. Much of Highland lays low, so there are few elevated spots that provide scenic outlooks.

The Van Til family settled in the Highland area in 1903, seven years before Highland became incorporated as a town. George Van Til served as a town councilman during most of the 1970s. He compared the town to girls who sometimes are underestimated because they are not "knock-outs." Van Til said that upon further examination, there can be much more to a person than superficial qualities. He looks at Highland the same way.

Van Til believes that Highland, like Chicago, is a town of diverse neighborhoods. He spoke of different churches of different faiths standing almost next to each other in the Main Square Park and downtown area. He said this diversity adds to Highland's appeal.

At one time, steelmaking fires from the open hearths lit up the sky across the Region. Tens of thousands of people in Northwest Indiana worked directly in the industry or in other manufacturing concerns. However, employment in steel slowly eroded and then plummeted in the early and mid-1980s. Many small factories that fed off the larger mills are long gone. Steel companies contracted and laid off long-time workers by the hordes. The larger nearby cities of Hammond and Gary suffered due to loss of population, a declining tax base, and long-term economic slumps.

In the early 1980s, home foreclosures were a common occurrence in Lake County, Indiana, and many houses were abandoned by families who saw their life savings depleted due to an unemployment rate that hit double digits across the country. Northwest Indiana was caught off guard as the nation's economy shifted from industrial to service-based.

Highland survived this economic downturn. The town's housing situation was more stable, and homes sold quickly as families wanted to move into the town. Highland fared better during the 1980s in relation to neighboring communities that suffered economic devastation and declining property values.

Lake Michigan helped form the geographical town called Highland. Some 20 miles to the east are the majestic sand dunes. On a clear day, one can stand by the vastness of Lake Michigan and catch a panoramic view of the steel mills that still provide an economic base for Northwest Indiana. Off in the distance and to the north is the skyscraper-filled Chicago horizon. When the conditions are extremely clear, the tower of the 100-story John Hancock Center can be spotted at its northern position on Chicago's Michigan Avenue.

Even as the town has grown and changed from its rural beginnings, it still has something that remains the same: the 1,547-acre Hoosier Prairie Nature Preserve established in 1976. "The Prairie," which also borders adjoining Griffith, is an environmentally protected area where deer, raccoons, and other wildlife exist without fear of being hunted or trapped. Author Dan Helpingstine once turned around in his backyard to find himself standing nose to nose with a rather large deer; it was the middle of winter, and the animal was searching for food. Hoosier Prairie has 350 different types of plants and is protected from any other economic development. The Prairie provides a scenic outlook and the opportunity for Highland residents to see and encounter various wildlife in close quarters.

Highland, like so many other communities, has changed and evolved with time. However, one of its enduring qualities has been its stability. While many corporate businesses have moved in, local entrepreneurs still thrive as they compete. The town's government has had its arguments and controversies but has avoided scandals and has had public servants provide decades of dedicated service. Spurts of population growth have stopped, but the town maintains a steady number at about 24,000.

The concept of "small-town America" provides an idyllic image of simple but peaceful and secluded places where problems are small and people know each other in a non-intrusive way. This is a myth, of course. No town is untouched by the problems of a diverse country or a dangerous world, and Highland is no exception. However, Highland does provide a sense of community for its residents. This book uses photographs to show the development of this town that grew and adjusted along with the changes surrounding it.

One

BEGINNINGS

Indiana was admitted to the Union as the 19th state in late 1816. Although Highland was not incorporated as a town until 94 years later, nonnative settlers arrived in the town before the Civil War. A significant portion of those who migrated to the area were Dutch who had made a short trek from Munster.

A historical marker that stands in a business parking lot on Kleinman Road reads: "Dutch immigrants after 1850 began moving to this area because of similarities to their homeland. They helped to locate ditches to drain water from the extensive marshes leaving rich land to expand successful horticultural activities."

As with many early European settlers in the New World, 19th-century Hoosiers wanted to practice their religion without persecution. According to the US50.com website, "many denominations have been cultivated here and contribute to the make-up of Indiana life. Today, over 7,000 churches can be identified that service about half of the population." In today's Highland, there are a variety of different denominations in town, and some are extremely close to each other.

Highland was still sparsely populated when it was incorporated in 1910 with slightly more than 300 residents. As images presented in this chapter will show, the town began to evolve as transportation and economic conditions changed. Railroads were developed, factories were opened, and the coming of the automobile changed many things.

In looking at some of the names of early Highlanders, readers may recognize names associated with the town's educational and business history. This chapter will also help illustrate how Highland became a modern American town.

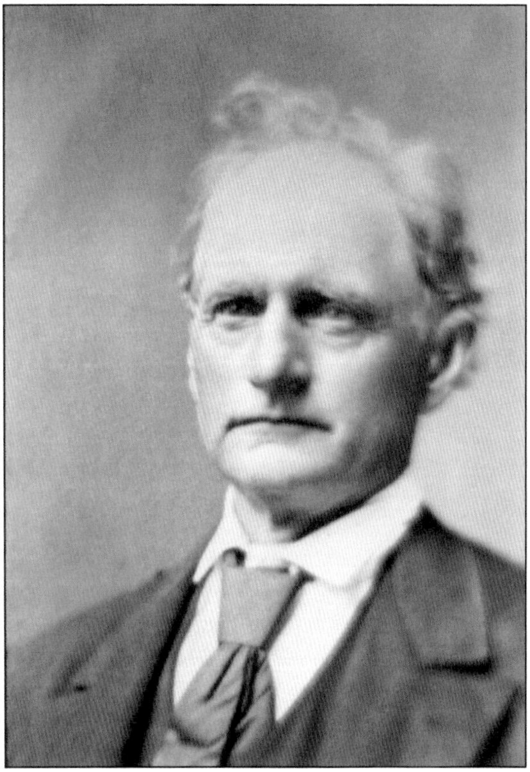

Pictured is Michael Johnston, the first white settler of Highland. He and his wife, Judith, migrated to the town in 1847. When they moved to the area, the nearest neighborhood was several miles away in Munster.

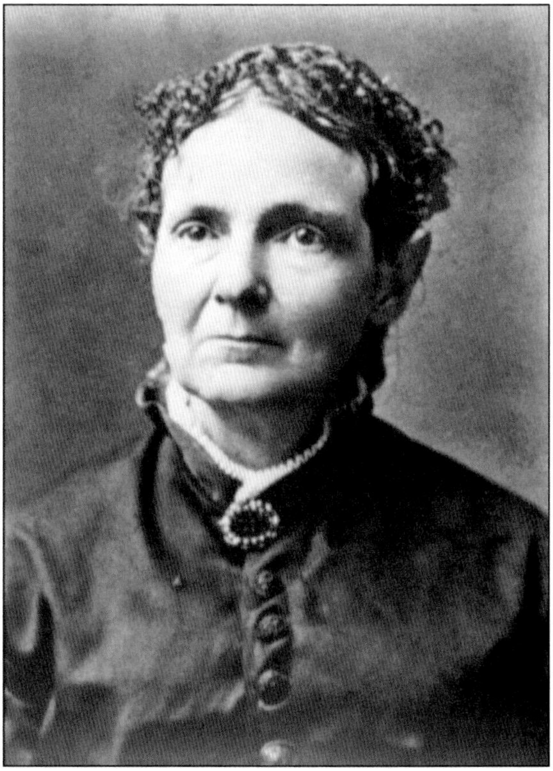

Judith Johnson was the first schoolteacher in Highland. The elementary school on Fifth Avenue is named for her. The mission statement of the school reads, in part: "Our vision for the Johnston Elementary School students is they be provided with the atmosphere, materials and expertise for their highest possible achievement."

In his 2001 pictorial history of Highland, Matthew Figi describes Roderick Johnston as "the first pioneer child born in Highland." He was the son of Michael and Judith Johnston, and was born in 1848.

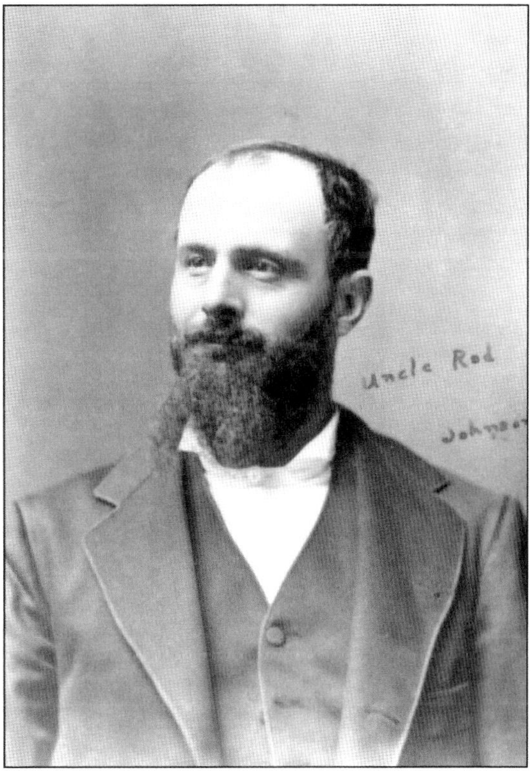

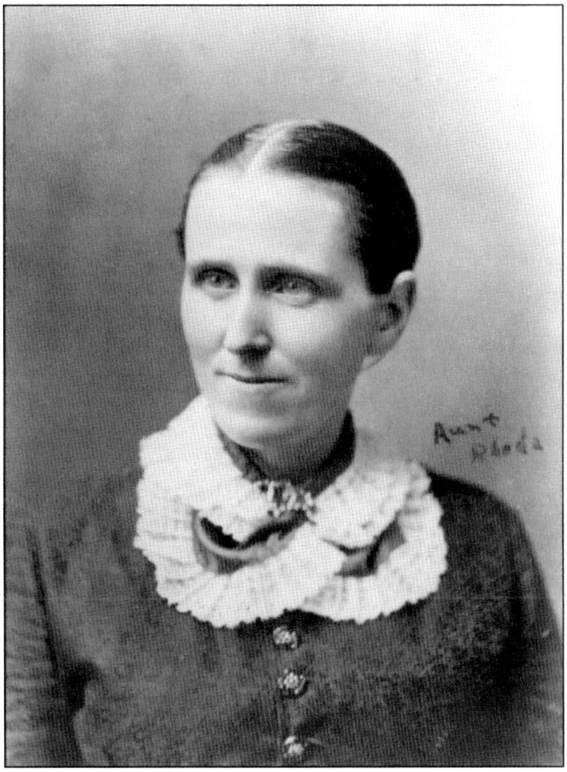

Rhoda Johnston operated the first general store in Highland toward the end of the 19th century after her husband Roderick "Rod" passed away. The store also included a post office and was a prototype general store of its time.

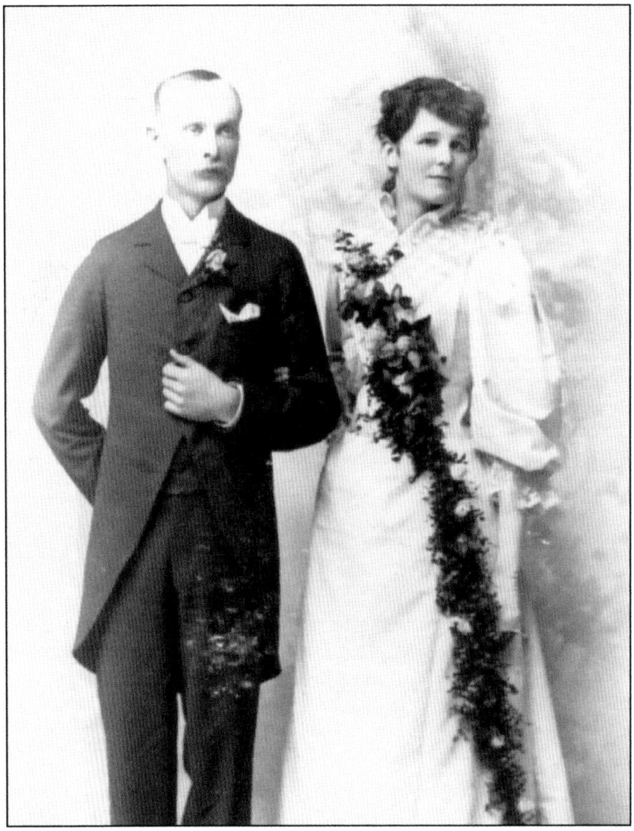

This is the wedding picture of Joseph Douthett and Grace Johnston. The couple married in 1894. Their reception was considered a major social event in Highland. They were married by E.T. George, reverend of a nearby Griffith church. The event took place 16 years before Highland incorporated as a town.

The Zandstra family is pictured here in the 1920s. The Zandstras are still a prominent family in Highland and still operate a farm and nursery on Kennedy Avenue.

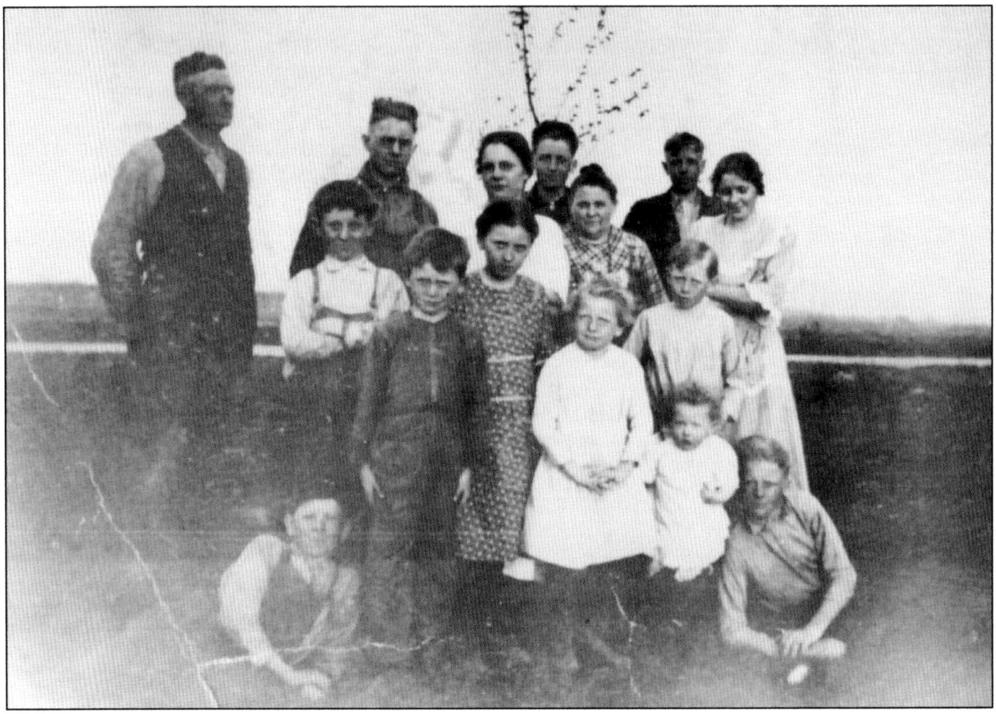

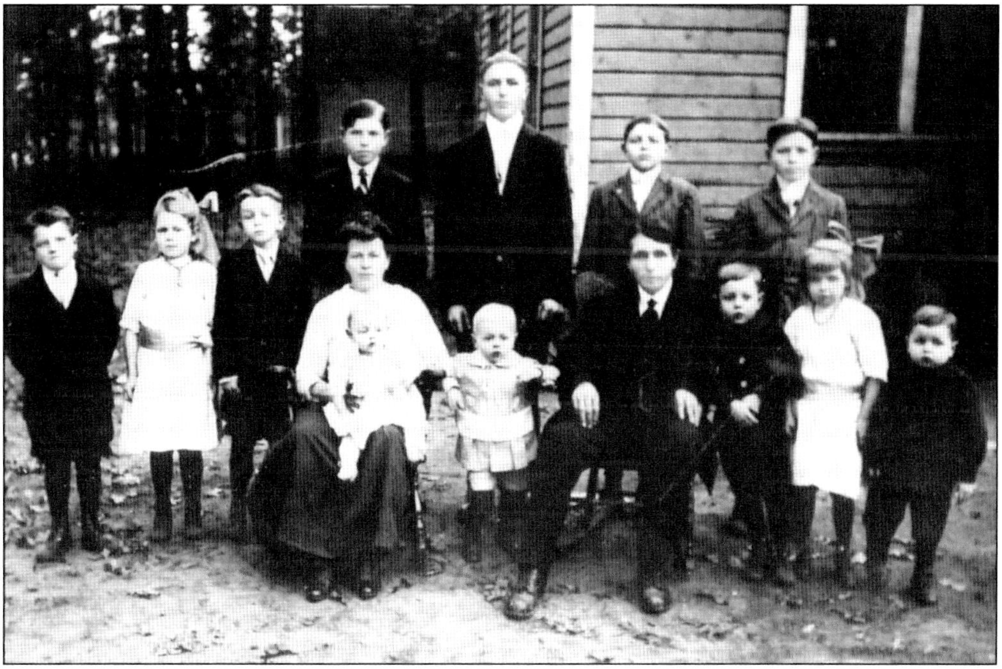

This is a 1918 photograph of the large Kuiper family that had immigrated to the United States from Holland. Dutch immigrants became a significant portion of Highland's population, and members of the Kuiper family have contributed to Highland as business owners and community leaders. Today, Konnie Kuiper sits on the town council.

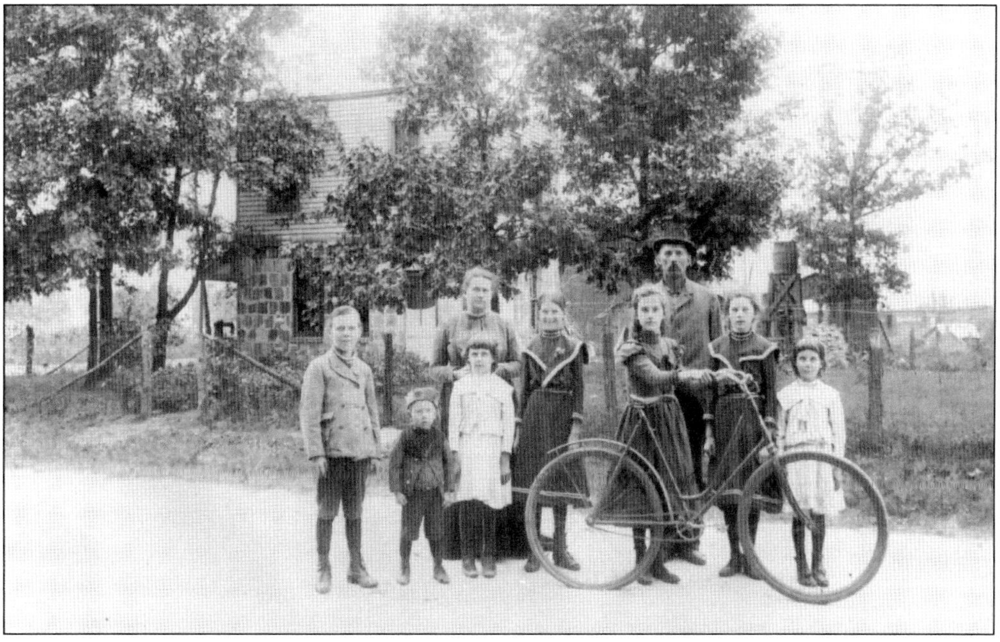

Pete and Iola Jansen are shown posing with family in 1905. The girl holding onto the bike is Mildred Merkley. The elementary school located at 9340 Fifth Avenue is named after her, although it had been suggested that the school should be named after the recently assassinated Pres. John F. Kennedy. Merkley's teaching career spanned a lifetime.

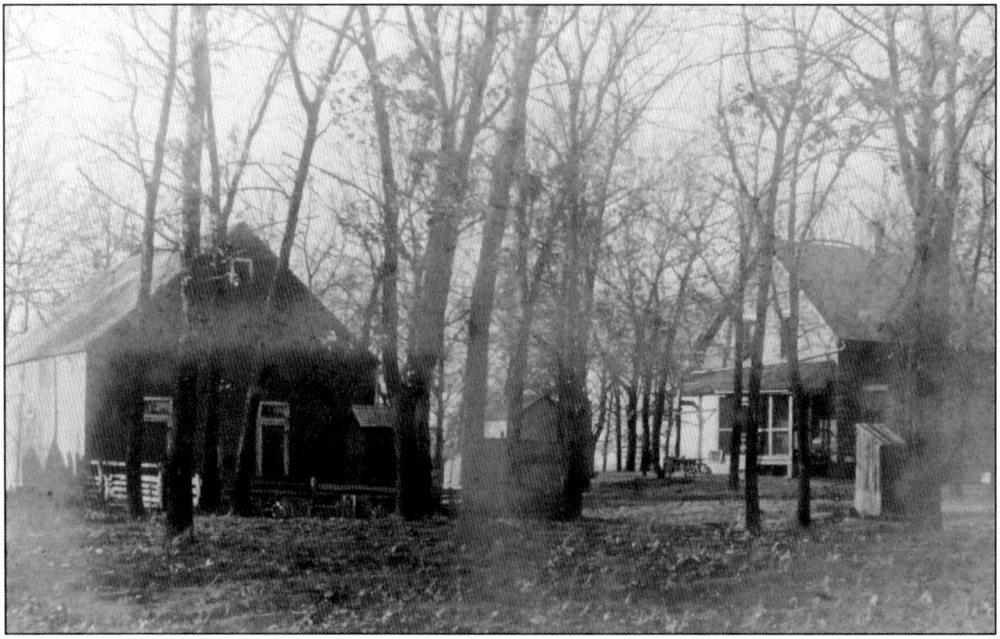

Here is a picturesque look at an early Highland home and barn amidst towering trees. The Garnt Huizenga homestead, an early 19th century property, stood on the edge of what is now Wicker Park. The Ridge Road home cost $1,250, and the barn was built for $350.

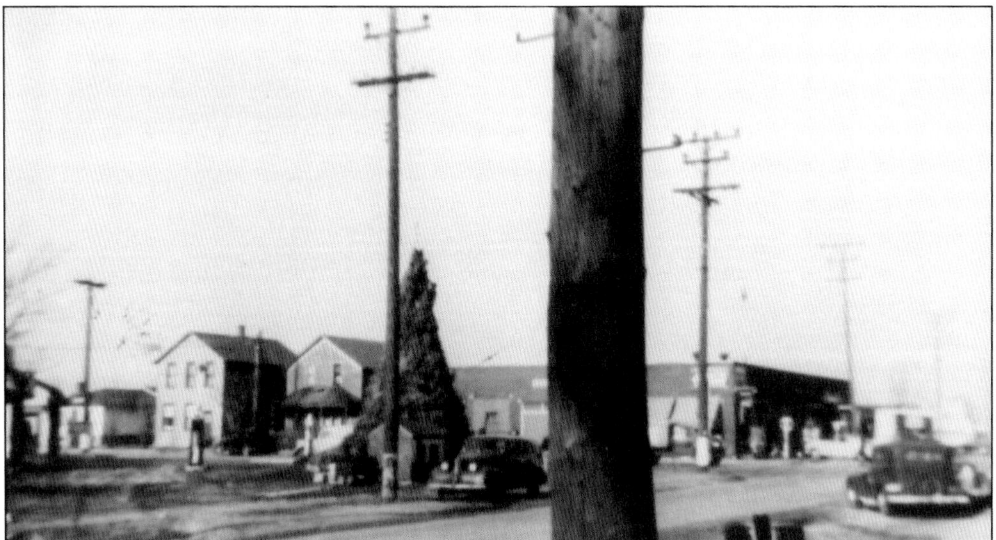

Highway Avenue is pictured as it appeared during the 1940s.The tall tree in the background looks similar to the trees growing in Main Square Park today, although a gas station now sits at this location at the corner of Kennedy and Highway Avenues.

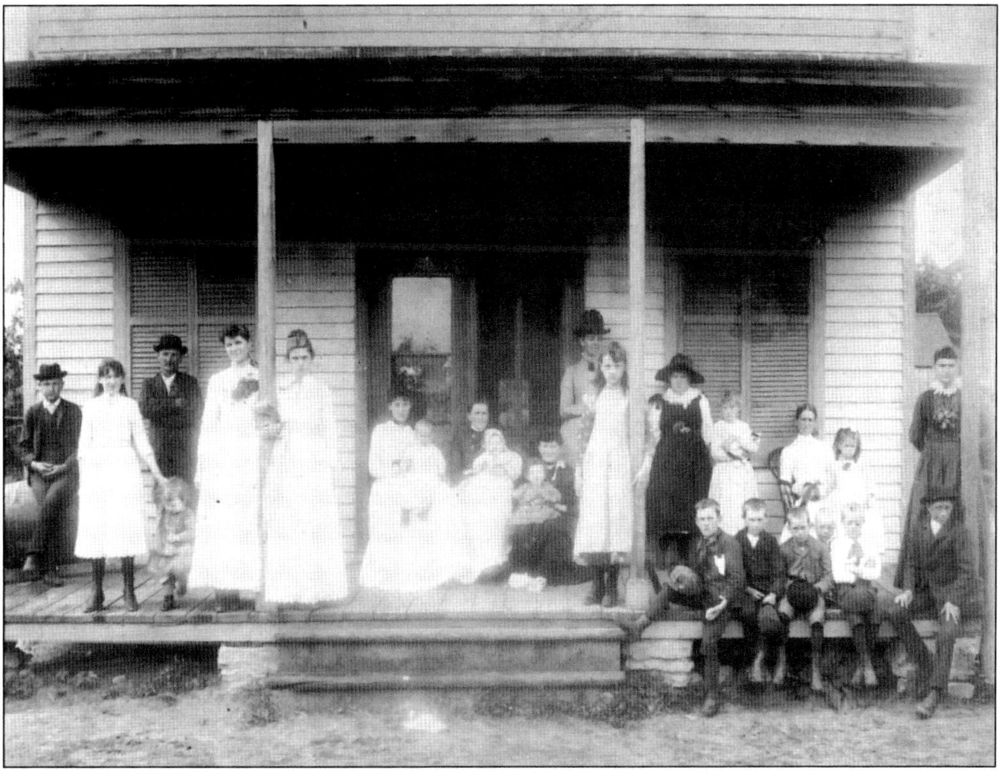

Rhoda Johnston's general store is pictured here sometime during the late 1880s. The building was located on what is now Highway Avenue in the parking lot next to Traditions Restaurant and very close to the intersection of Kennedy and Highway Avenues.

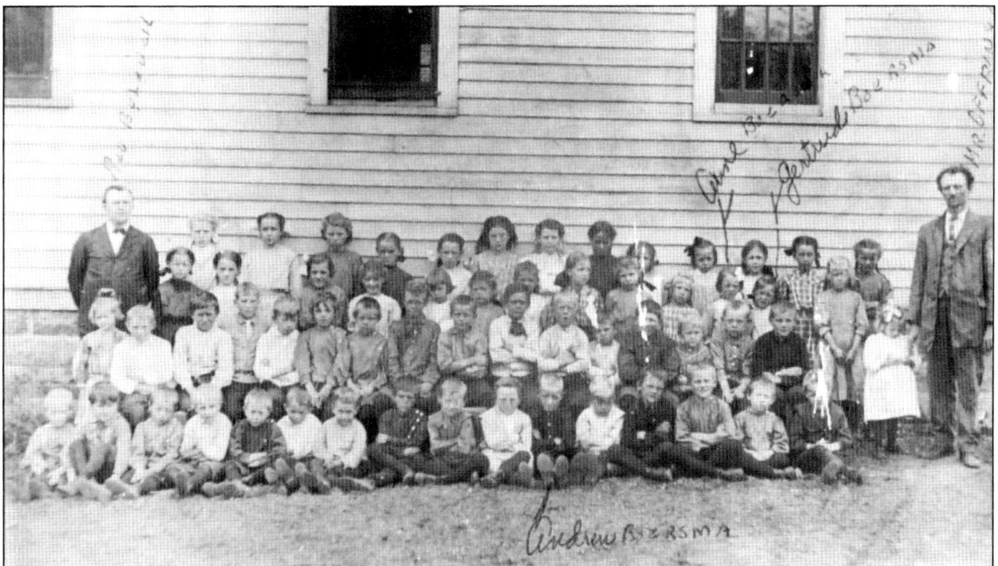

This is the entire student body of the Highland Christian School in 1915. The school had opened six years earlier. The school is now a large facility sitting on Ridge Road directly across from Main Square Park. Its serves students from pre-kindergarten through the eighth grade.

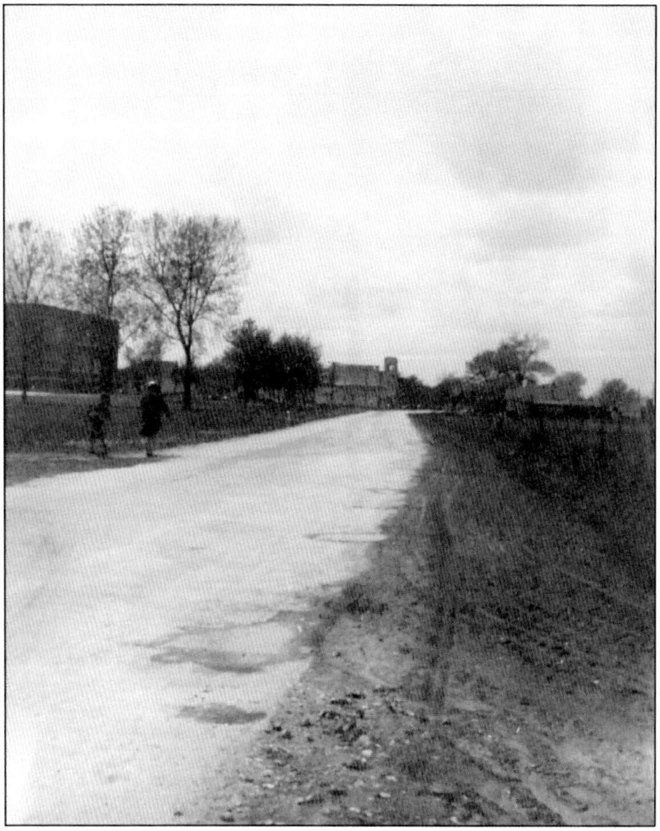

Here is another old stretch of Highway Avenue looking a little on the empty side. Today, this avenue is a hub for small businesses and social activity in the town; there is little vacant land.

This is Ridge Road during the early development of Highland. Today, Ridge Road is not only one of the main thoroughfares through town, it is also a conduit to the bordering communities of Munster and Griffith and heads straight west into Lansing, Illinois.

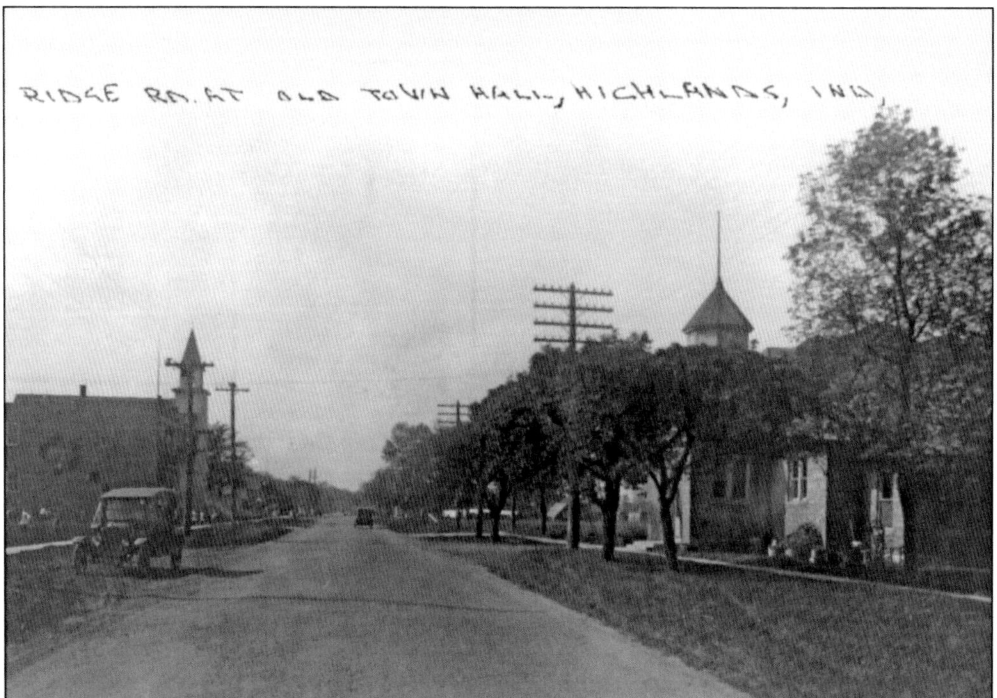

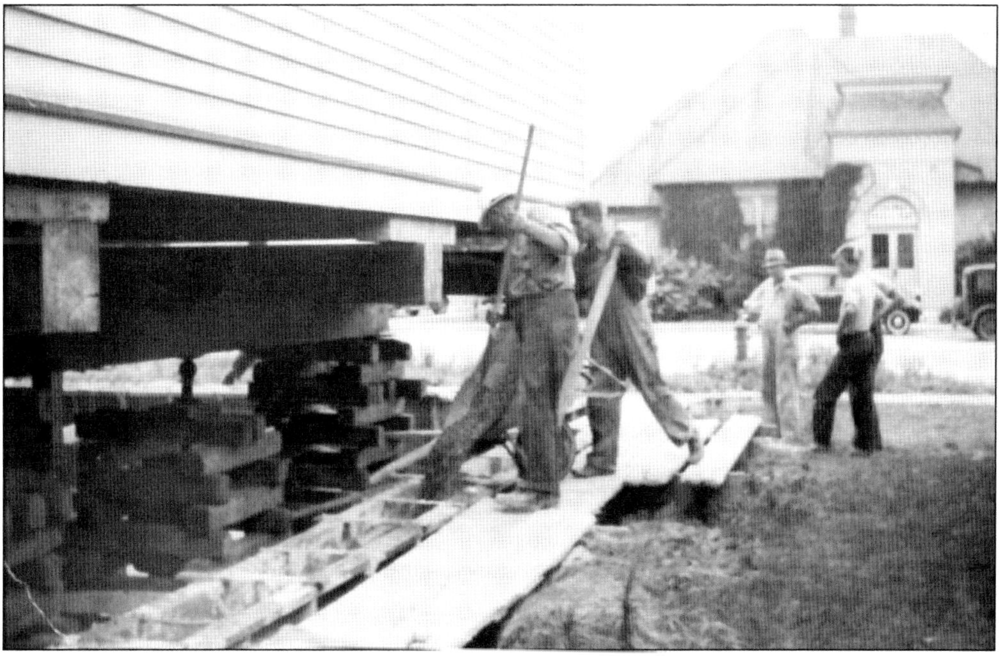

This 1939 image shows the Christian Reformed Church as it was being moved across the street on Highway Avenue. In the background is the old Town Hall. That spot is now home to the Central Fire Station. The Town Hall now sits on Ridge Road, although there has been talk of constructing a new town government building.

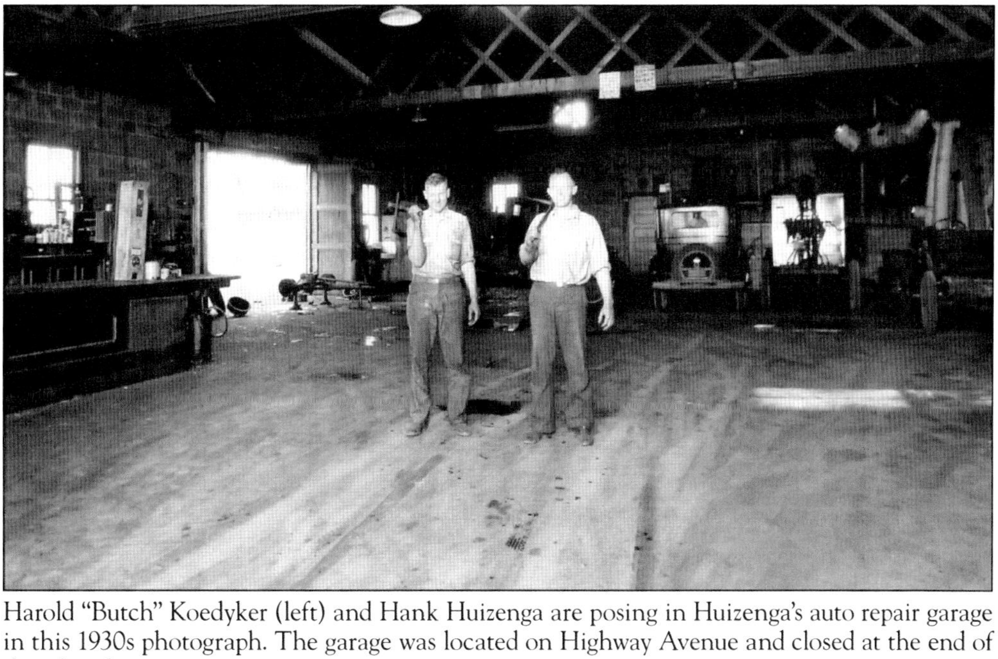

Harold "Butch" Koedyker (left) and Hank Huizenga are posing in Huizenga's auto repair garage in this 1930s photograph. The garage was located on Highway Avenue and closed at the end of that decade.

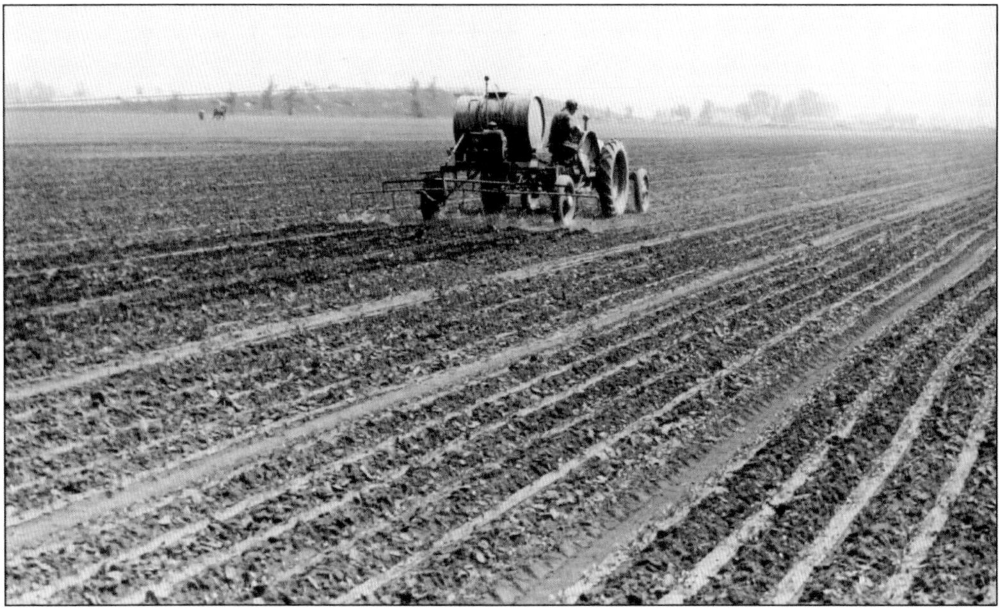

The Zandstra family's Highland farm is pictured here in the early 20th century. A Meijer megastore now stands here. The change is an indication of how Highland is evolving from its agricultural origins. The Meijer property was developed on this site during the late 1990s.

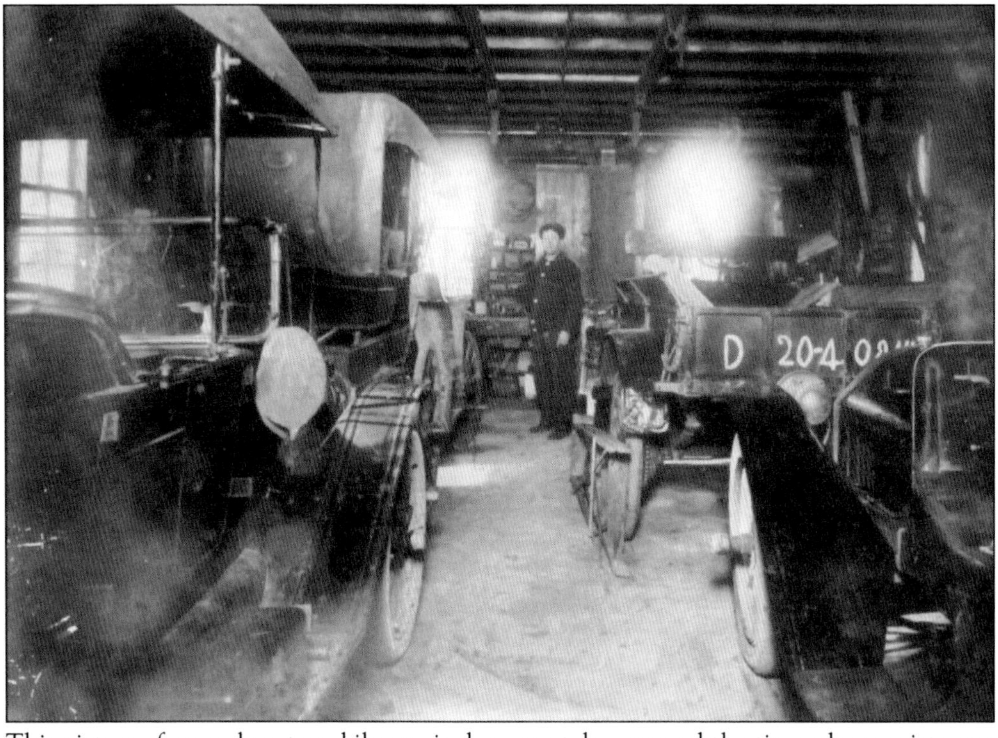

This picture of an early automobile repair shop was taken around the time when society was transitioning from the horse and carriage to the automobile. Mike Grimmer is the proud owner shown in this 1917 image. His garage was at the corner of Highway and Kennedy Avenues where Apex Construction is now located.

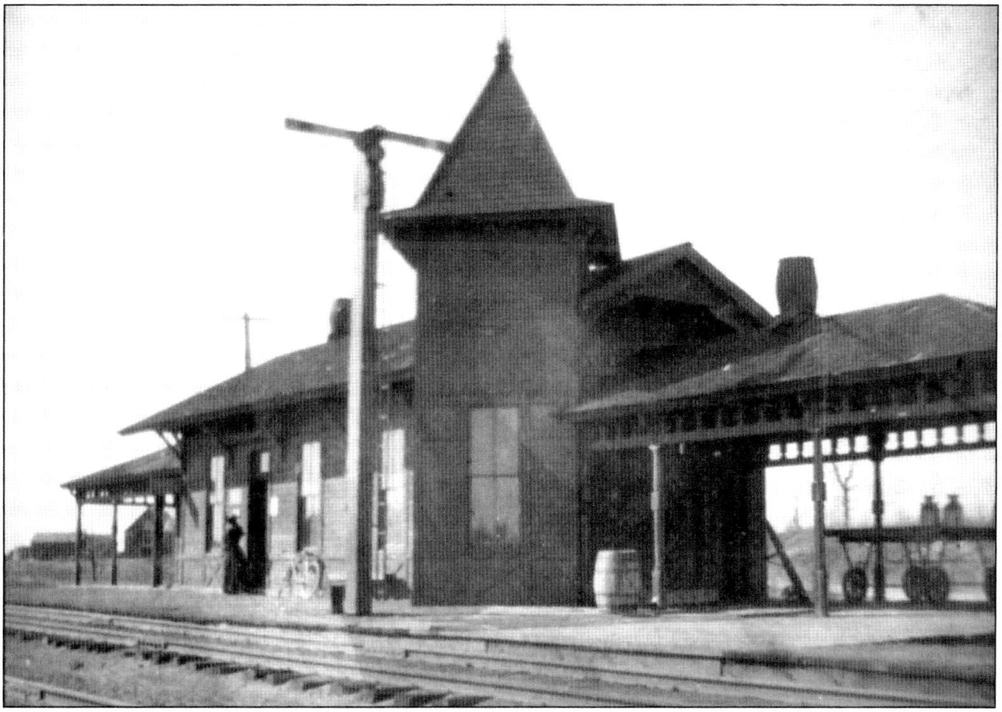

One person is shown standing at Highland's first Erie Railroad station before 1907. The station was destroyed by fire in 1908 and was later rebuilt. The loss from the fire was estimated at $2,000, and the blaze occurred on a Saturday night. A coal-burning stove was the suspected cause.

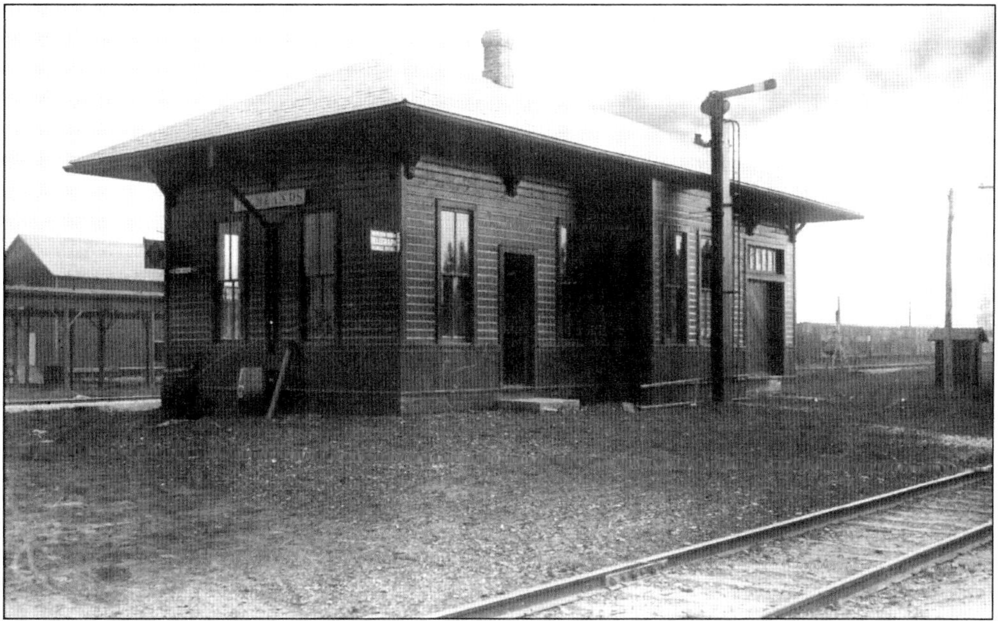

This downtown station was built in 1910 and served the Erie and Chesapeake Railroads. The Erie Railroad began operations in the 1830s in the northeastern part of the United States and expanded westward. The Chesapeake started in West Virginia in the late 19th century and made its way to Indiana by the early part of the next century.

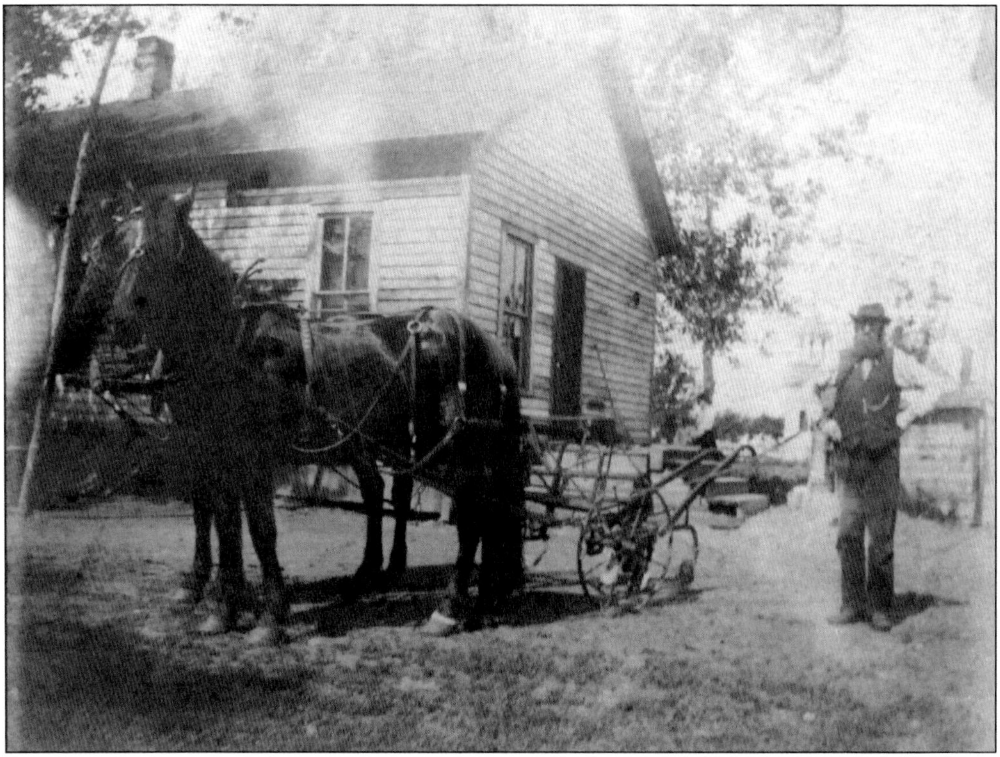

This early 20th century farm is pictured before the advent of corporate agriculture. Dutch immigrant Nick Kikkat is standing behind his home, which is still standing at 2925 Highway Avenue.

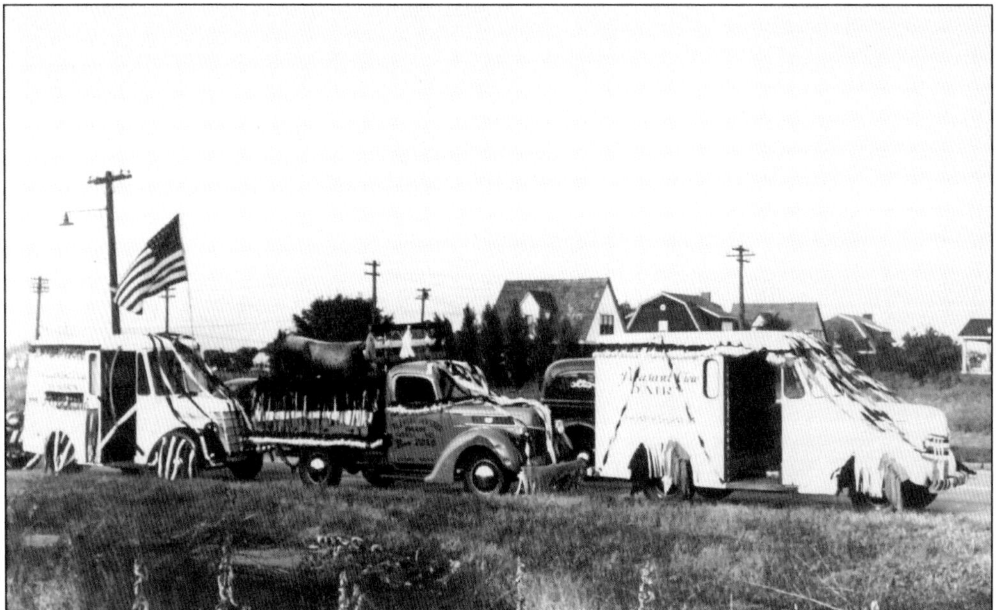

Leading the way in this small procession is the Pleasant View Dairy truck. The vehicles were part of a parade that made its way through downtown Highland. The town traditionally holds parades on the Fourth of July and during the Christmas season.

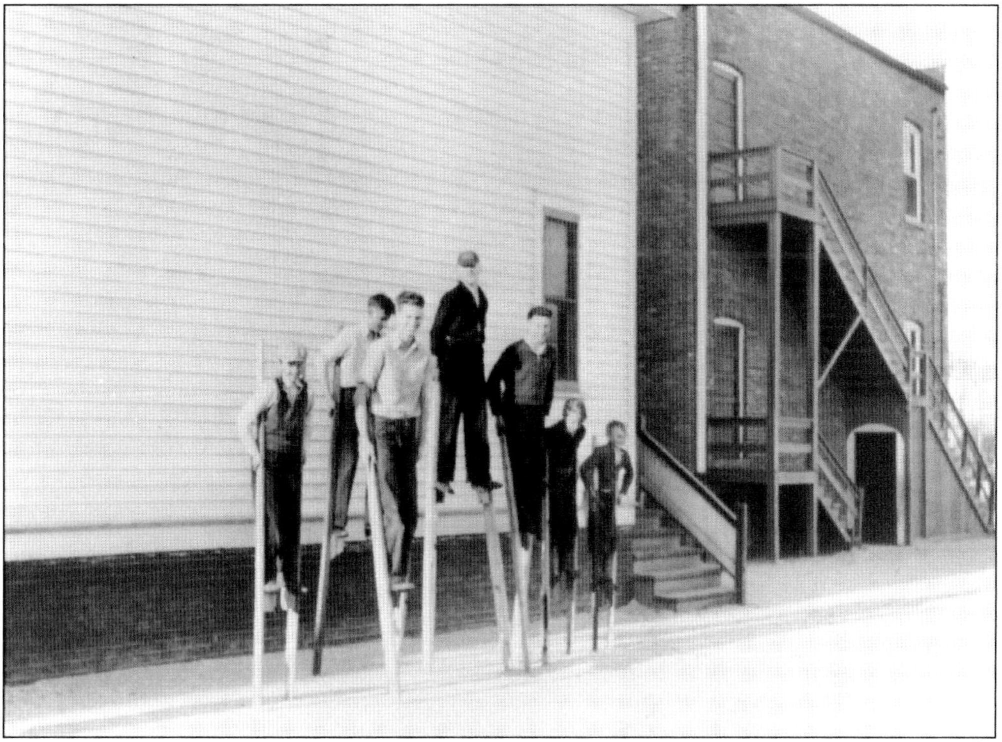

Clarence Van Til, Ivan Van Til, and Jake Scheeringa are among the youngsters having some fun on stilts near the original site of the Christian Reformed Church (the brick building at right) in this 1920s image. This site was eventually occupied by Midwest Bank.

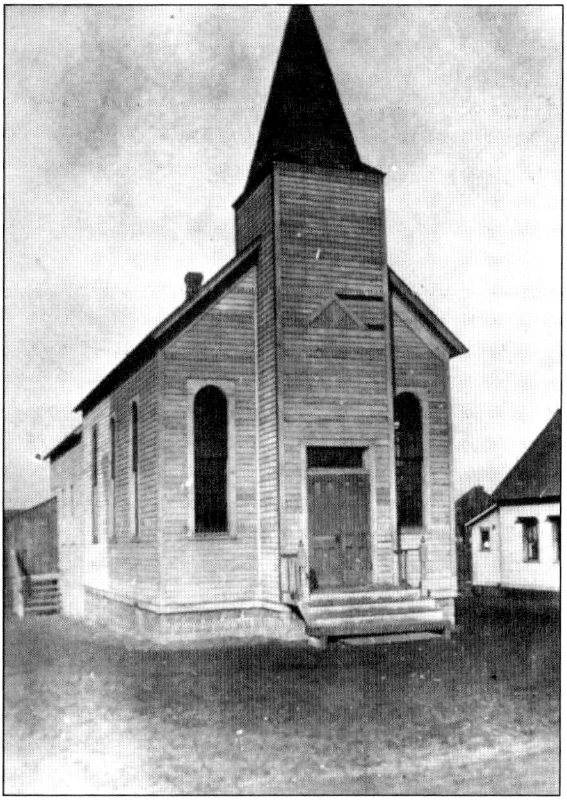

Schoon's Church was the earliest church in Highland and was built by Jacob Schoon in 1891. He maintained his church and congregation until the beginning of the 20th century. The church was located just west of the present-day Highland Branch of the Lake County Library on Jewett Avenue. It was later known as the First Christian Reformed Church.

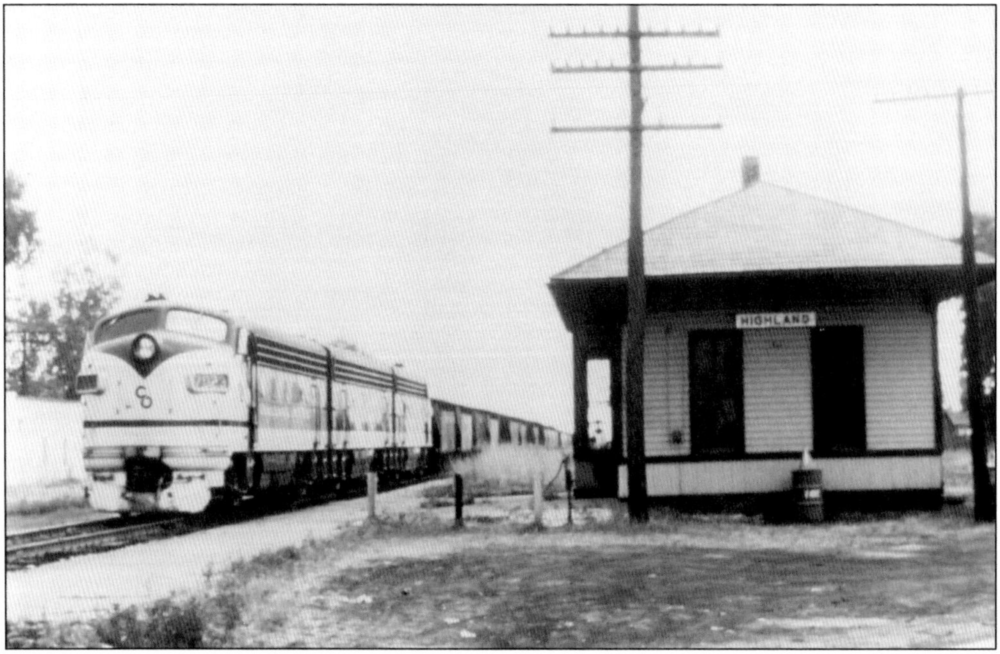

This locomotive once barreled through the center of Highland. Train traffic still runs through the town, although it is more common in the neighboring town of Griffith. This photograph was taken in August 1952. The depot, built in 1910, replaced one that burned down in 1908.

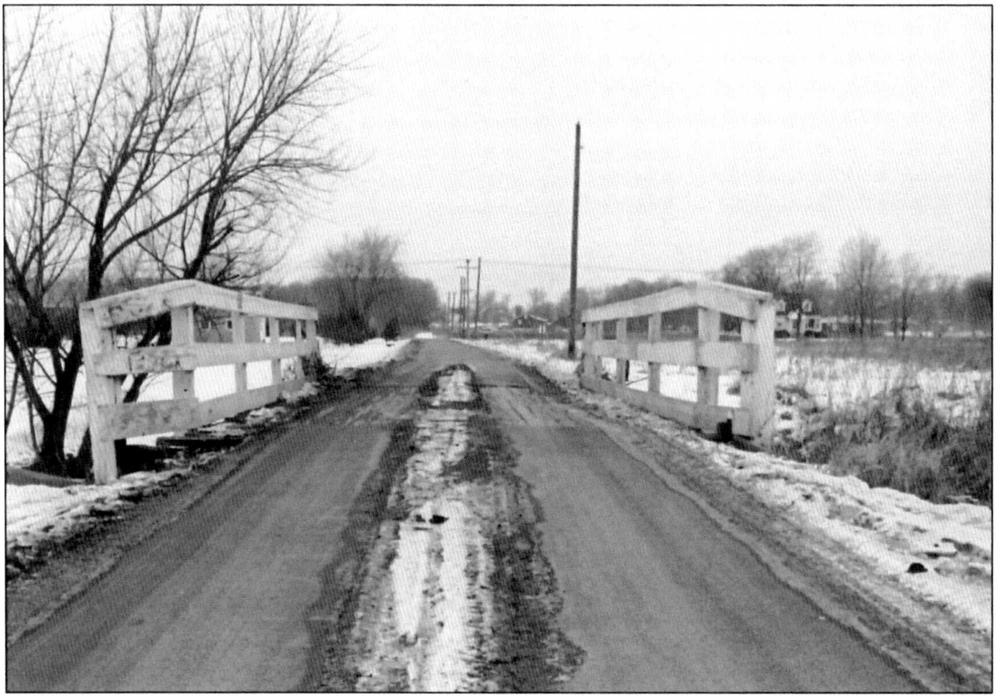

This rustic image shows what appears to be an isolated country road. This road now borders the protected Hoosier Prairie on Main Street.

An early motorist is getting ready to brave driving after what looks like a healthy snowstorm in Northwest Indiana. One wonders how this vehicle would have negotiated the storm of 1967.

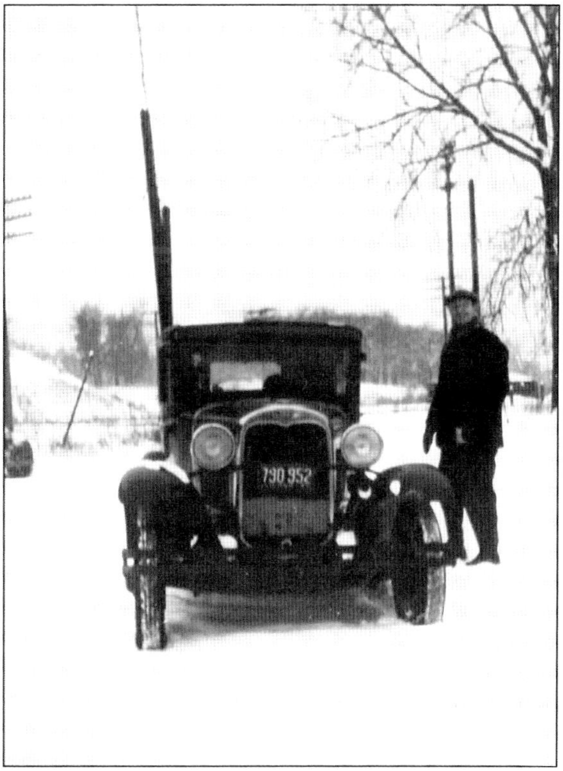

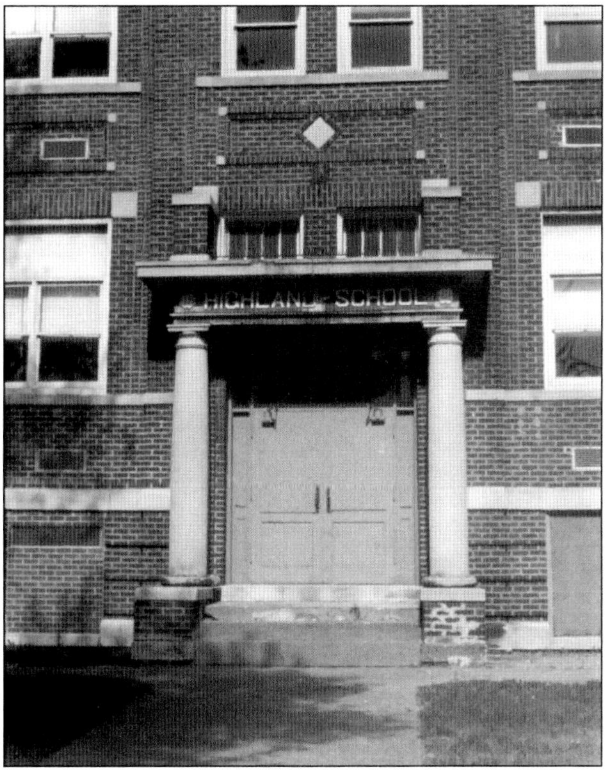

This is the epitome of an old-fashioned brick school building. The site that was once home to the Highland Main School is now Main Square Park. The school was built in 1915 and closed in 1972.

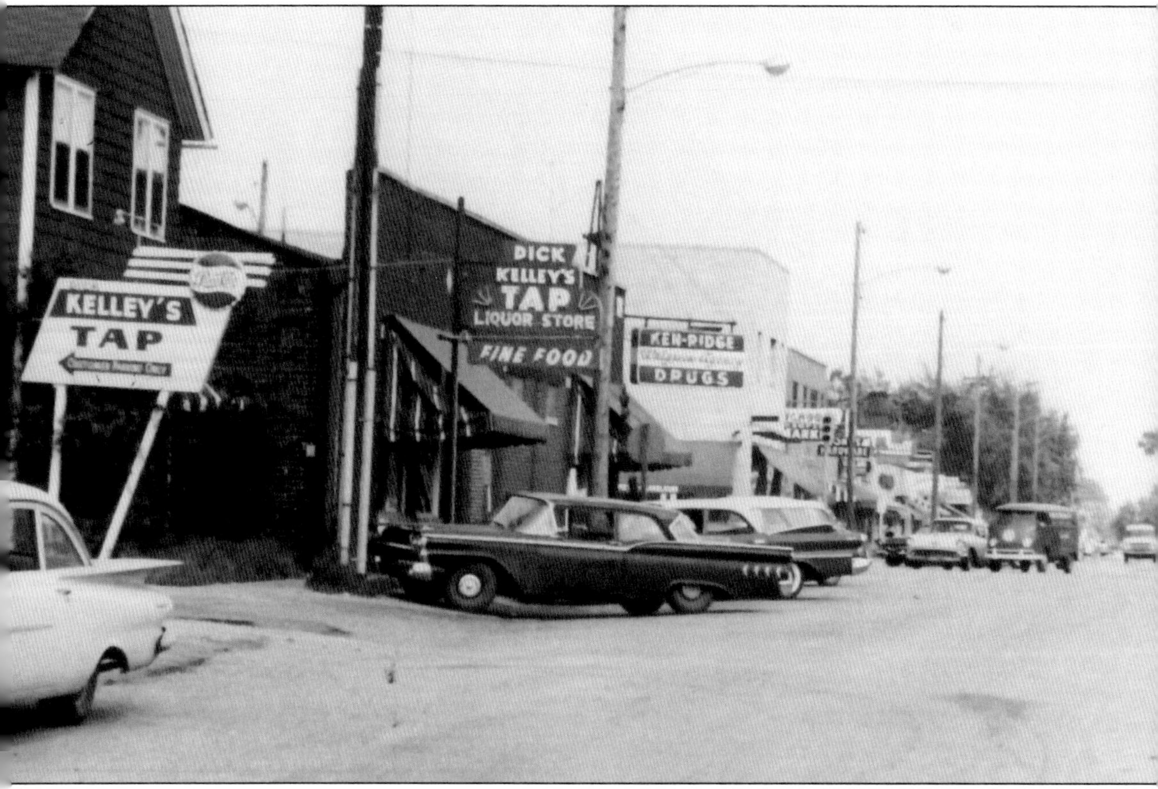

If the huge Ford parked diagonally in front of Kelly's Tap is new, this photograph shows Highway Avenue in 1959. Kelley's Tap and Ken-Ridge Drugs have been gone for some time now. The Ford appears to be a Galaxie 500. Ford used the name as a way to associate the car with the United States' entry into the space race. The gas-guzzling model went out of production in 1974 just as a massive energy crisis hit the country and the world.

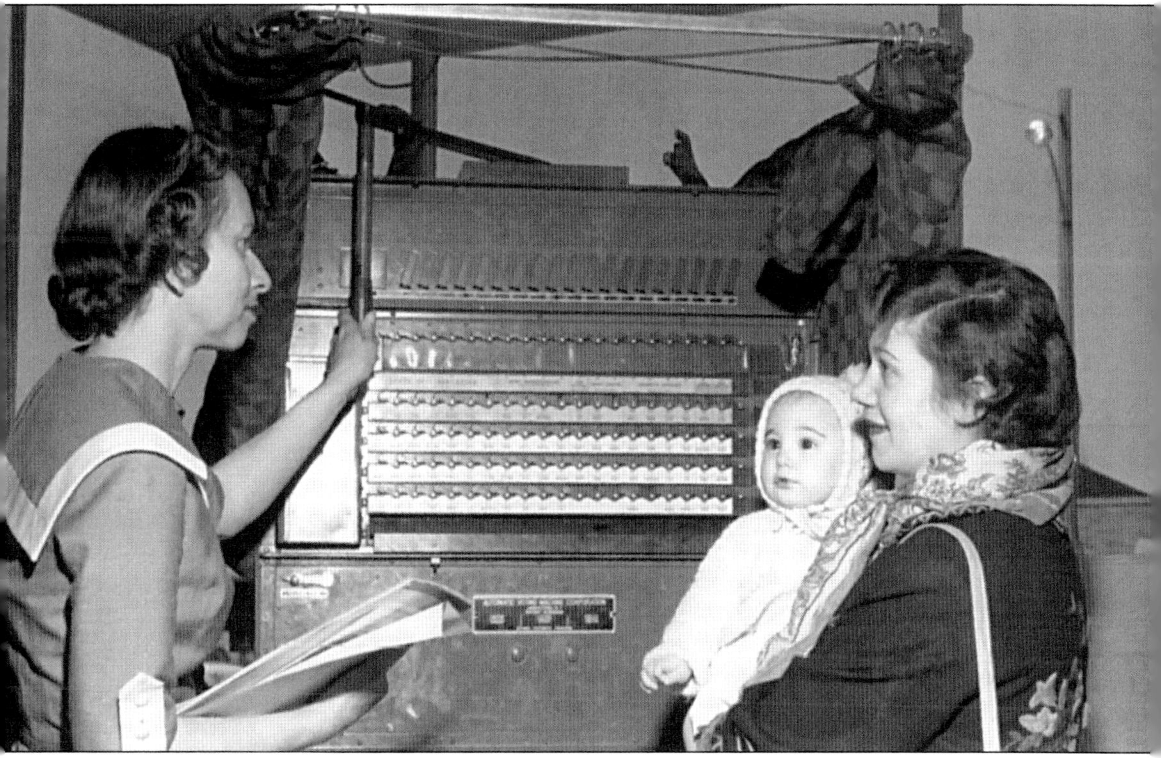

Chicago Tribune writer Mike Royko used the "Indiana No-Place" slur, but most of the time, dead Hoosiers did not vote (as deceased Chicagoans often did). This picture shows a 1958 voting machine that was hand-operated by levers. The large lever pulls the curtain closed to protect the voter's privacy. In 1960, Republicans charged that fraudulent votes from Chicago helped deliver Illinois for John F. Kennedy.

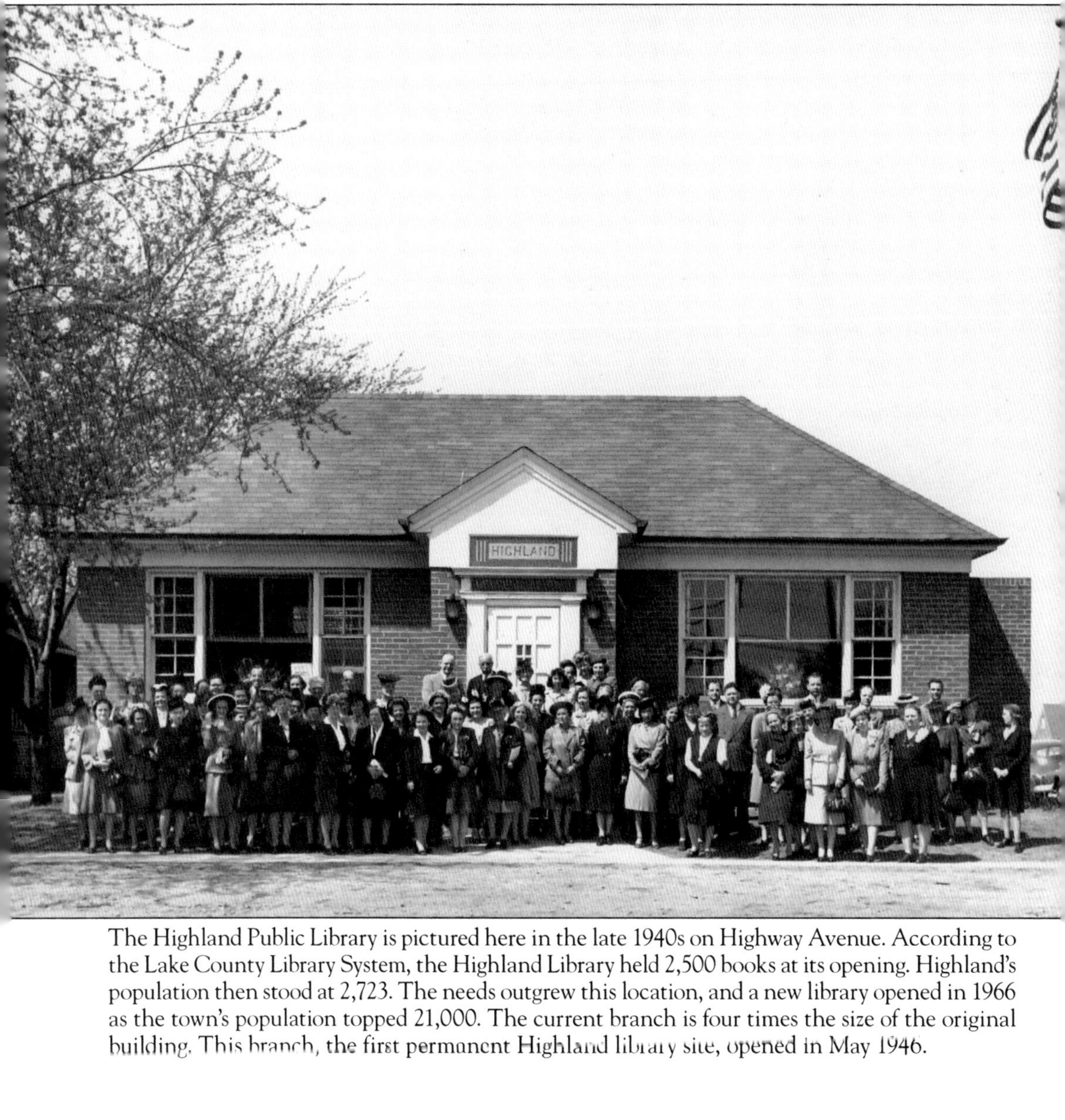

The Highland Public Library is pictured here in the late 1940s on Highway Avenue. According to the Lake County Library System, the Highland Library held 2,500 books at its opening. Highland's population then stood at 2,723. The needs outgrew this location, and a new library opened in 1966 as the town's population topped 21,000. The current branch is four times the size of the original building. This branch, the first permanent Highland library site, opened in May 1946.

Two

Small Businesses and the General Store

General Store: *A retail store in a small town or rural community that carries a wide variety of goods, including groceries. In the United States, the general store was the successor to the trading post, which served pioneers and settlers. The general store served as a meeting place for the members of the community, of which the storekeeper was an important member not only because he supplied material goods but because he was also the source of news and gossip.*

This entry from the *Encyclopedia Britannica* describes the type of general stores that are depicted in some photographs in this chapter and the lifestyles in small towns like Highland around the start of the 20th century.

The general store symbolizes how towns grew and developed in the United States. Over the course of the Industrial Revolution, big businesses and corporations grew and extended their influence on society. Yet small businesses remained the backbone of developing communities, especially rural ones.

Mark Hines owns and operates the Town Club Restaurant, which has been in business since 1947. He told the authors that when the Town Club first opened, some customers still used a horse and carriage on their night out. At the time of this writing, the Town Club was getting ready to celebrate its 70th anniversary. According to Hines, the Town Club faced challenges when corporate chains brought their eateries to Highland since families only have so much in their budget to patronize restaurants. This meant that some folks had to put off returning to the Town Club as they tried other eating establishments. Hines believes the Town Club has endured because it has not changed. "We are still an old-fashioned dinner house," he said.

This section will briefly examine the small, local business ventures in Highland. Some have vanished as institutions, others closed or moved, some burned to the ground, and others have remained a part of the community. In some ways, these types of businesses have taken on the role of the general store.

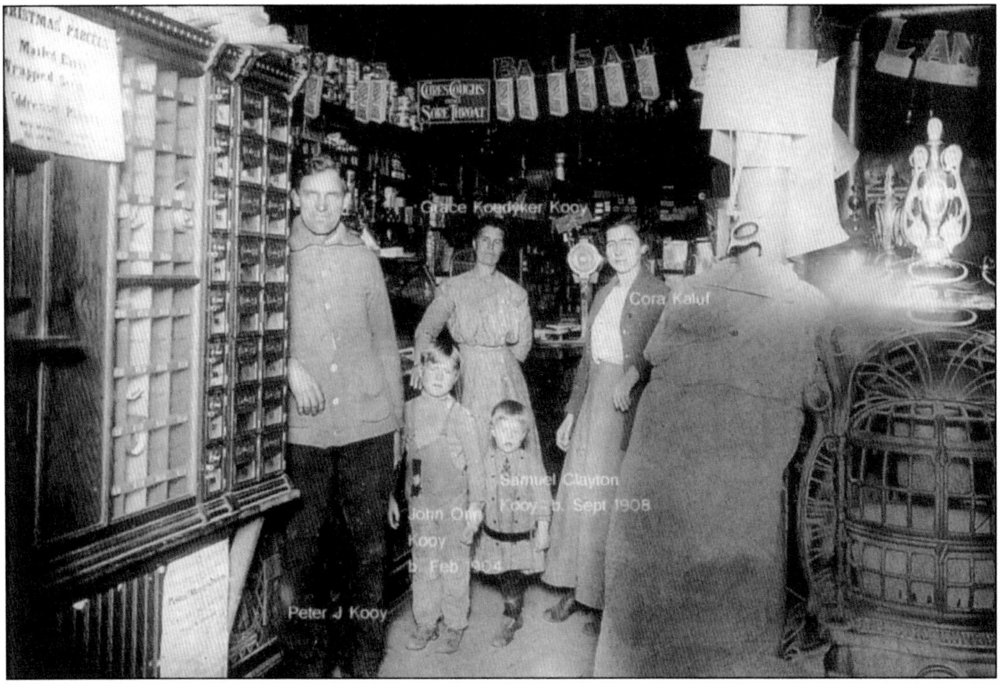

In Peter Kooy's grocery store around 1910, post office boxes are to the left, and there are a variety of goods available, including a remedy to cure common cold symptoms. From left to right are Kooy, sons John and Samuel, wife Grace (rear), and niece Cora Kaluf.

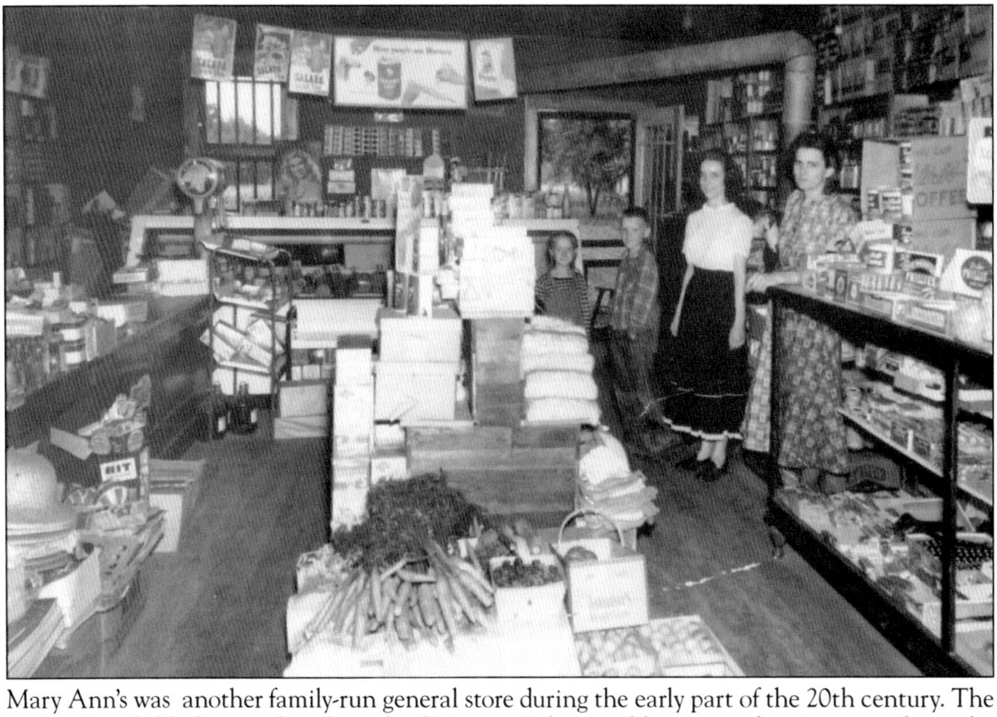

Mary Ann's was another family-run general store during the early part of the 20th century. The easily identifiable logo and trademark of Morton Salt is visible on an advertisement above the meat counter in the back. Today, salt still showers upon the umbrella-carrying girl.

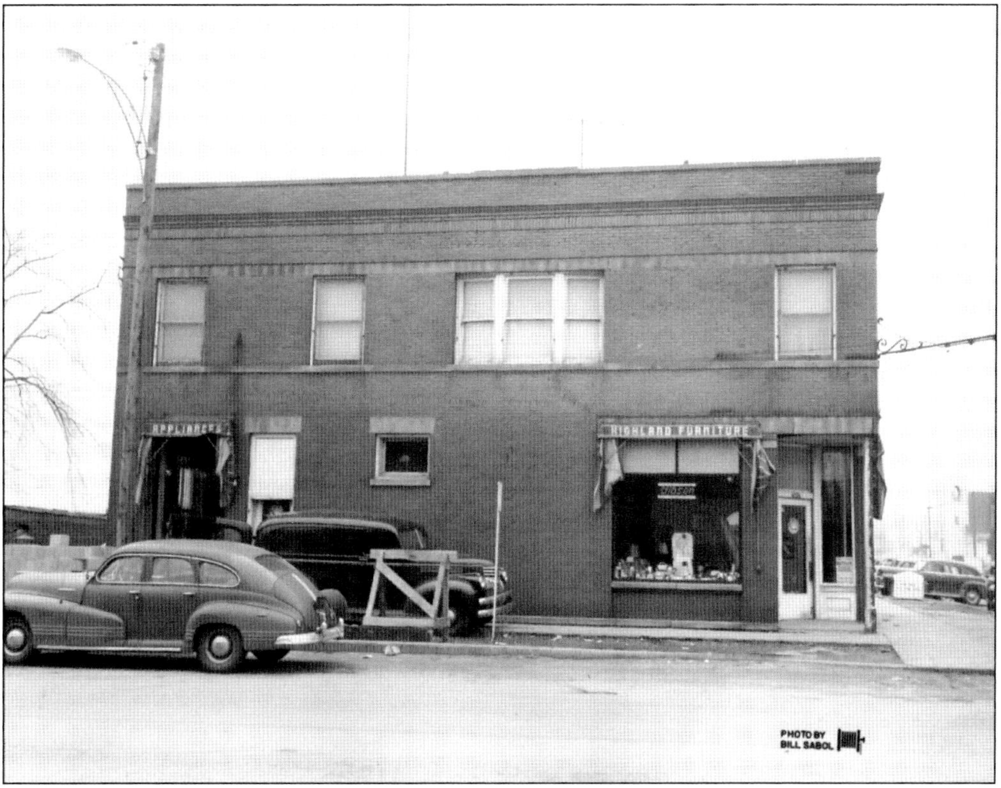

The Highland Furniture Store stood on the corner of Highway and Kennedy Avenues in 1950. It was one of several businesses to occupy the northeast corner where Exotic Aquatics now sits and where the Highland Department Store once stood. Jim and Maxine Marciniak ran the Highland Furniture Store and improved it by installing an elevator.

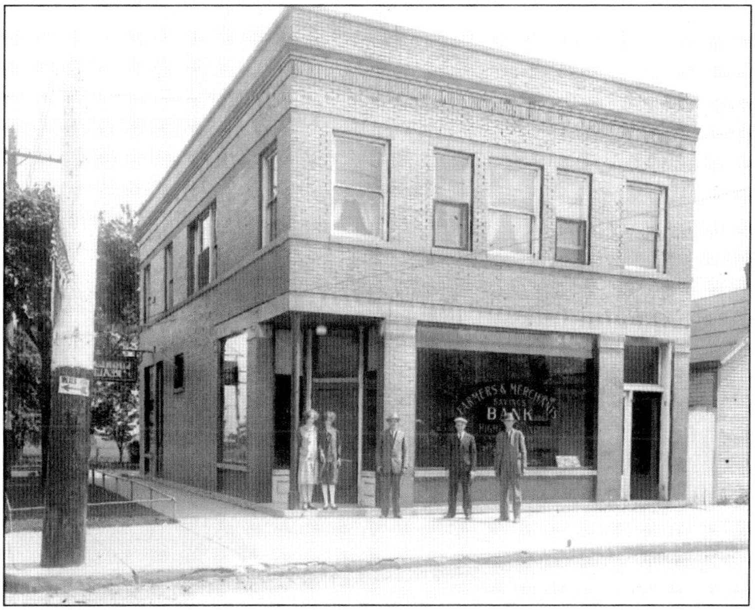

The Farmers and Merchants Bank is pictured in downtown Highland sometime during the 1920s. Many banks like this did not survive the Depression; this bank remained open until 1932. A small sign pointing the way to Wicker Park is nailed to the telephone pole at left.

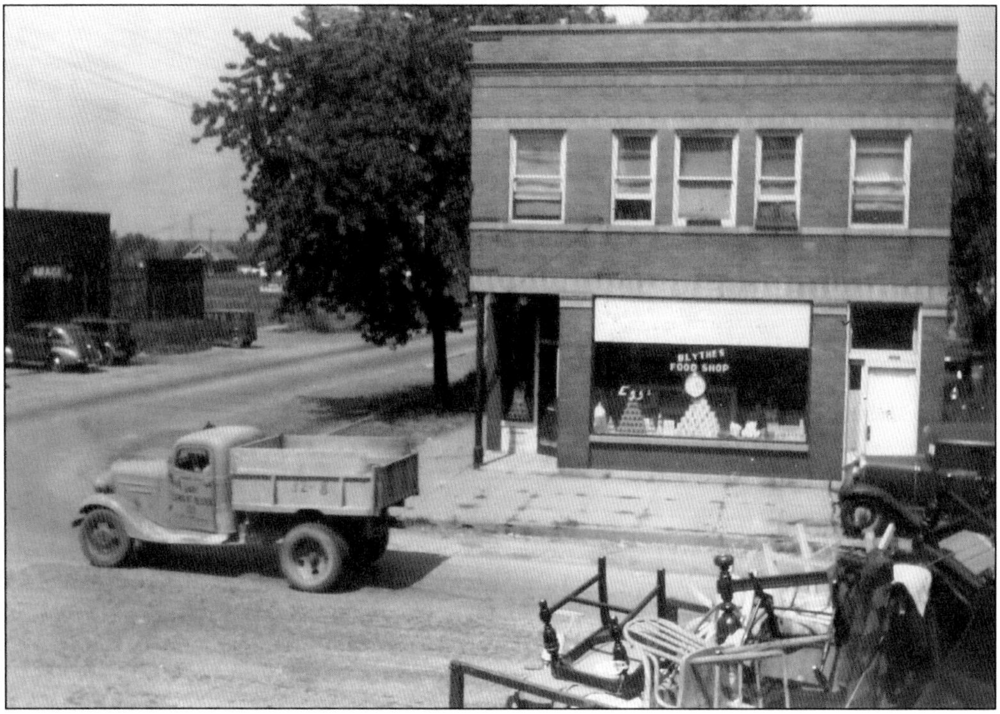

A truck ambles past Blythe's Food Shop sometime during the 1930s on Highway and Kennedy Avenues. This corner evolved and changed through the decades, including the Highland Department Store expansion.

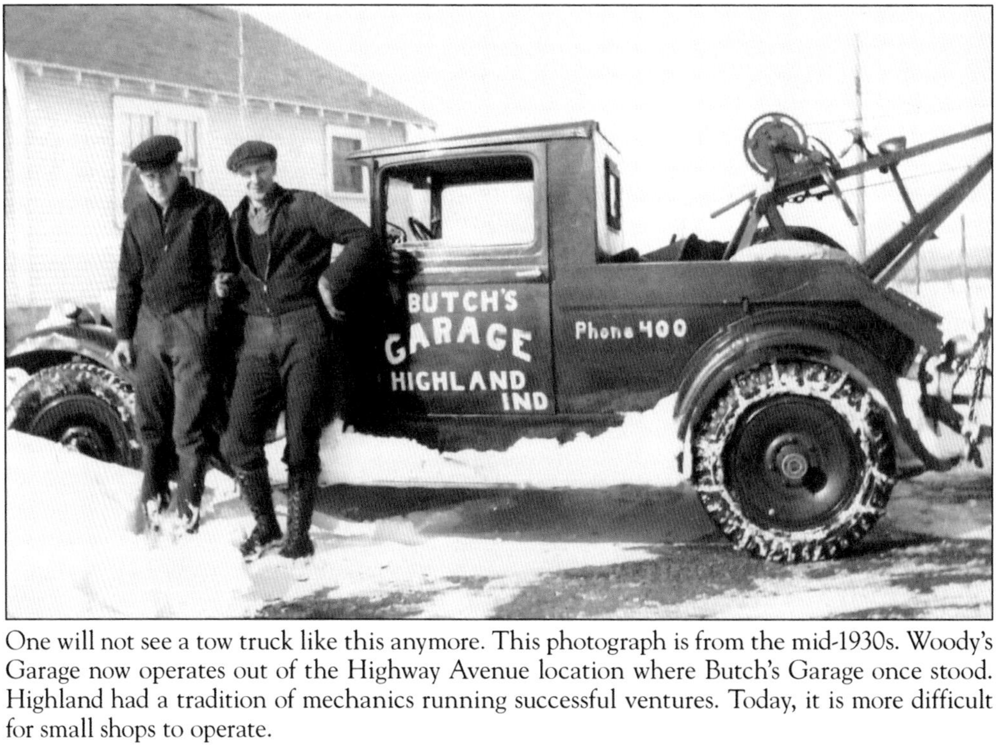

One will not see a tow truck like this anymore. This photograph is from the mid-1930s. Woody's Garage now operates out of the Highway Avenue location where Butch's Garage once stood. Highland had a tradition of mechanics running successful ventures. Today, it is more difficult for small shops to operate.

Highland businessman Everett Farmer is acting as if he is looking for water with a divining rod. Farmer's family operated Farmer & Sons Well and Pump Service before sewers were installed in Highland. The business moved south as the town developed and modernized. A Wendy's now occupies the old Farmer business site on the corner of Forty-Fifth Street and Kennedy Avenue.

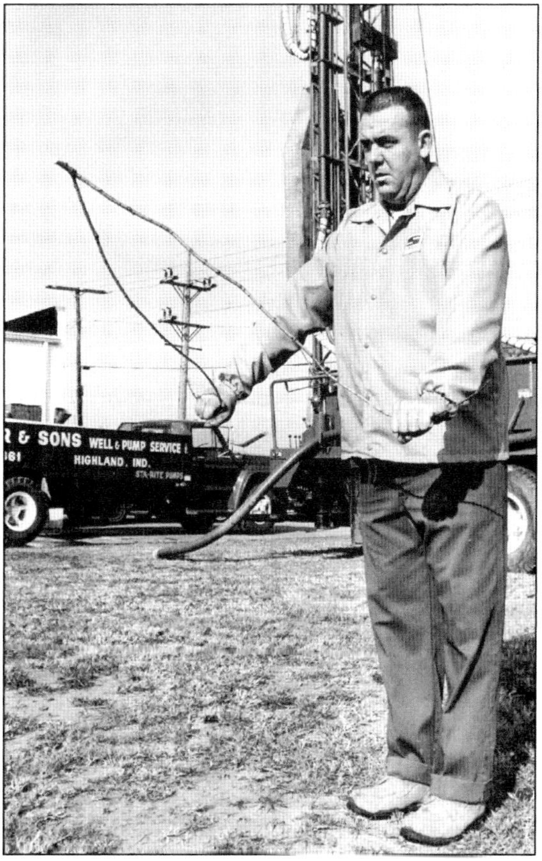

This 1950s image shows a specialty shop filled with kitchenware. Pyrex was in vogue at this time, as was Flatware and Ovenware. These types of shops are now mostly incorporated into modern department stores.

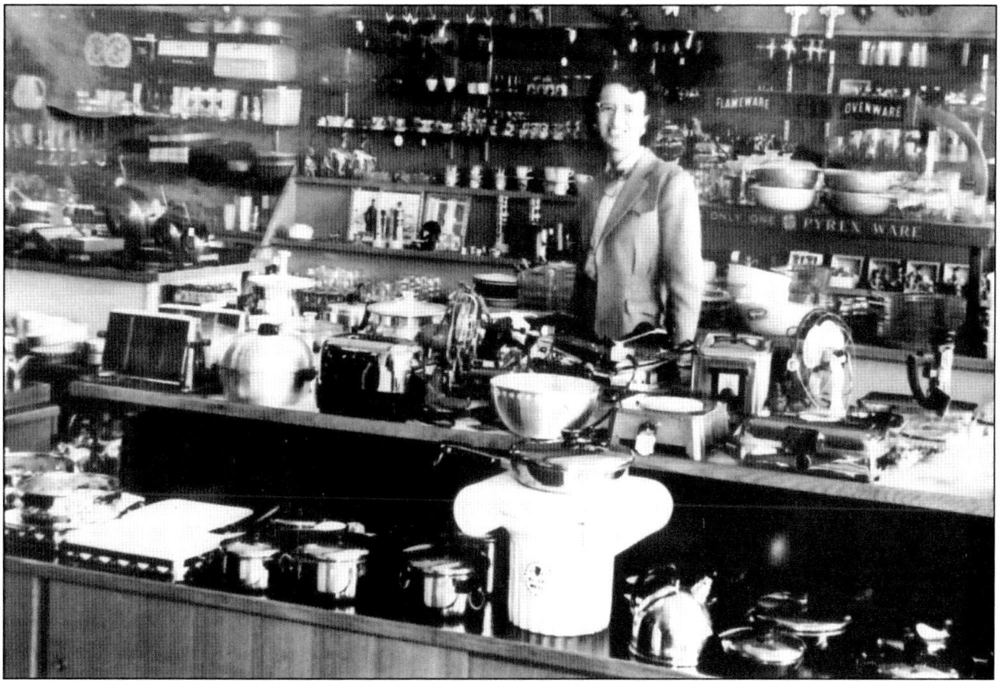

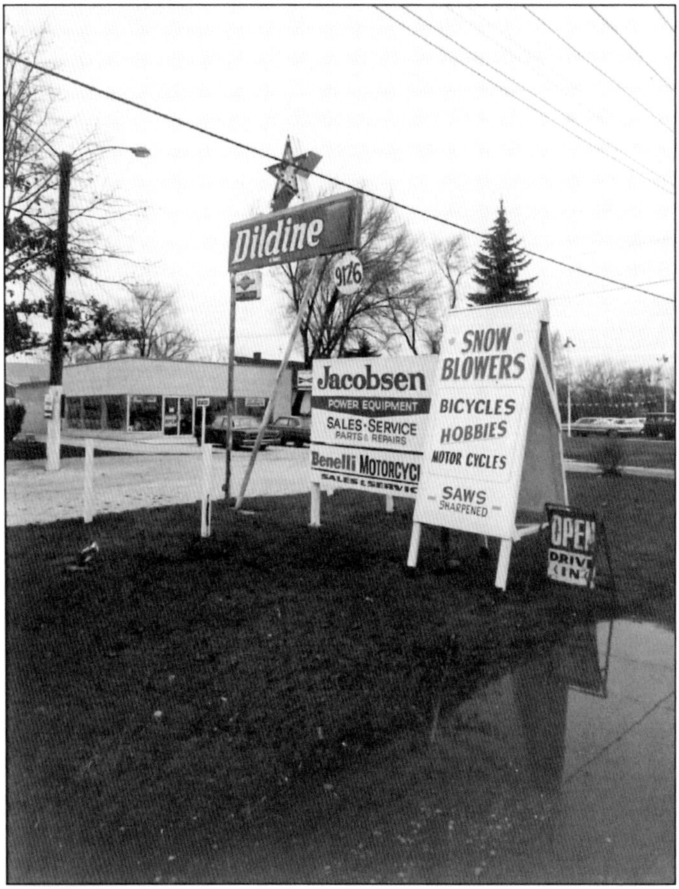

This photograph shows a power equipment store during the 1960s. Dildine has long since left Highland. Many residents took their mowers and other lawn equipment to shops like these for repairs. Bicycles and hobby items were sold there as well. Ridge Cycling helps fill this need for modern cyclists. It is located on Ridge Road.

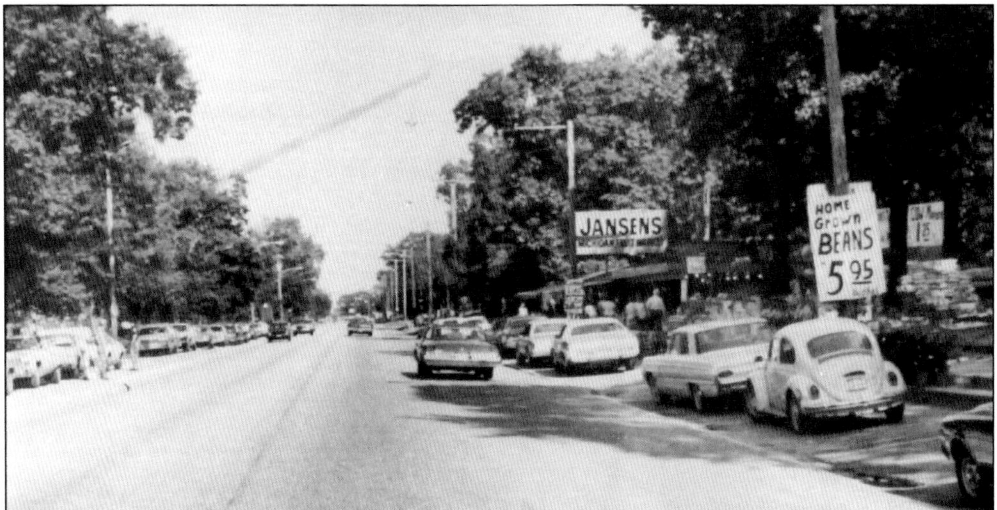

Jansen's Produce Market is shown on Ridge Road during the 1960s. Jansen's gave the town a small rural touch even as its population increased and Highland began to have a more urban flavor. Jansen's was directly across the street from Wicker Park. The business also grew its own trees in Michigan for sale in the winter as Christmas trees.

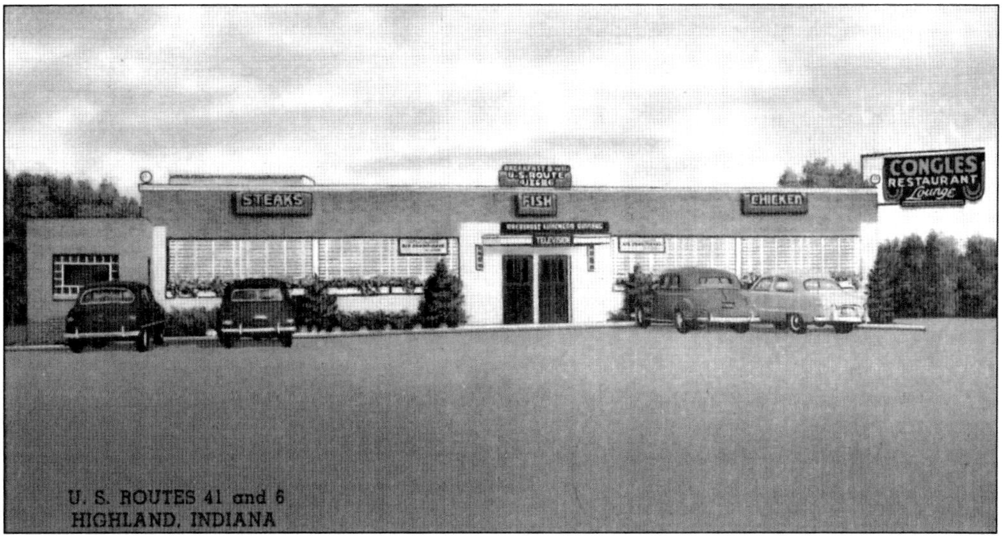

This is a postcard advertising Congles Restaurant. Although shown in black and white here, the original 1950 card was brightly colored with a deep blue sky. Although postcards like these are now sold online for prices up to hundreds of dollars, in 1950, this card was sold for far less than $1. This restaurant sat on the current site of the Highway of Flags monument.

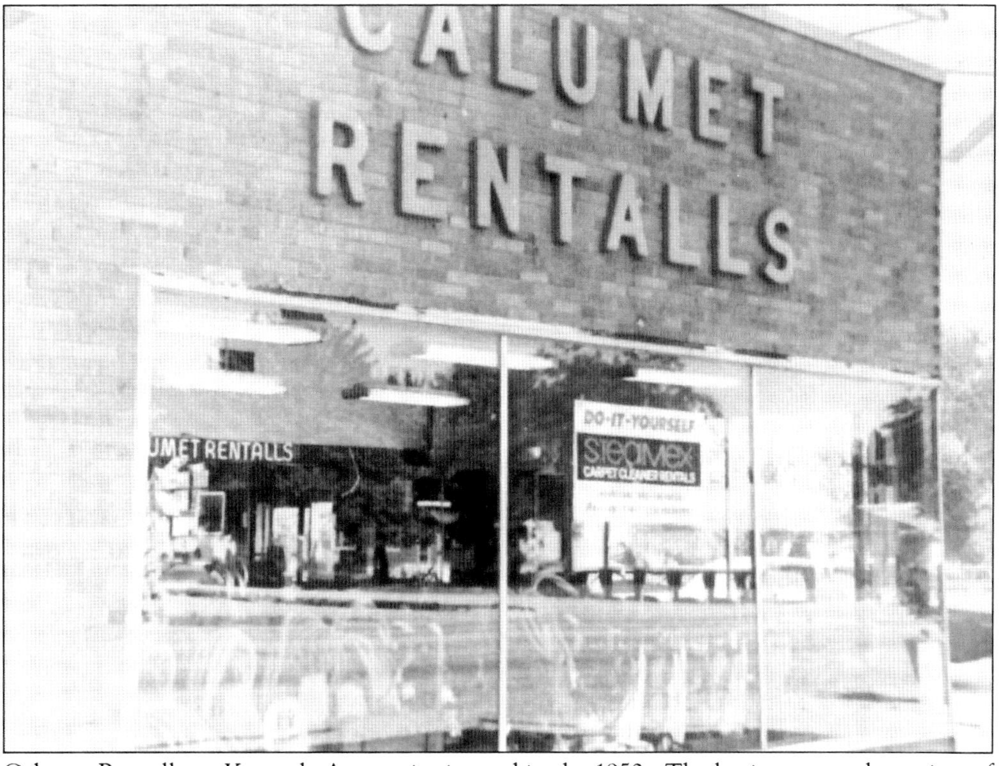

Calumet Rentalls on Kennedy Avenue is pictured in the 1950s. The business rented a variety of equipment. Aide Rentalls opened in 2002 at this site, which is three doors down from the former Town Theatre.

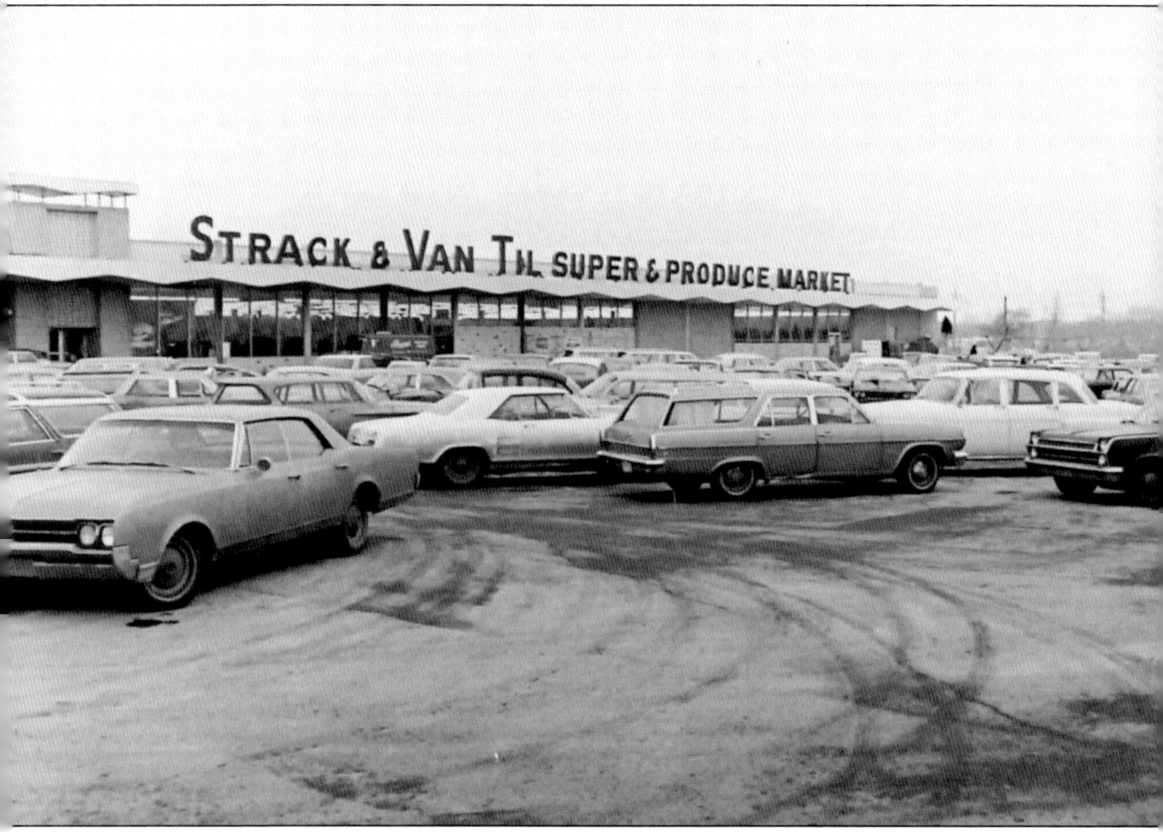

The Strack and Van Til Super & Produce Market is pictured here in 1968. Around this time, grocery stores began to include produce in their stores in large amounts. Strack and Van Til was a viable local business in Highland and the surrounding areas for decades starting with Nick Van Til and Ernie Strack's partnership in 1958. In 2017, the situation surrounding the stores' names changed (see the following page).

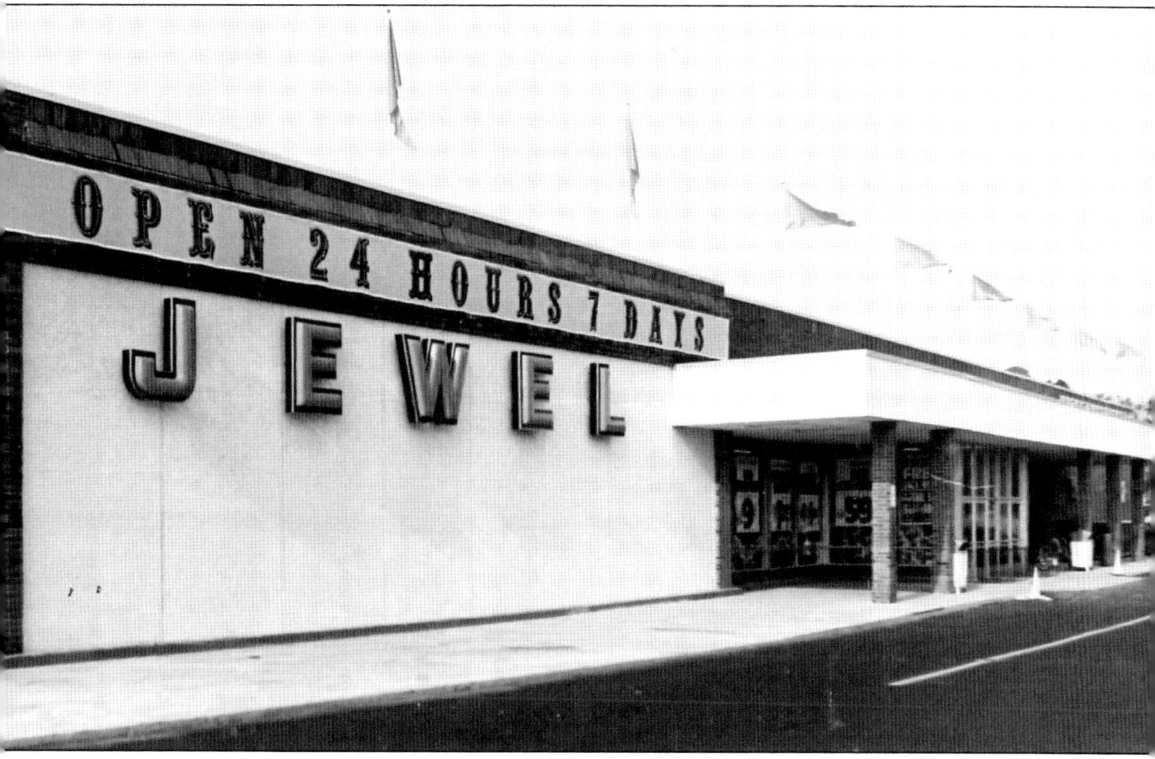

Jewel Food Store is shown here in the 1970s. Jewel eventually moved out of Highland, but as of this writing, its corporate structure was in the process of acquiring Strack and Van Til assets. Central Grocers, the corporate owner of Strack and Van Til, announced it was filing for Chapter 11 bankruptcy in the spring of 2017. Jewel had made a bid to buy 19 Strack stores for $100 million and promised it would keep Strack and Van Til employees after taking ownership. Jewel was not able to complete the acquisition, and the Strack family purchased its former assets. The grocery business has become a great deal more competitive since the early days of the general store.

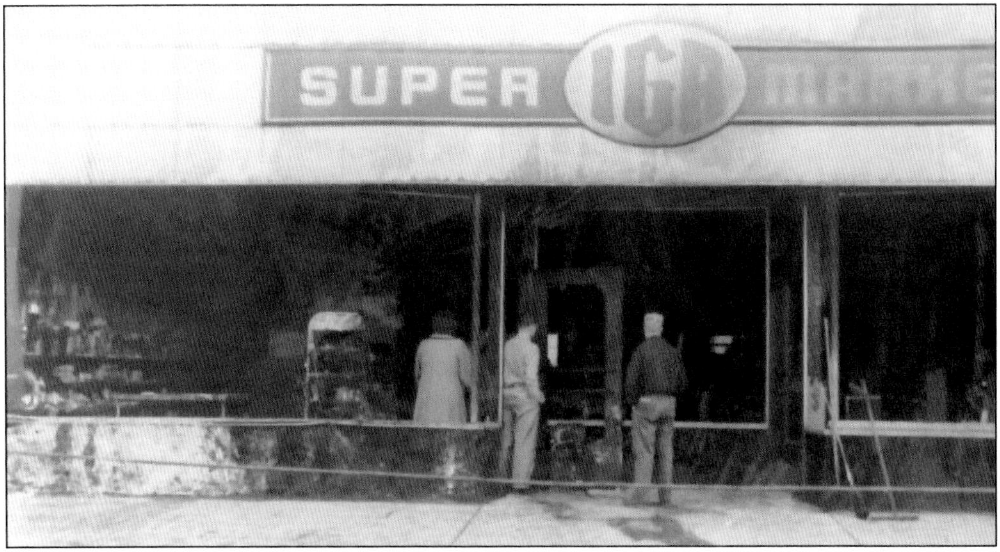

This is a mid-20th century IGA grocery. Business at IGAs was forgiving. Customers were allowed to run tabs that were settled at the end of the month. This is a rarity in the 21st century. The store was located on Highway Avenue where the Fagen & Miller Funeral Garden now stands.

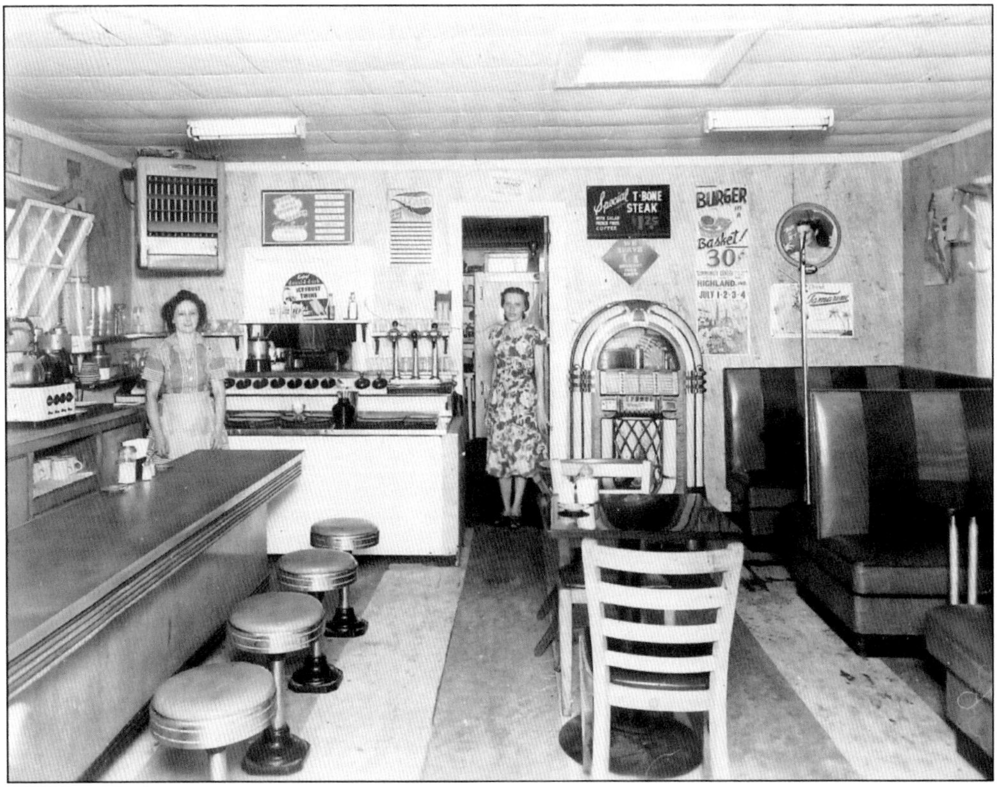

The inside of Ada's Café is shown here during the 1950s. The café, run by Ada (Whittaker) Sutter, was a friendly place where customers could get a T-bone steak for $1.25. Ada's husband, Heine, owned a service station called Heine's.

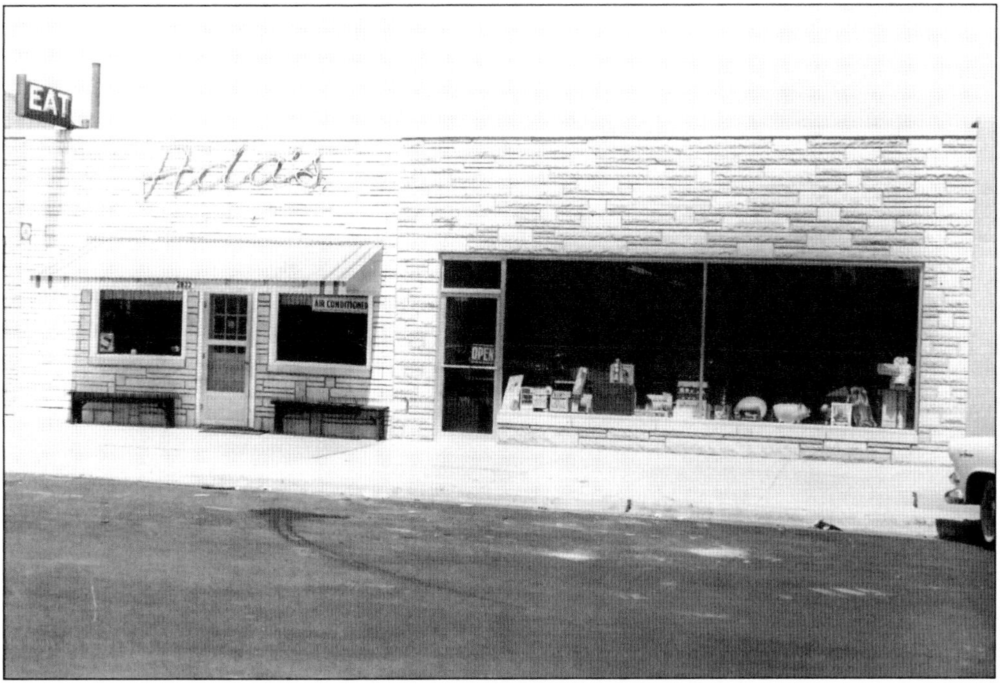

In this 1956 image, a sign that reads "Air Conditioned" hangs in the upper corner of a front window. At this time, it was not always a given that restaurants and other businesses had air conditioning. The frosty artwork on these signs conveyed the comforting thought of escaping the heat and was a useful marketing tool.

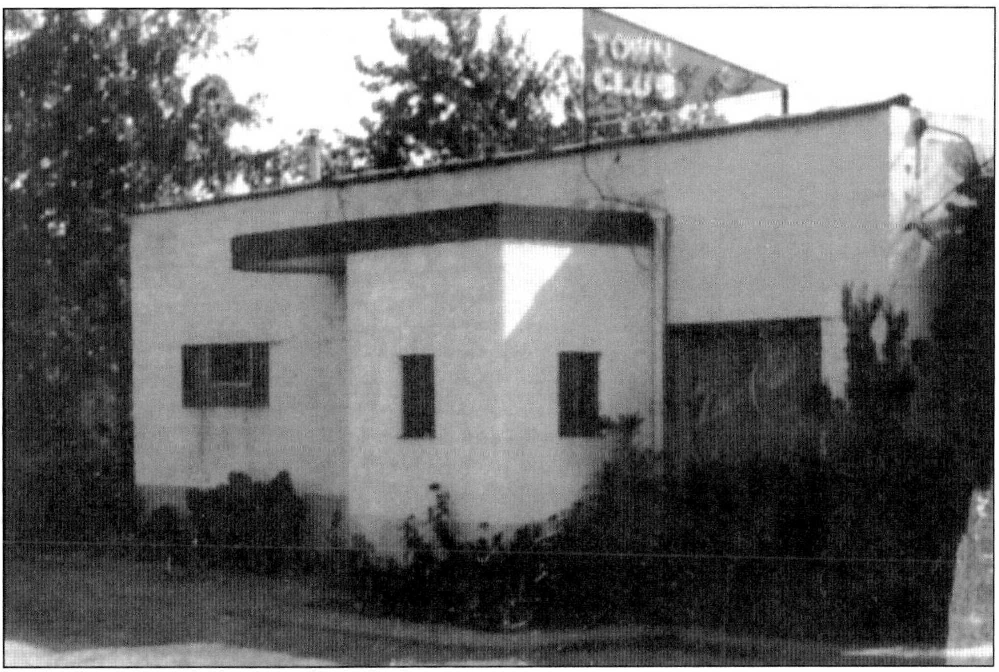

Here is an early photograph of the Town Club restaurant, the second-oldest such establishment in Highland. It is entering its eighth decade and is a real fixture in the town.

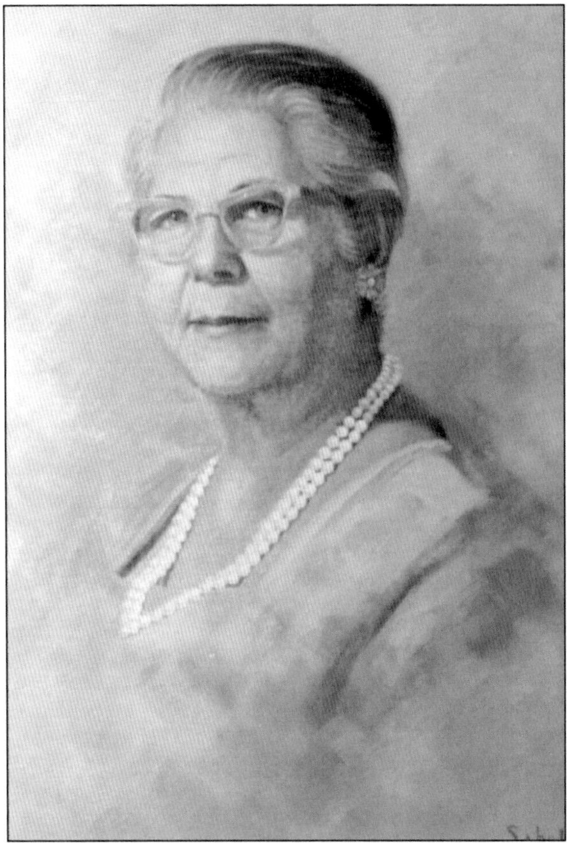

This is Anna Puntillo, who opened Mama Puntillo's restaurant in 1965. The restaurant, named in her honor, operated on Forty-Fifth Street for almost 20 years. The business was a popular place to host banquets.

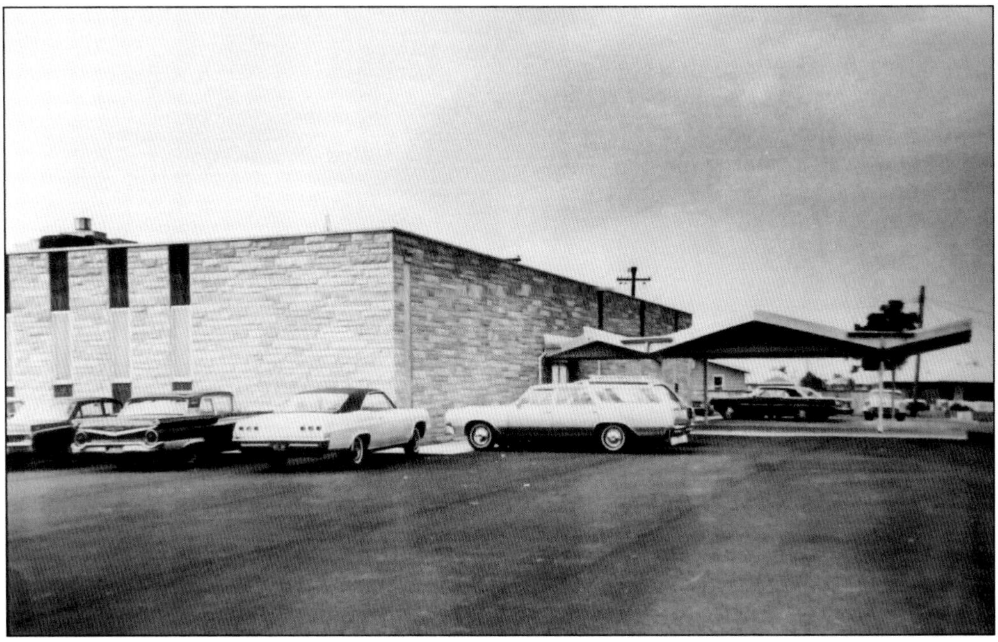

This is Mama Puntillo's. Two other proprietors operated at the site after it closed in 1984. The building then fell into disrepair and had to be razed due to flooding in the basement.

In this 1953 photograph is Julius Szur (left), Bill Blink (right), and his daughter Bonnie. Szur owned the original barbershop in town. Some barbershops faced challenges during the next decade, when young men emulated the Beatles and let their hair grow.

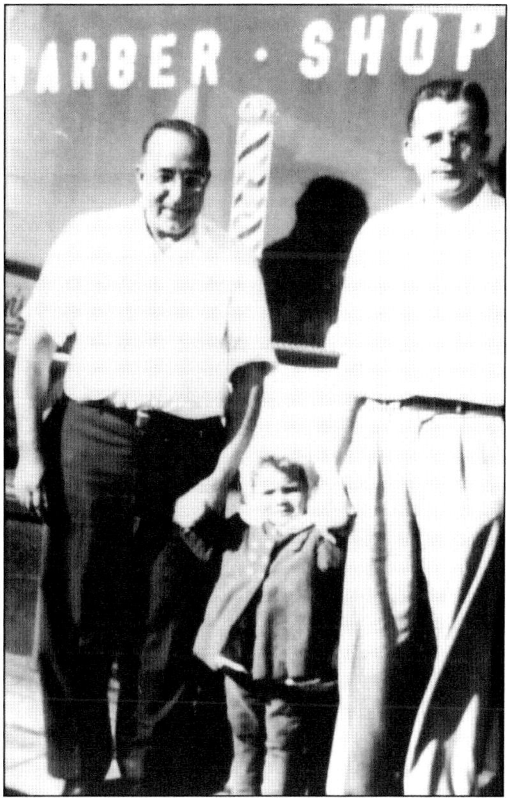

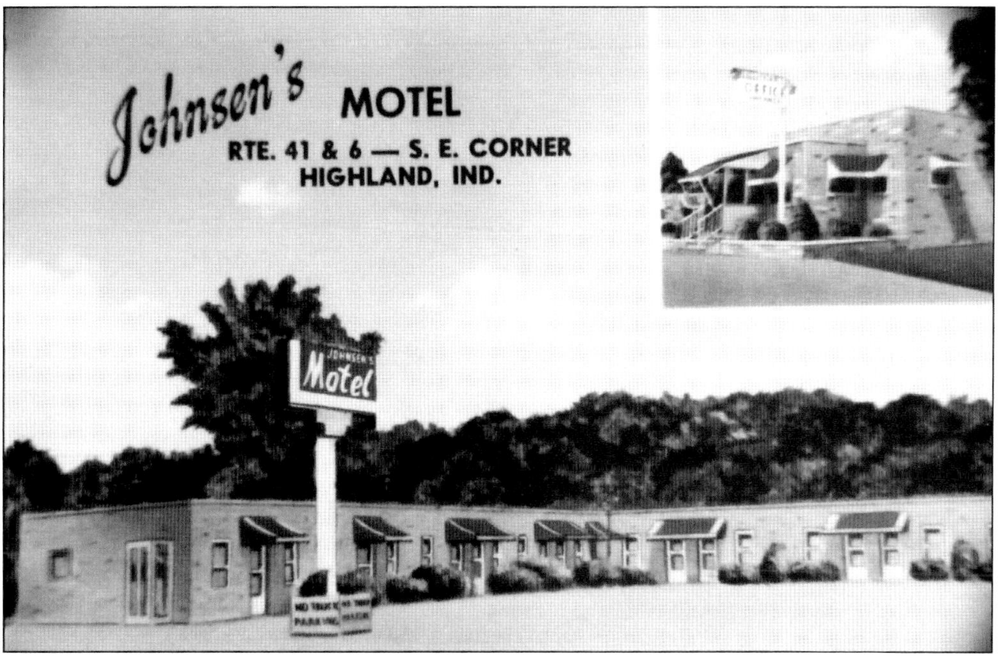

Motels like Johnsen's were once prevalent on US Route 41. That changed as the interstate system developed. Now, a traveler can drive for miles and miles on Route 41 and see only remnants of past motels long out of business.

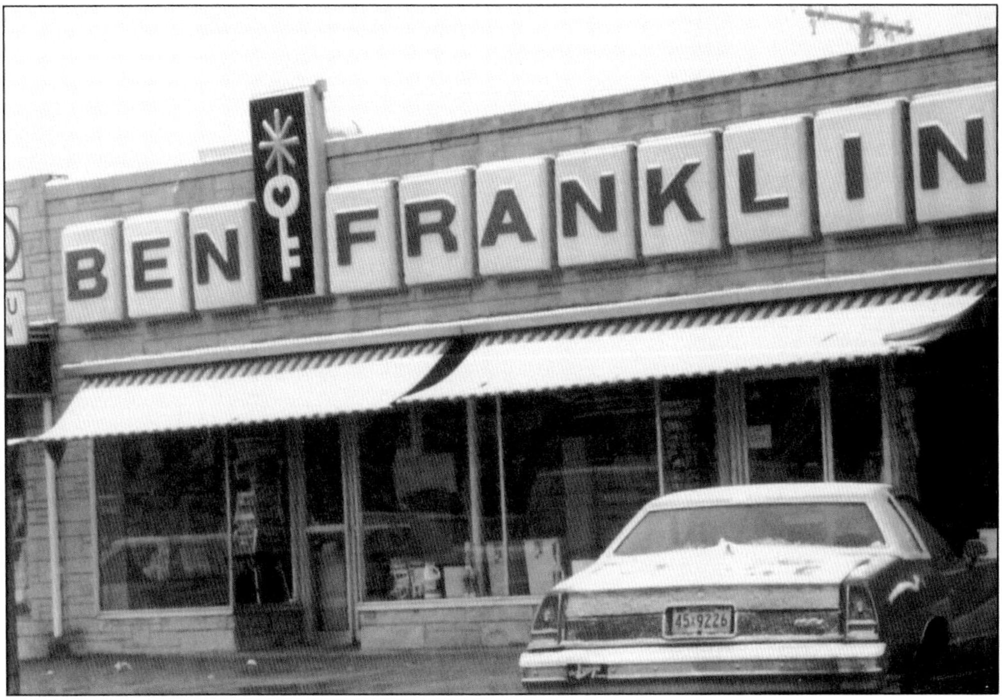

The Ben Franklin Store on Highway Avenue is shown here in 1984. Before Jo-Ann Fabrics or Michael's, there was Ben Franklin. At one time, Ben Franklin had 2,500 stores in 47 states. One estimate now lists 112 sites nationwide, with four in Indiana. None of the four are in Highland.

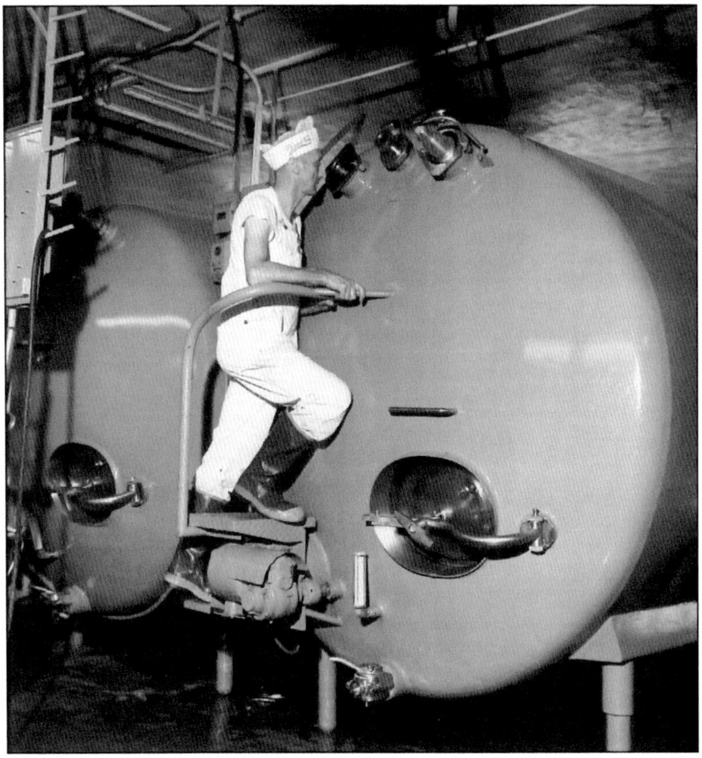

An unidentified worker is pictured inside the Pleasant View Dairy, which has been in operation since 1948. In a *Northwest Indiana Times* story from 1996, Bill Leep, one of the owners of Pleasant View Dairy, described his workforce: "Everyone who works here, lives here. Our kids are in your kids' classes." The Leep family has been a large part of the Highland business community in various ways for decades.

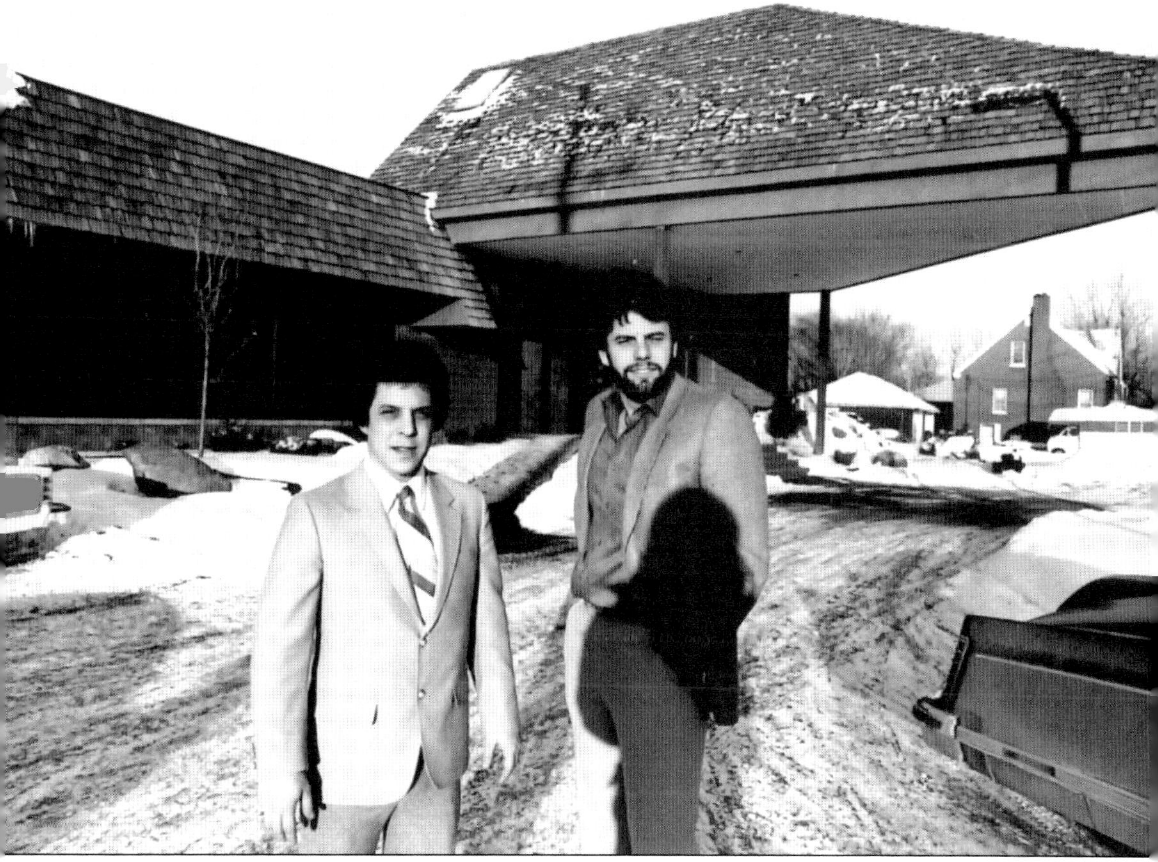

This 1982 photograph shows the optimistic managers at a restaurant called Courtney's on Forty-Fifth Street. They picked a bad time to open an upscale establishment. By the end of 1982, the national unemployment rate had risen to over 10 percent. Locally, thousands of steelworkers were laid off, and many never returned to their jobs. Courtney's closed, and several other businesses tried to make it at the large building at this site. The most recent was a place called Zuni's, which closed at the end of 2016 during the holiday season.

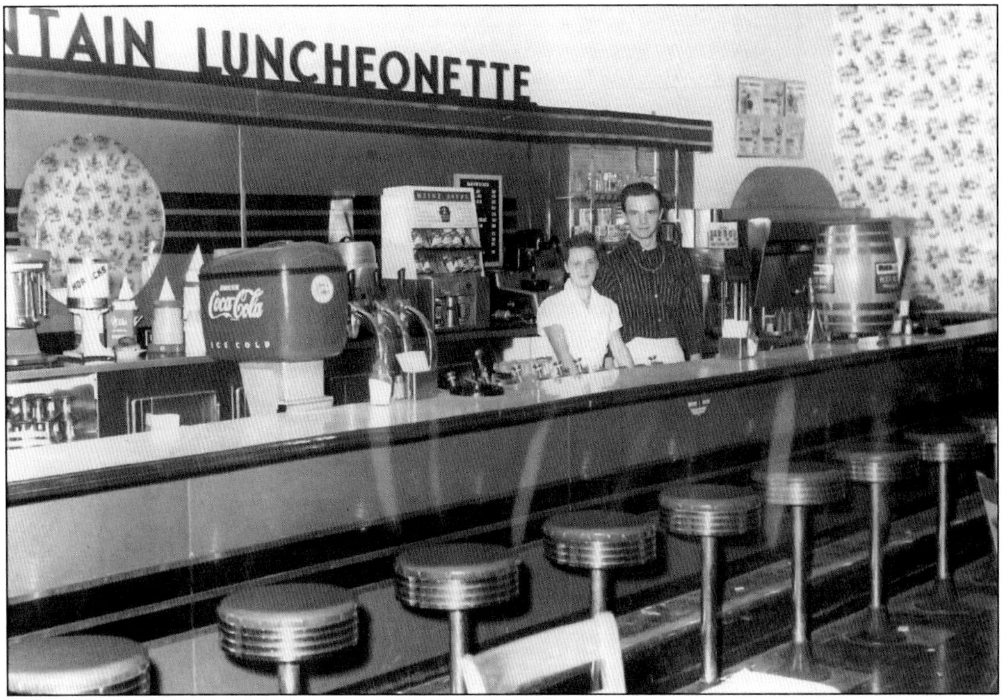

This image brings back memories of the late 1950s and early 1960s. This soda shop was located in the middle of Ken Ridge Drugs. Dining areas like this provided a casual place for people to socialize.

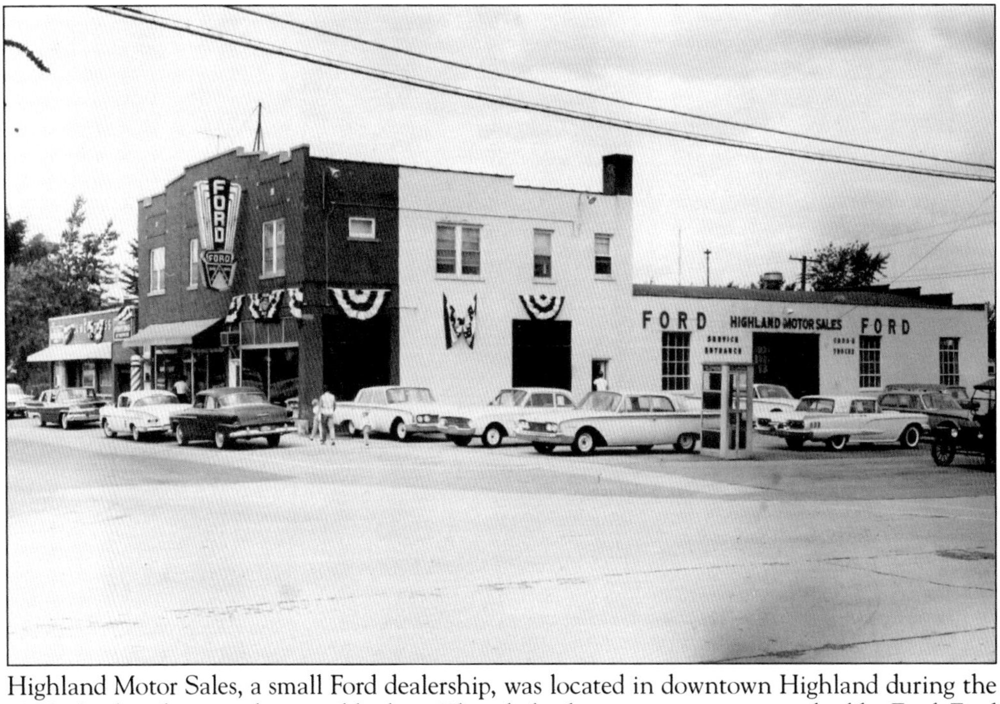

Highland Motor Sales, a small Ford dealership, was located in downtown Highland during the 1960s. In this photograph, a good-looking Thunderbird is sitting next to a much older Ford. Ford stopped production of Thunderbirds in 2005.

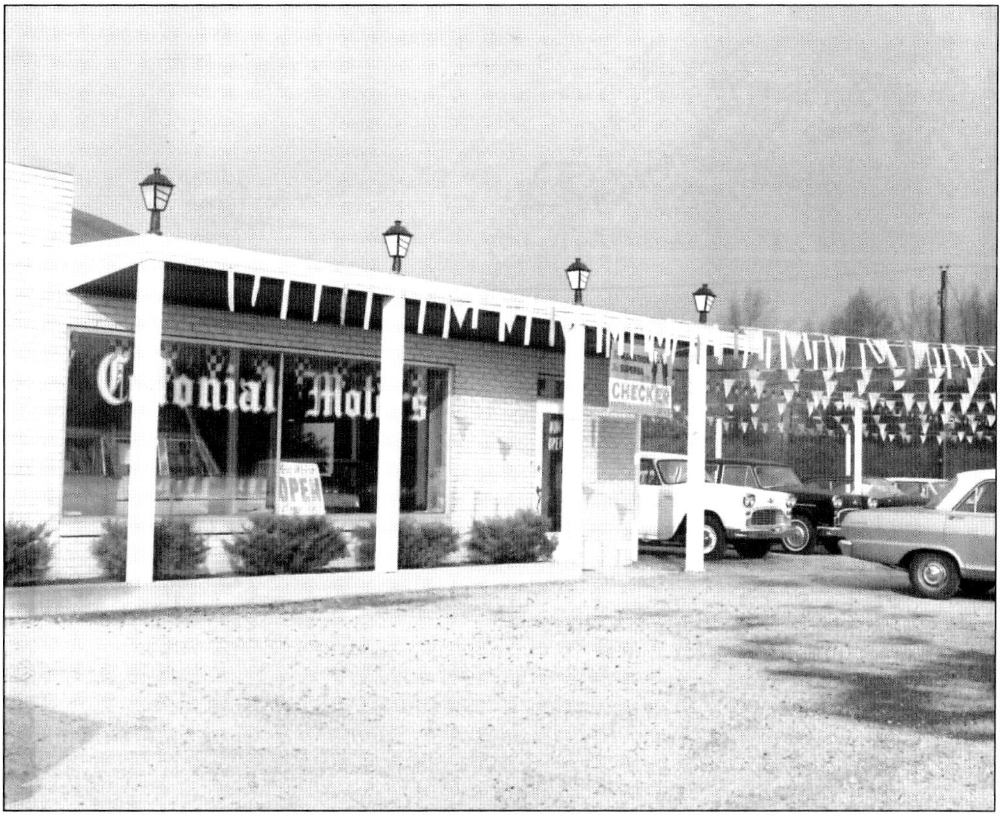

Colonial Motors was a small dealership located on US Route 41. In the second row are Checker Motors cars, which were often used as taxis in the 1960s.

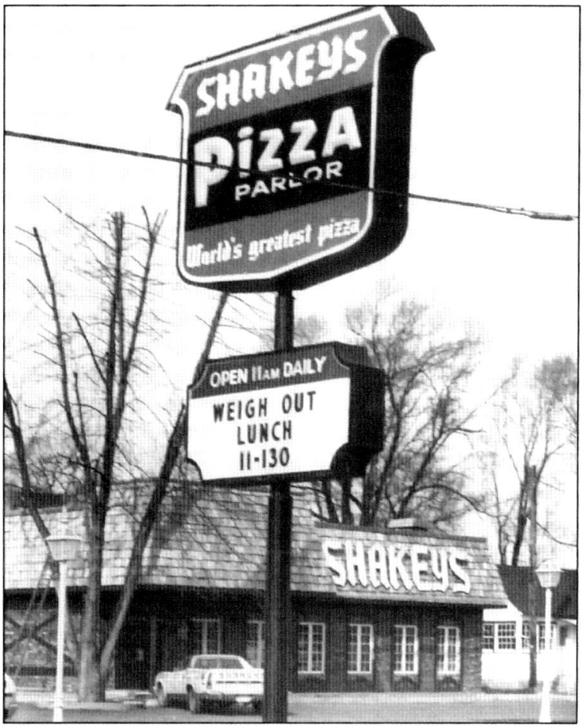

This sign refers to the practice of a "weigh out lunch," in which lunch prices were determined by weight as a lunchtime diner put his or her plate on a scale. Shakey's Pizza, which opened its first location in Sacramento, California, has been in business for over 60 years. However, there has been no Shakey's in Highland for a long time.

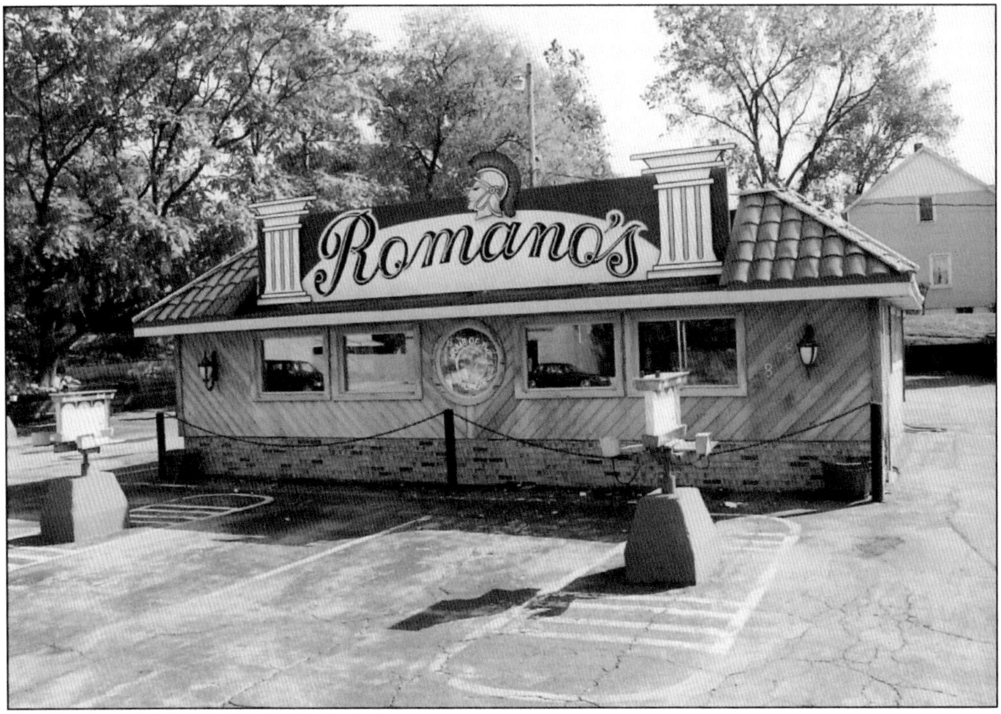

Romano's was a Ridge Road fixture starting in the 1940s. Patrons could eat from their cars drive-in style if they chose. Romano's, which has now been owned by three generations, has moved to a site in Griffith. A restaurant called Amici's opened at this site, and the owners remodeled the building. The Romano family moved to Highland from West Virginia in the late 1930s.

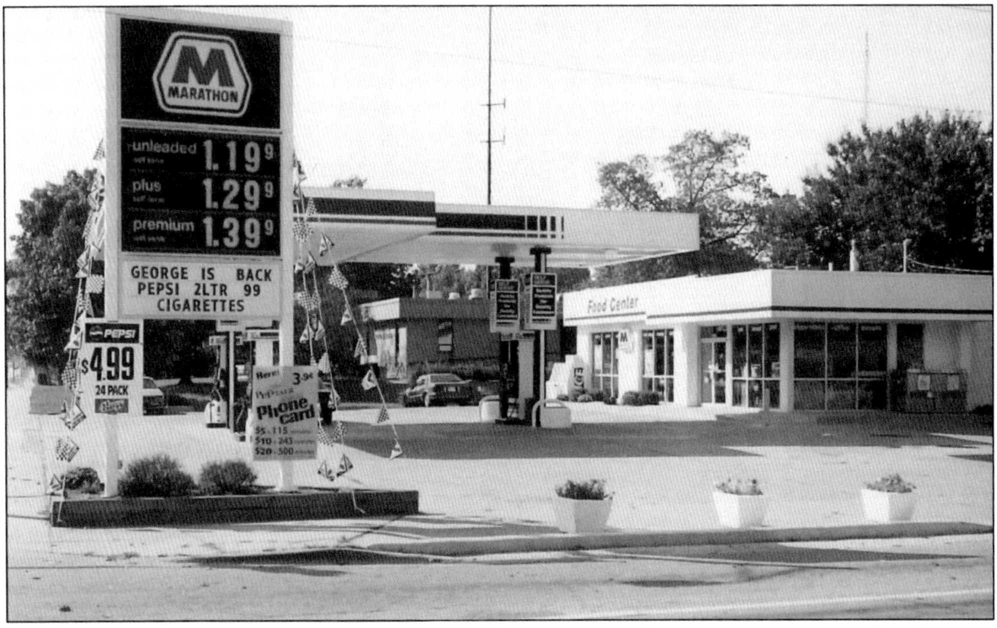

The Marathon station on Ridge Road is pictured at a time when gas prices were a bit cheaper. It is not known who "George" was, but he was back from somewhere. The station is still at this corner but under different ownership. The Highland Town Hall is visible in the background.

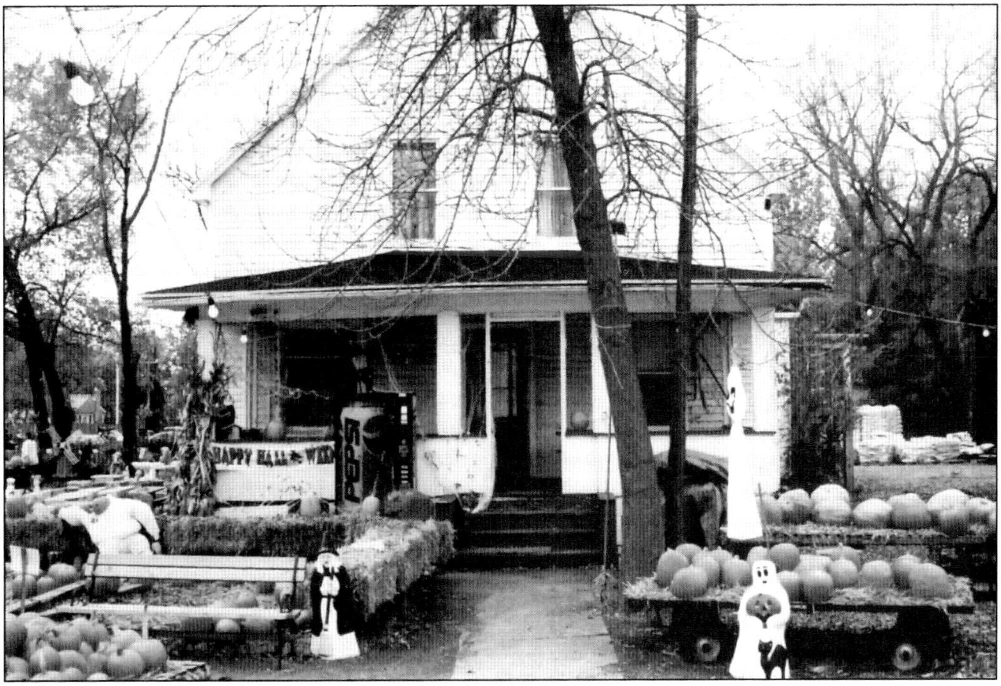

This is a front view of Mary Ann's Garden Center, a locally owned business on Ridge Road. This enticing fall scene features Halloween decorations. After Mary Ann retired, her business was sold to a local landscaping and garden center.

The *Calumet Press* building is shown here at its Kennedy Avenue site. The small weekly newspaper described itself as "A Voice of the Ridge." Former Highland clerk-treasurer Paul Doherty described media outlets like the *Calumet Press* as vital to maintaining an informed community. The paper stopped publishing in 2004. Other small newspapers in the area also folded in this era when the Internet started to dominate the media.

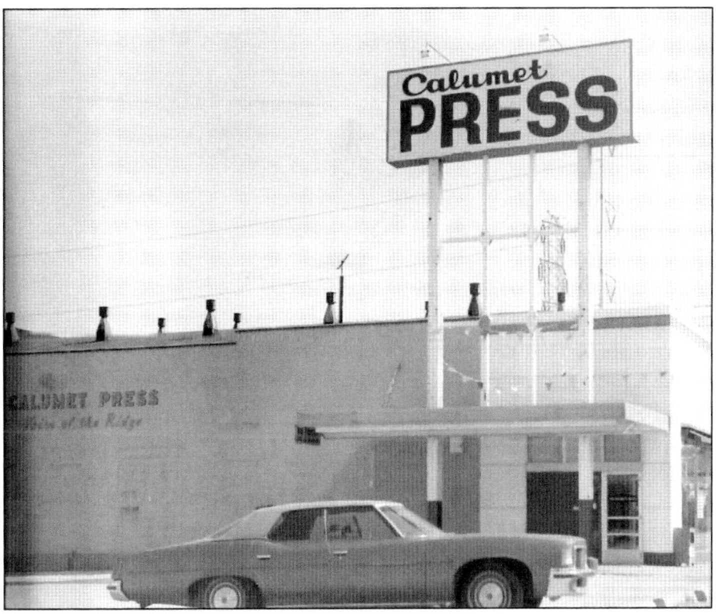

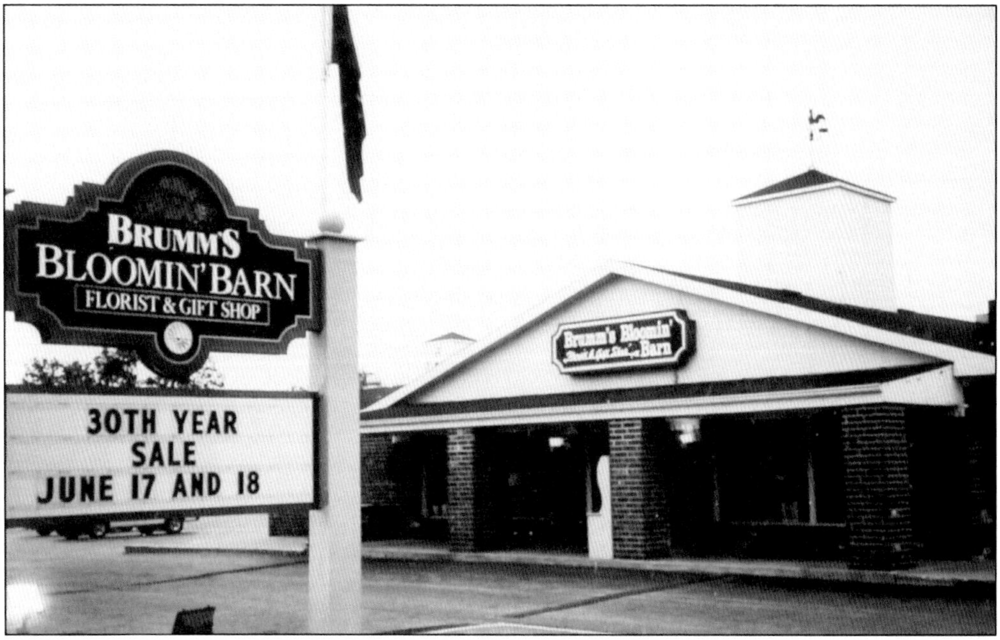

Brumm's Bloomin' Barn was founded by Jerry Brumm and his wife, Nancy, in 1970, when Forty-Fifth Street was a two-lane road. The shop has been at this location for all of its 47 years. Brumm's Bloomin' Barn, like many small businesses, feels the crunch of competition from chain stores and Internet businesses. Jerry Brumm recalls when Highland had "dollar days" throughout the town that attracted customers to local businesses like his.

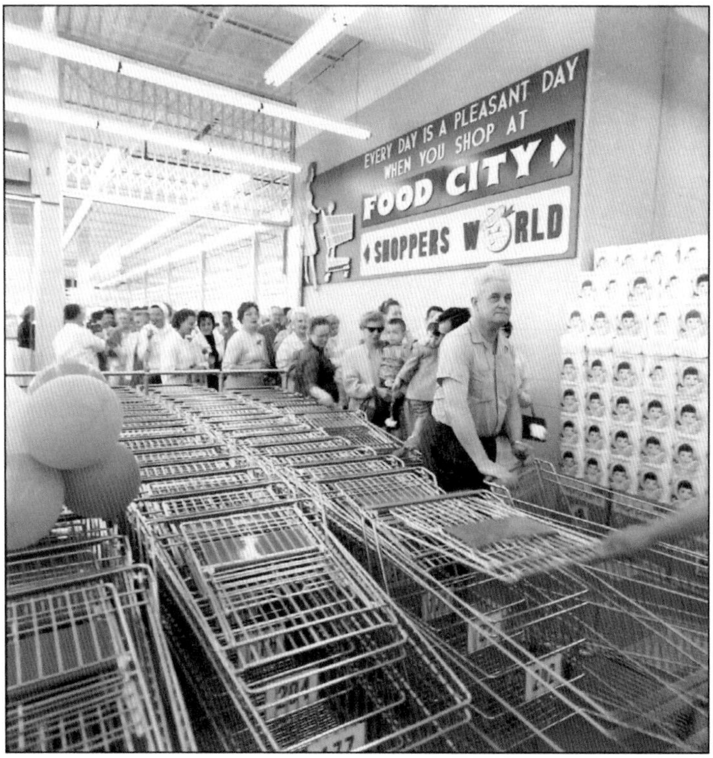

Grocery shoppers are shown eagerly entering a food store in the mid-1960s. Today, many people take "mega-marts" for granted, but 50 years ago, large grocery stores were just coming into being. This store was connected to Shoppers World. These businesses operated adjacent to the Topps location.

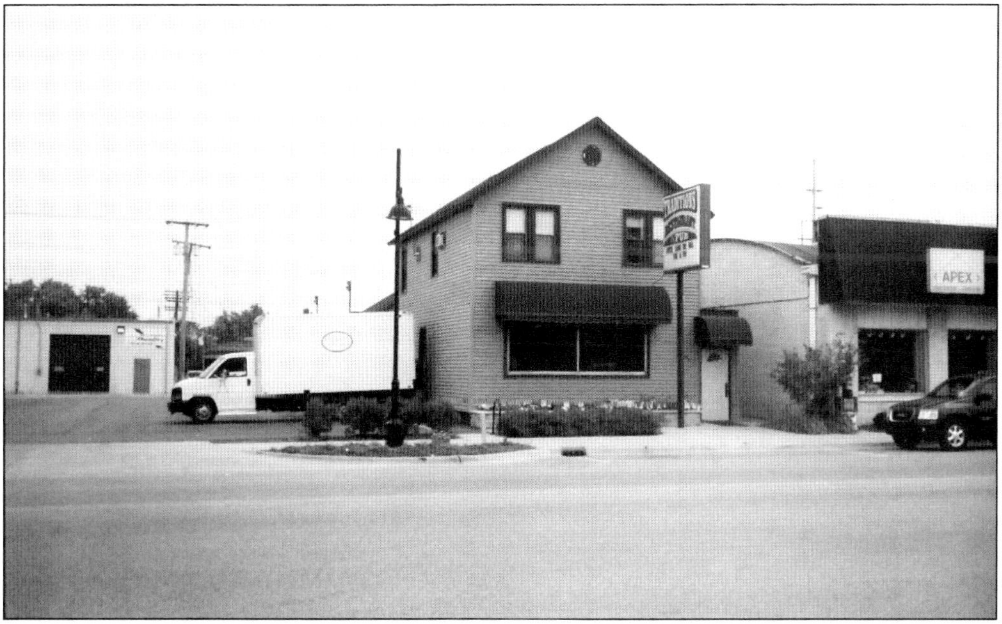

Traditions Restaurant and other restaurants at this site have been operated by seven different sets of owners since 1910. The building, erected in 1896, has gone through renovations inside and out and was moved one door to the west from its original location in the early 1920s.

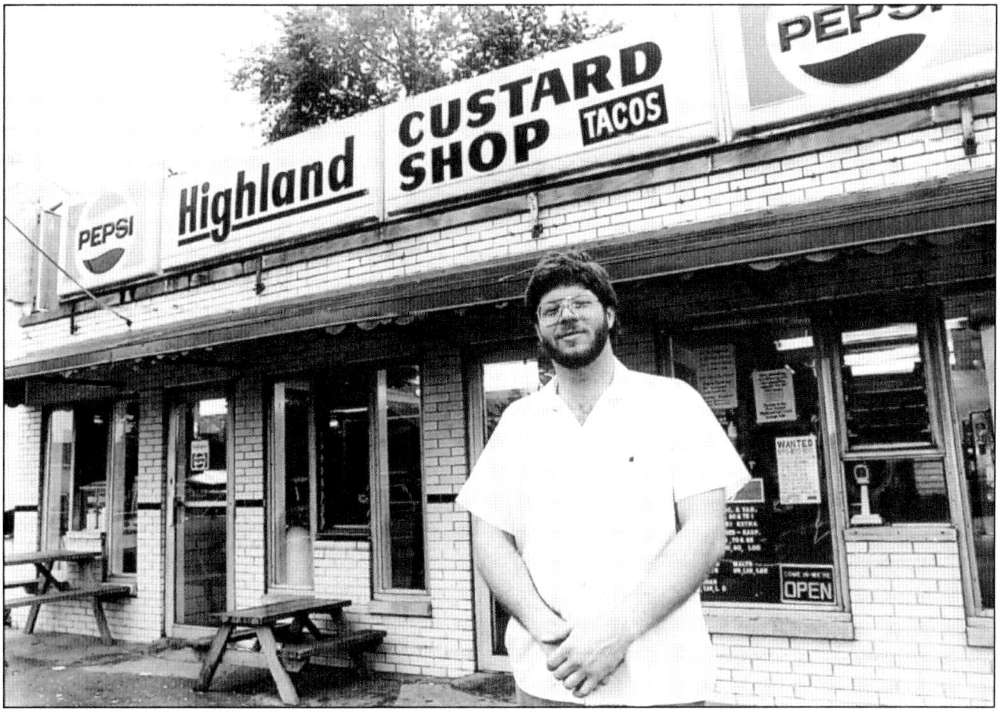

Every small town seems to have a friendly fast-food/ice cream shop like this one. Pictured here is Tom Porter, who operated the Highland Custard Shop from 1982 to 1994. After 1994, it became an Italian restaurant called Anthony's, which provided a cozy and sometimes boisterous place to eat.

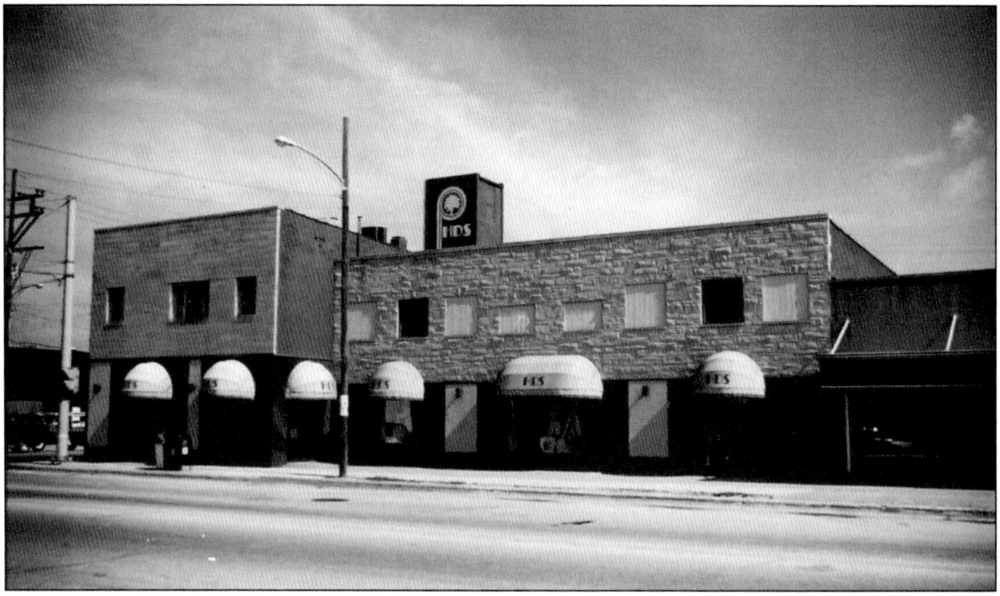

At one time, the Highland Department Store dominated one side of Highway Avenue downtown. The store closed in the early 1990s, and several businesses now occupy the space.

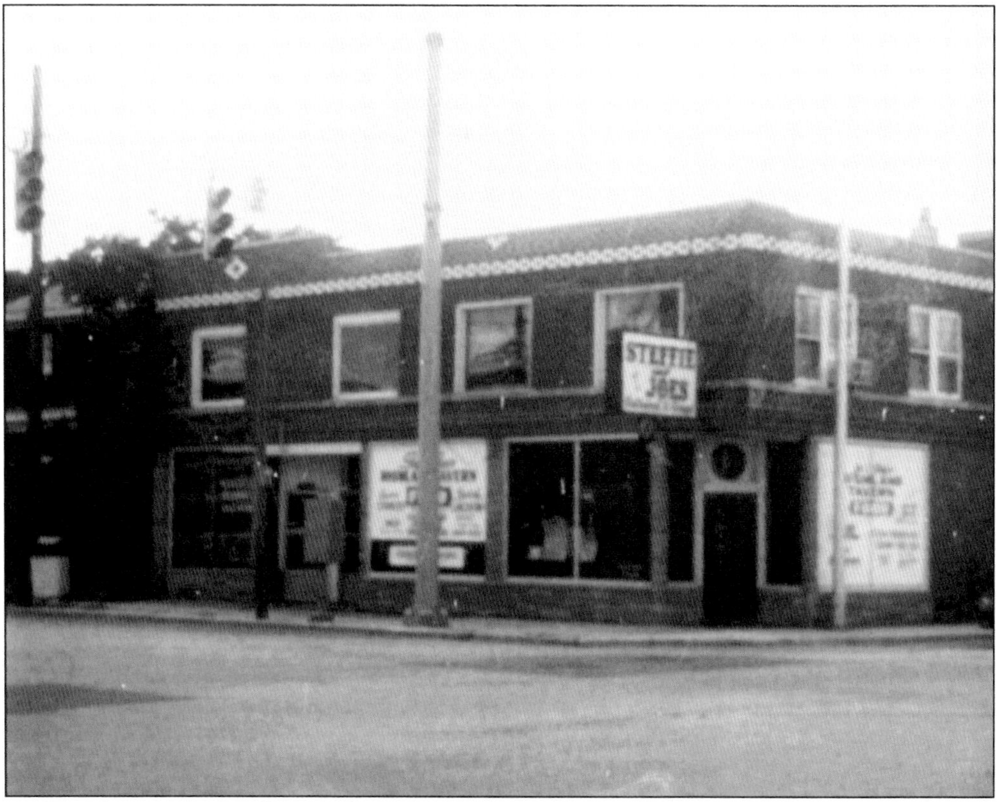

Steffie and Joe's was a locally owned restaurant on the corner of Highway and Kennedy Avenues. The site is now a town parking lot that serves businesses operating in the small downtown area.

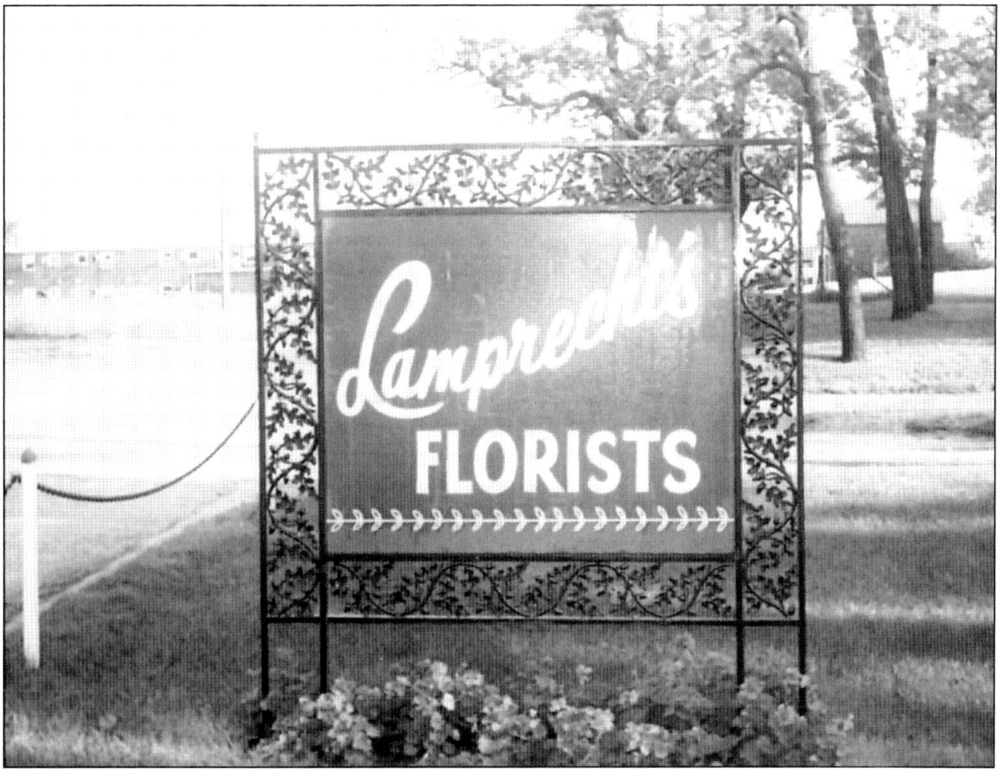

Lamprecht's was a Highland institution for over 92 years. The business, located on Kleinman Road, was opened by Charles and Hattie Lamprecht in 1923 and closed in the spring of 2016.

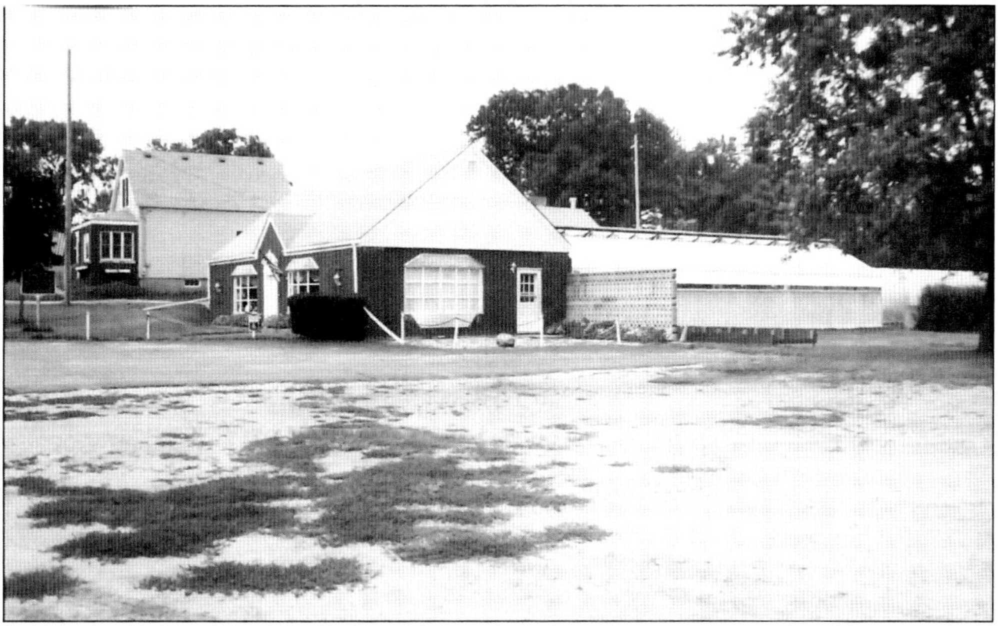

The Lamprecht's building (center) is shown here before its 2016 closing. The building was razed, and a crematory now sits in its place. A historical marker describing Dutch immigration to Highland still sits on the spot.

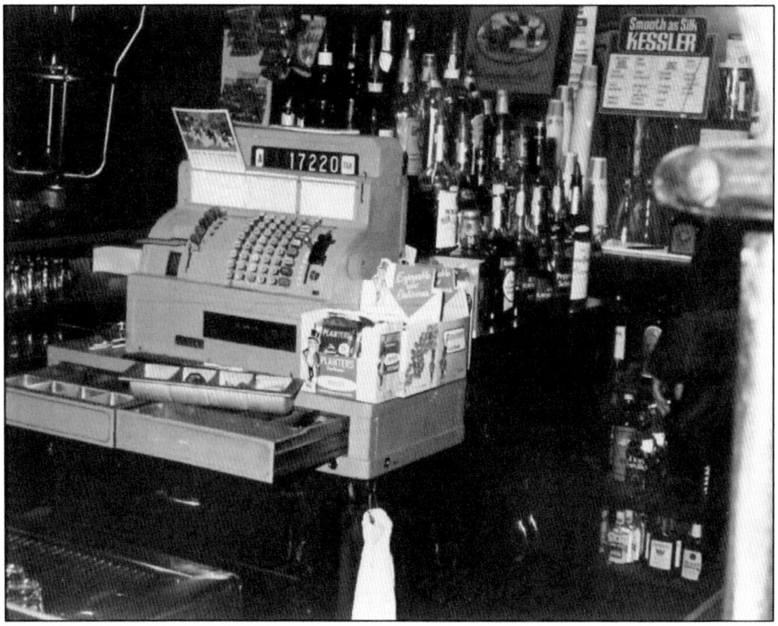

This cash register is of a type that is rarely seen or used these days. The exact business where this particular model was located is not known, although based on the Kessler "Smooth as Silk" sign and the many bottles in the background, it was likely a bar.

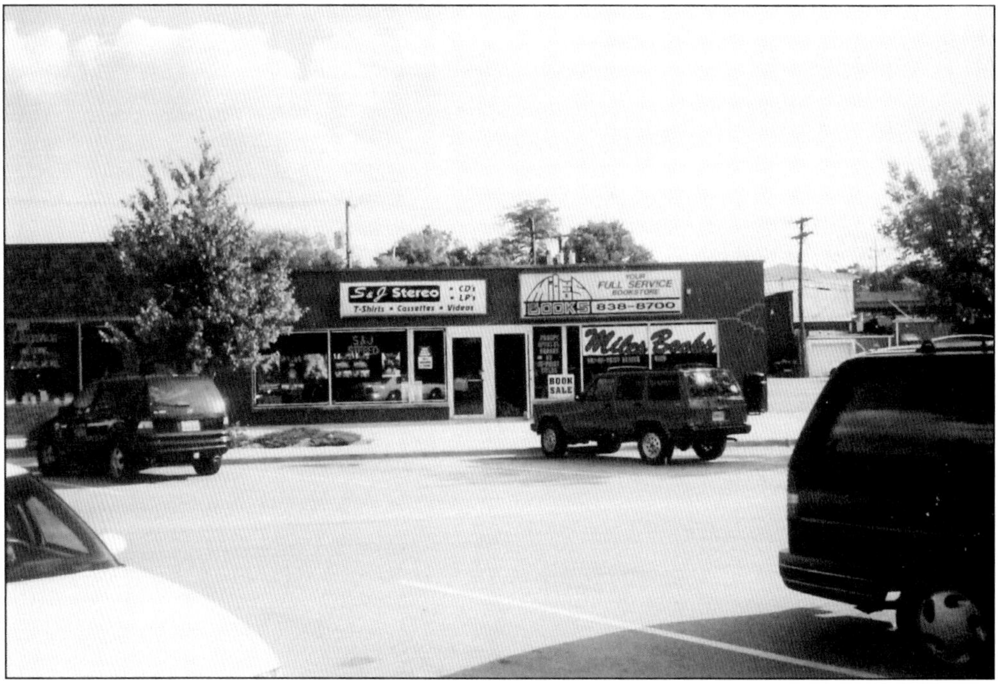

Here is a small section of downtown Highland in the 1980s. S&J Stereo no longer operates in Highland, although it still describes itself as the "last great record store in Indiana." Miles Books is one of the few remaining independent book stores in the area and now occupies a location on Jewett Avenue.

Three

"Keeping the Fire at the Shed"

This chapter's title has been the Highland Fire Department's motto since the early days, according to chief Bill Timmer. "Keeping the fire at the shed" referred to keeping the fire away from the rest of the farm.

Today, the challenges facing fire departments are different. Keeping the fire at the shed has, for all intents and purposes, become keeping the fire from the neighborhood or even keeping it from the town. Highland is now considerably more urban and contains neighborhoods crowded with houses. Fires that spread can do damage in different ways.

In 21st-century Highland, there are other firefighting worries. Home wiring can present its own challenges, and furniture can be more combustible. In the event of any kind of terrorist attack, the Highland Fire Department might have to face other kinds of fires with different dangers.

Chief Timmer told the authors in late 2016 that past fire fighters "wouldn't recognize the Highland Fire Department now." Timmer has been fire chief since 1990 and said the department has modernized with the times.

Now, a computer screen high on the wall in the firehouse shows the activities of fire departments across the county. Massive fire trucks dwarf the smaller vehicles of the past.

Chief Timmer is the only full-time employee of the department. It has been modernized, and Timmer believes it has maintained its tradition of having well-trained citizen firefighters. "We are still blue collar and hands-on," he said.

Before 1950, Highland's population was below 6,000. But as the baby-boomer generation came into existence, the town's population ballooned to nearly 18,000 by 1960. The town had made do with a volunteer police force, but that changed in 1956 with the hiring of a chief and four full-time officers. "We view our role more so as a 'guardian' rather than 'enforcers,' " said current Highland Police Department chief Peter Hojnicki. He has been chief since 2002.

"In many respects, Highland shares many of the same challenges that both rural and urban municipalities face across the nation," Hojnikci said. "Some of which include: the media's often negative portrayal of law enforcement, increases in criminal activity, and budgetary concerns. However, Highland has also been fortunate with a rich history of town fathers who have always had a 'we care' philosophy. In that same respect, the personnel of the Highland Police Department consisting of sworn, civilian and volunteers carry that same viewpoint."

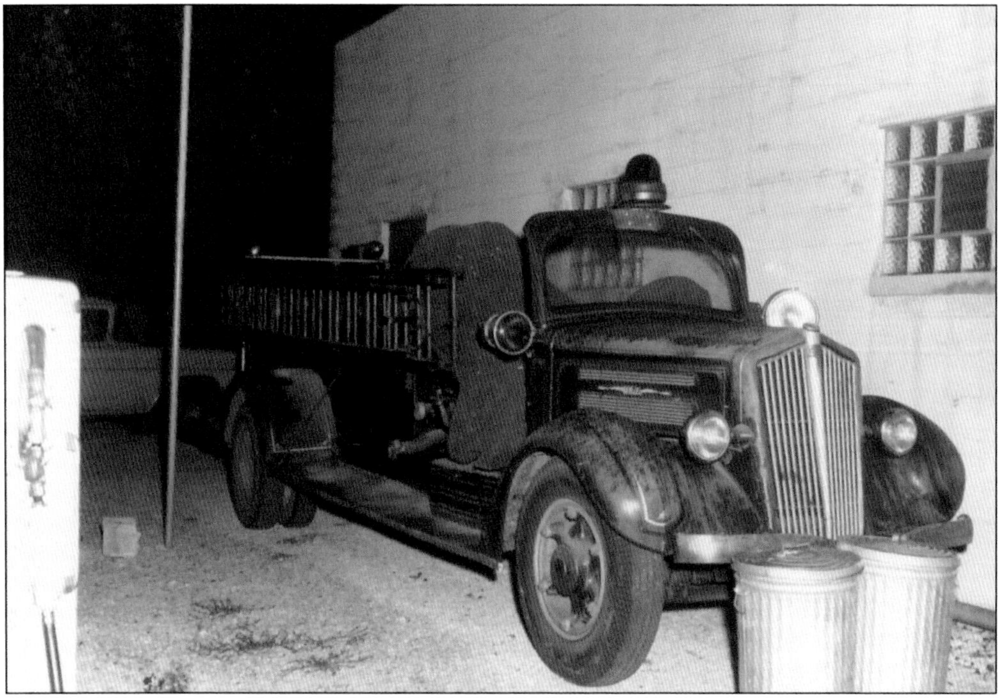

One of the first—if not *the* first—fire trucks in Highland is pictured here in the 1930s. The building it is parked next to looks nothing like the Central Fire Station that is now located on Highway Avenue.

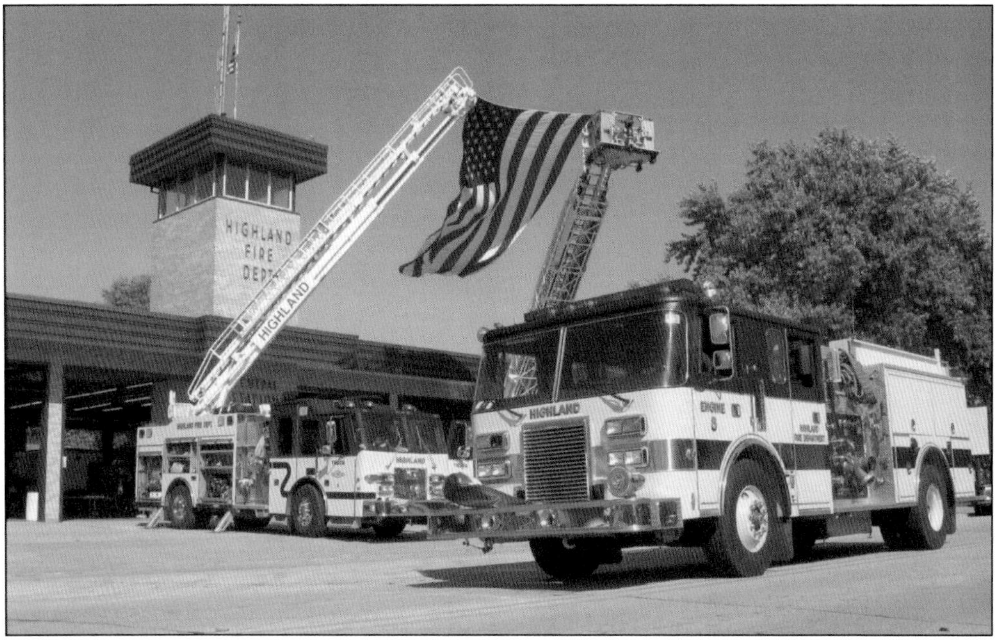

Highland Fire Department trucks are looming in the fall sun directly outside the Central Fire Station on Highway Avenue during a public open house in October 2011. These imposing vehicles are a little larger than the 1930s model shown at the top of this page. (Photograph by Theresa Pecsek.)

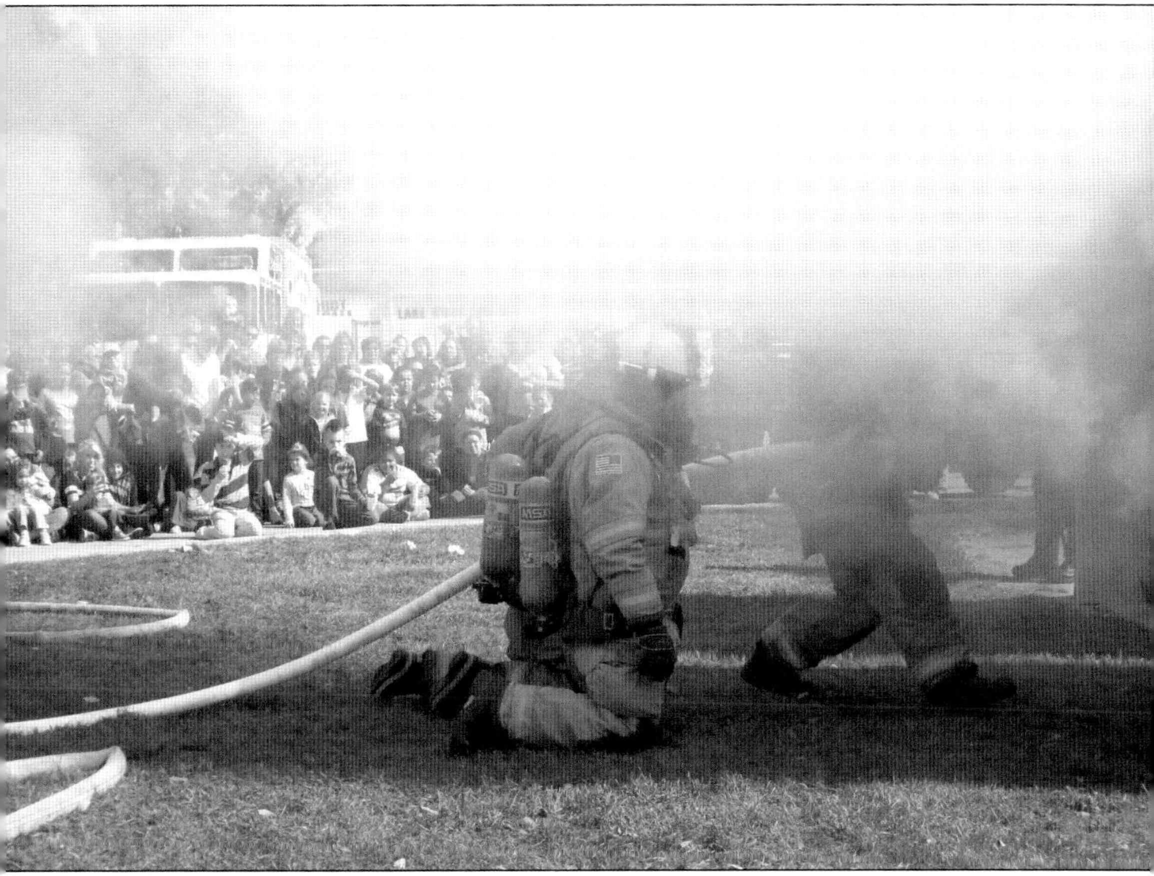

These Highland firefighters are demonstrating firefighting techniques at a public open house at the Central Fire Station on Highway Avenue. The flying water and high-tech outfits the firemen are wearing provide a strong image. The audience seems awed by the demonstration. The department has had to confront some large blazes over the years. This demonstration took place in October 2015. (Photograph by Theresa Pecsek.)

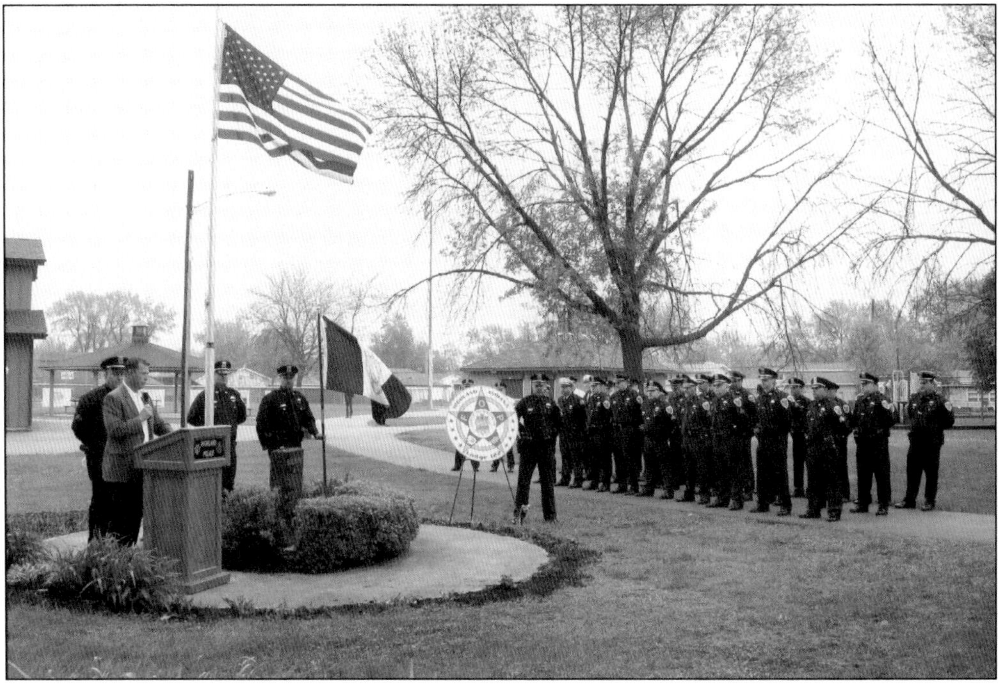

This May 9, 2015, ceremony at Markley Park was held in honor of Robert Markley, a Highland police officer killed in the line of duty. Ryan Markley, Robert Markley's son, is pictured speaking at the podium during the ceremony. (Photograph by Theresa Pecsek.)

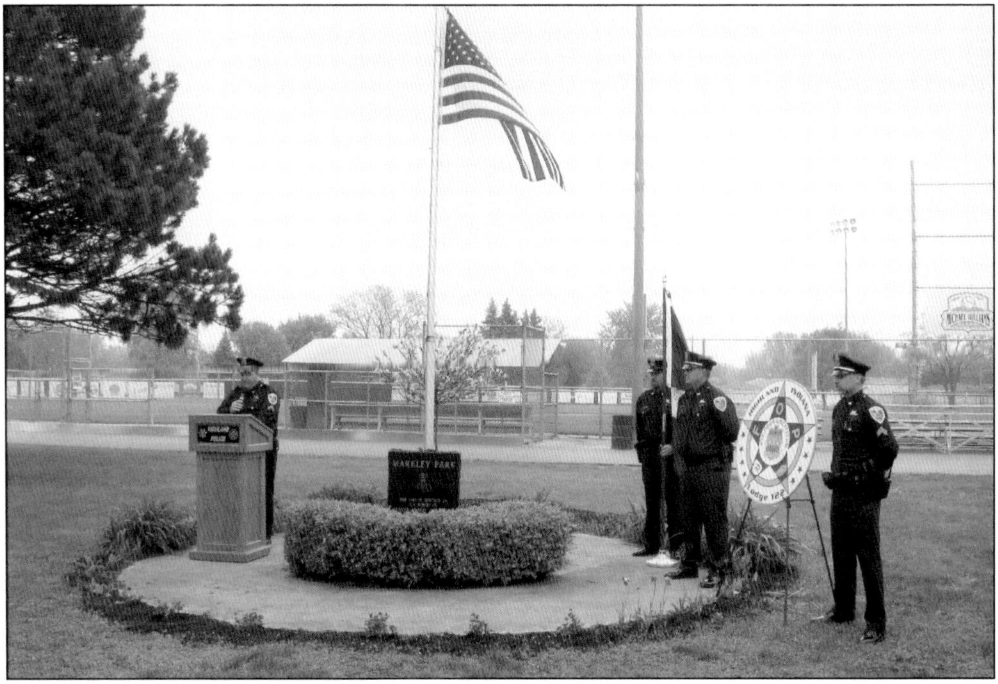

The inscription on the black stone reads: "This park is dedicated to the memory of Robert J. Markley who gave his life in the line of duty on March 10, 1978." Fortunately, no Highland police officers have been killed in the line of duty since then. (Photograph by Theresa Pecsek.)

This is a 1975 photograph of Highland Police Department officer Robert Markley. Three years later, Markley was killed in the line of duty when he was struck by a drunk driver. Markley was directing traffic, and died on March 10, 1978. He left behind a wife and son.

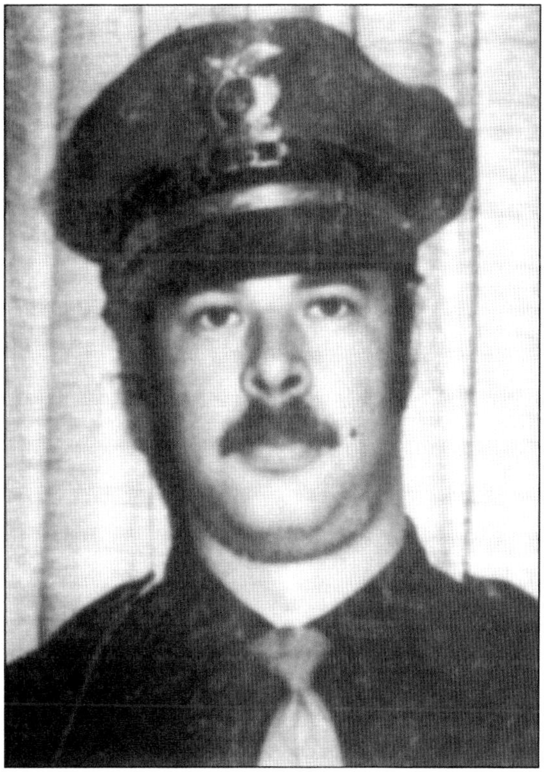

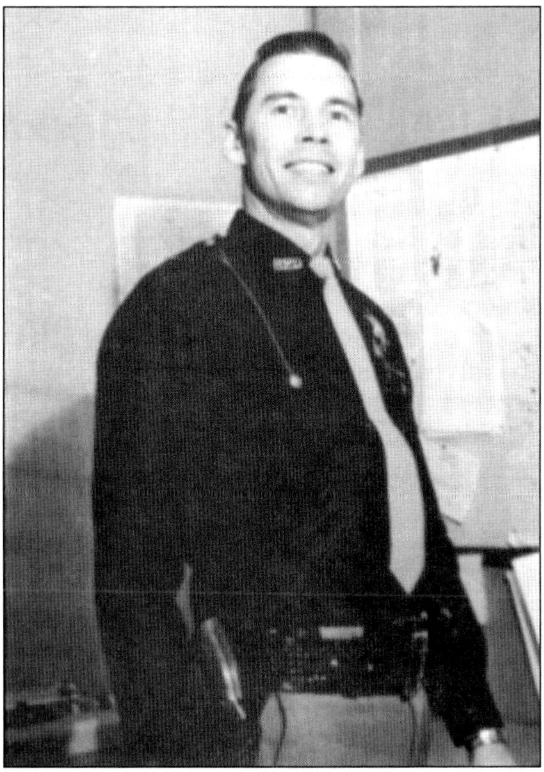

Highland Police Department officer Donald Sheppard was killed on November 12, 1971, during a routine traffic stop. Sheppard was shot and killed by a prisoner who had escaped from a Michigan City facility. He was on the verge of his 35th birthday. Sheppard was survived by a wife and three children. A town park is named in his honor.

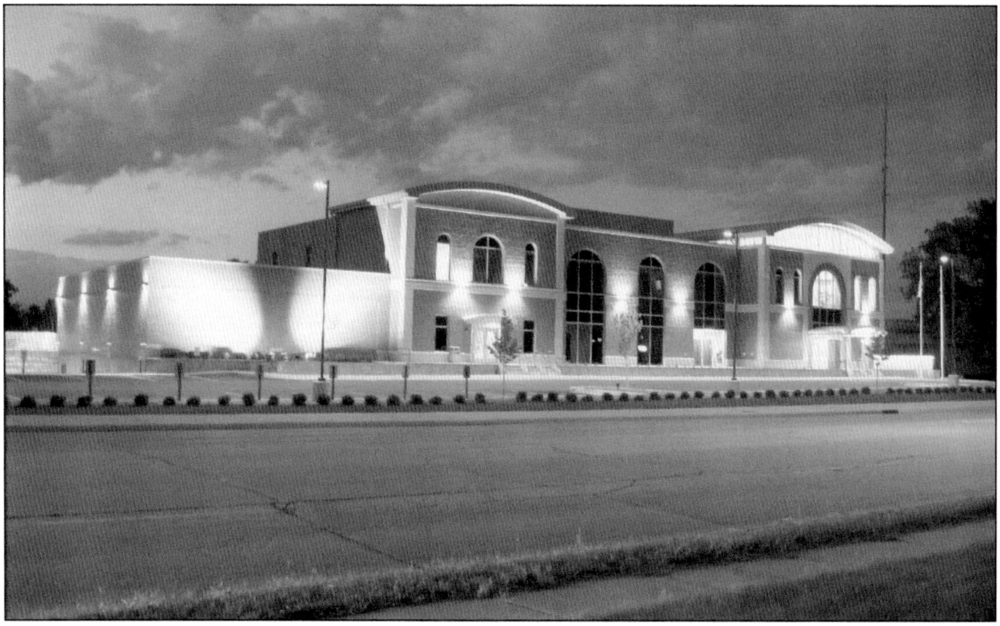

The current Highland Police Department headquarters opened on Ridge Road in February 2016. The former police headquarters was attached to the Town Hall. Some citizens think the station is a bit extravagant, while others believe its towering presence may serve as a crime deterrent. (Photograph by Theresa Pecsek.)

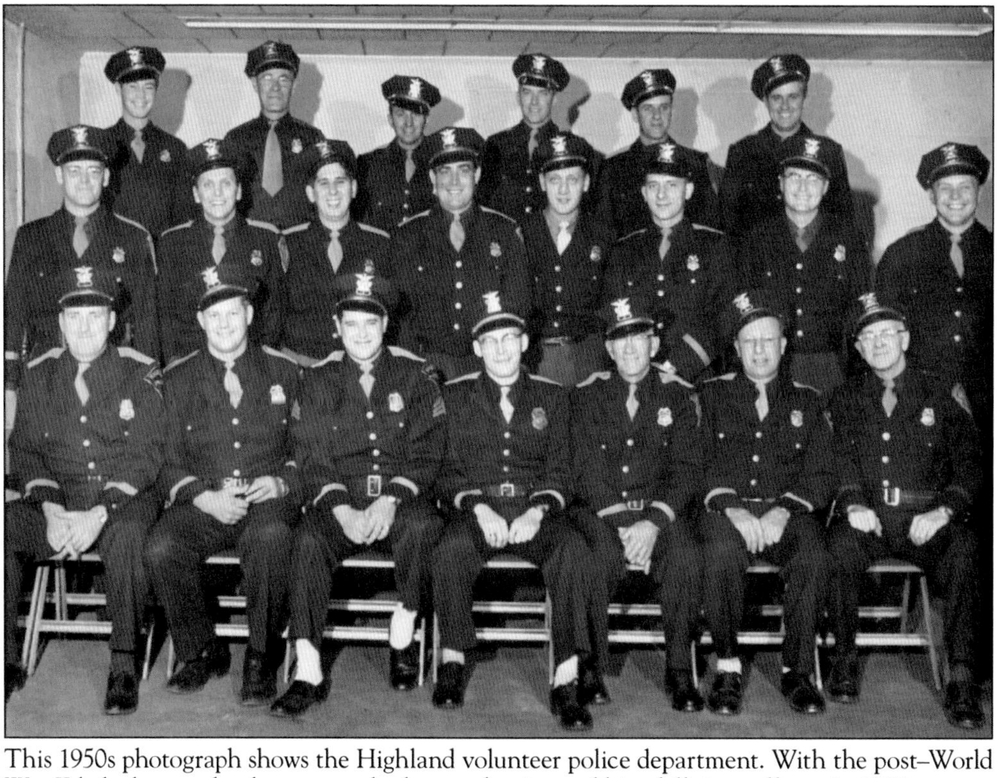

This 1950s photograph shows the Highland volunteer police department. With the post–World War II baby boom, the department had to modernize and hire full-time officers in 1956.

Grade-school students in Halloween costumes learn about the Highland Civil Defense. This photograph was taken at the height of the Cold War, when there were widespread fears about a nuclear attack by the Soviet Union. Children were taught to cover their heads and hide under their desks in case of a nuclear strike.

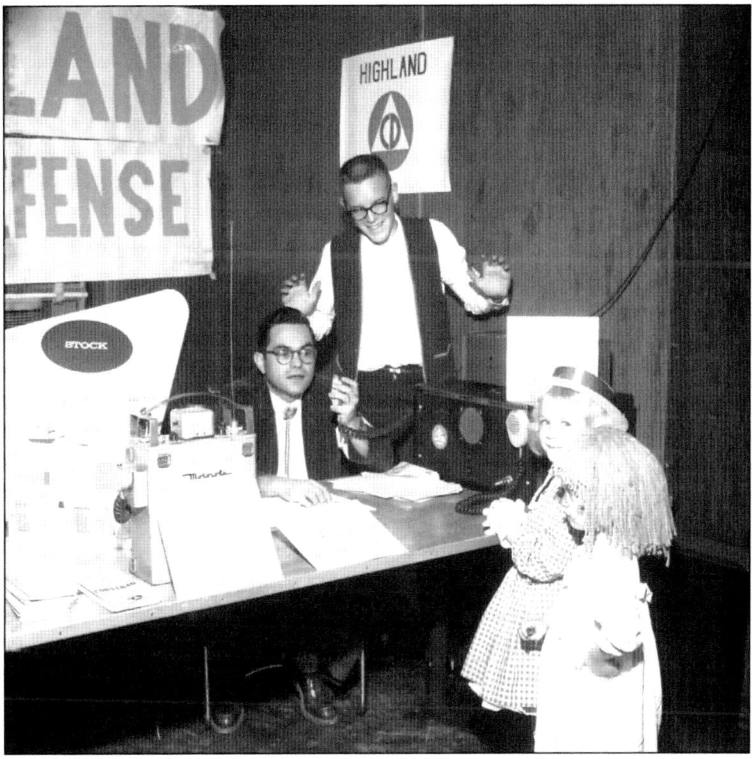

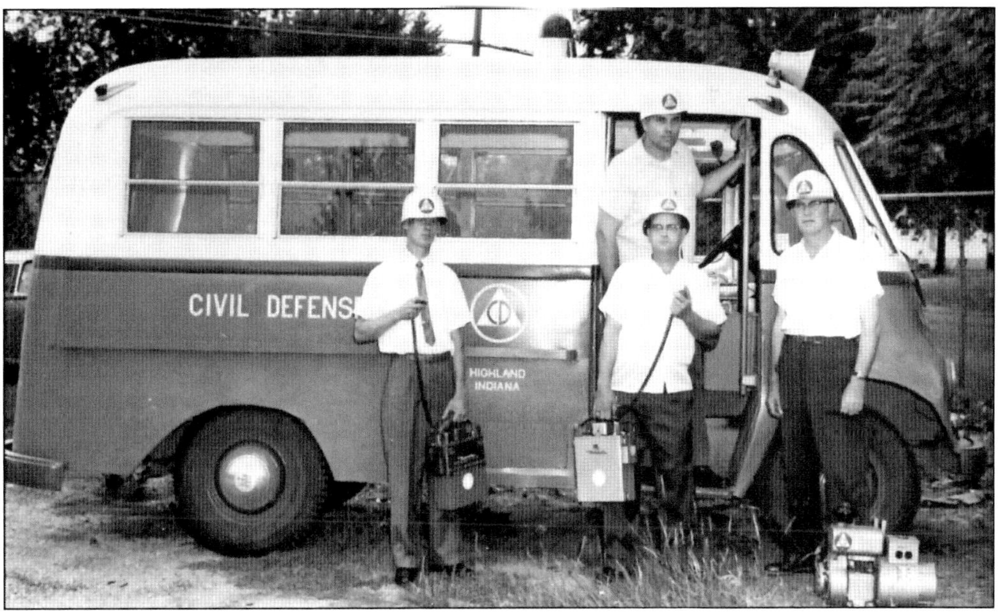

Civil defense officers are shown holding communications equipment outside a van during the tense times of 1967. Today, the civil defense function has been taken over by VIPs (Volunteers in Public Service), which augments the Highland Police Department.

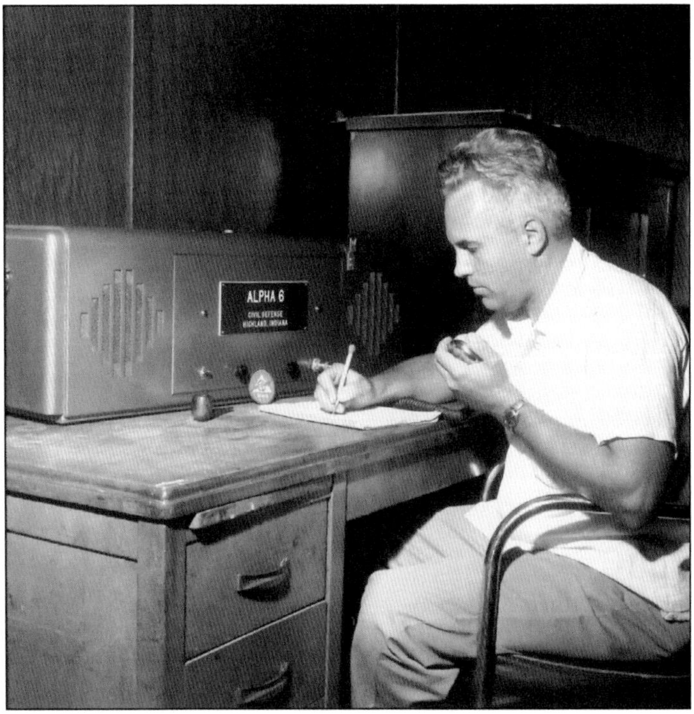

During the World War II and Cold War eras, the civil defense was to serve as a backup emergency communications system in case of an attack that most feared could come from the Soviet Union. Pictured here is Bill Swiss, communications officer.

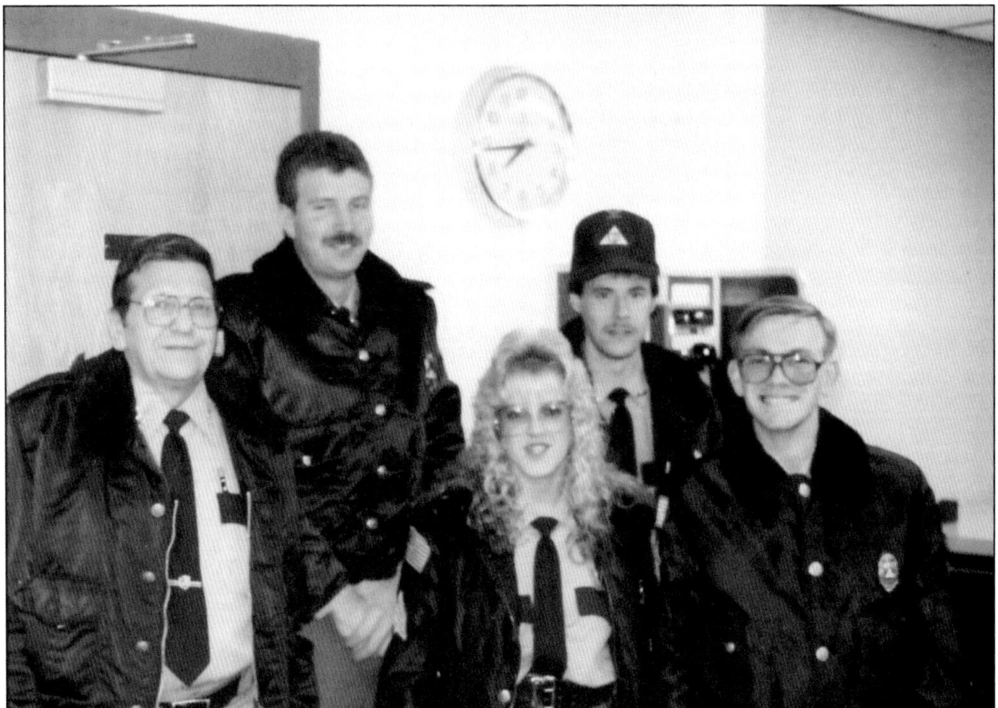

The Highland Civil Defense took on a slightly different role in the 1980s. This squad acted as a volunteer auxiliary to the police department. Joe Szendrey (standing at far left) headed the group.

Four

HIGHLAND AND WAR

Tragically, war affects all generations. World War II has been called the "good war" fought by what many have labeled as "America's greatest generation." The United States' involvement in that war spanned almost four years. The country was united against Hitler's imperialism and butchery in Europe and Japan's assault on the South Pacific.

The Vietnam War divided the country. Some Americans became wary as the war dragged on and wondered if the incursion into Southeast Asia was warranted. Others thought that dissent sabotaged the war effort and was unpatriotic.

The two Gulf Wars still await history's judgement. The events of September 11, 2001, still traumatize the United States.

Regardless of politics or point of view on any war or military action, Highland remembers and honors those who have served in the armed services with two monuments. The first is located on a walking/bike trail that surrounds Wicker Park. The exact spot faces the always-busy intersection of Ridge Road and Indianapolis Boulevard. The square granite structure is about four feet high and has a torch-like flame. The flame is always lit, much like the eternal flame that adorns the grave of John F. Kennedy. A semicircular metal piece attached to the back of the structure contains this inscription: "In Honor Of Those Who Served."

Across the street from the granite structure is an even larger monument. The "Highway of Flags" was dedicated on May 25, 1975. Nine flagpoles rest on a white, crescent-shaped cement base. The middle pole is the tallest and supports the American flag. Below it, the other, slightly shorter eight poles list the names of eight governors. The monument dominates the busiest corner in Highland.

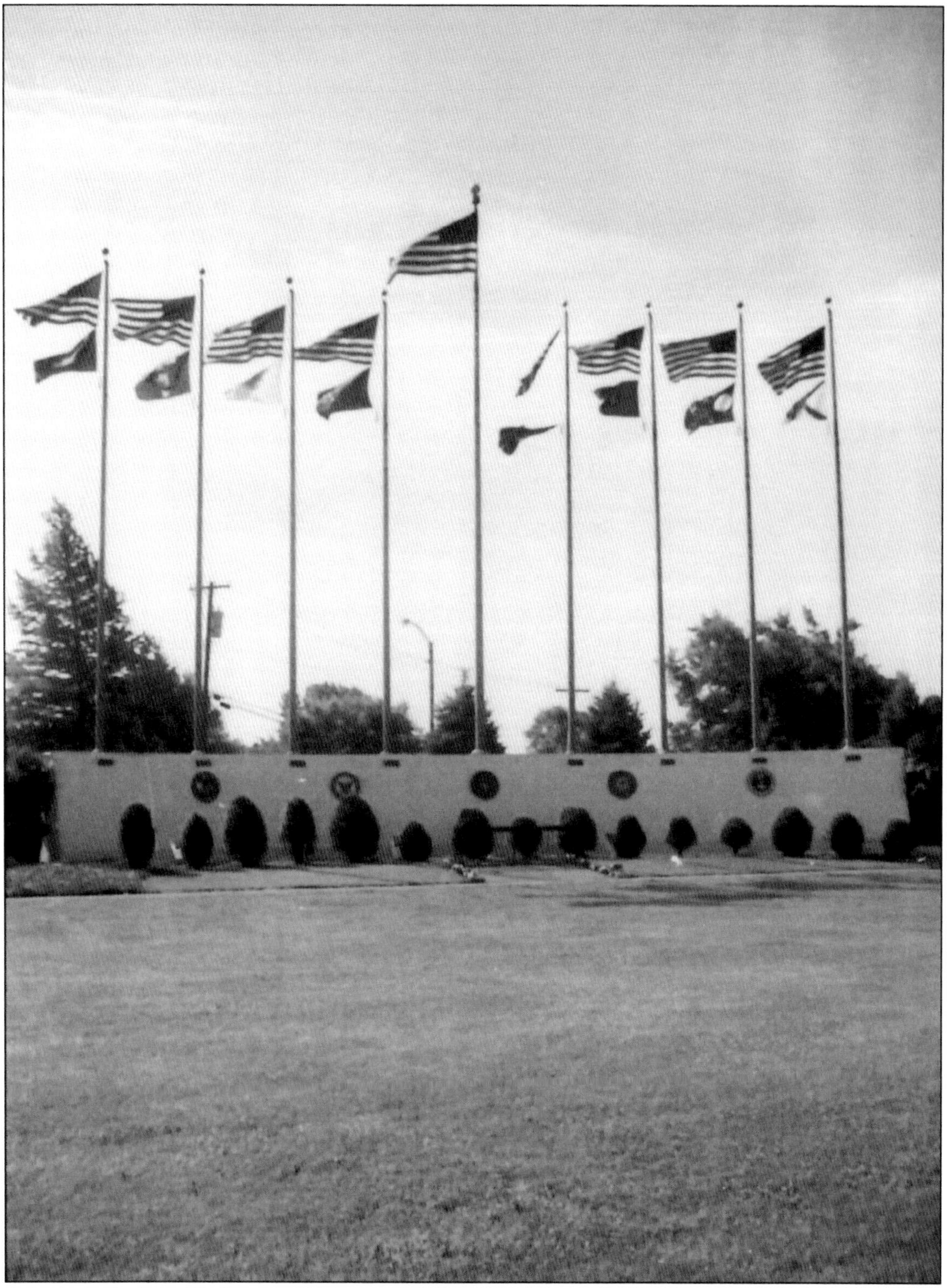

A full view of the Highway of Flags Veterans Memorial on a bright day reveals its majesty. The memorial, which can be seen from a distance when driving south on Route 41, is often a site of ceremonies and small protests.

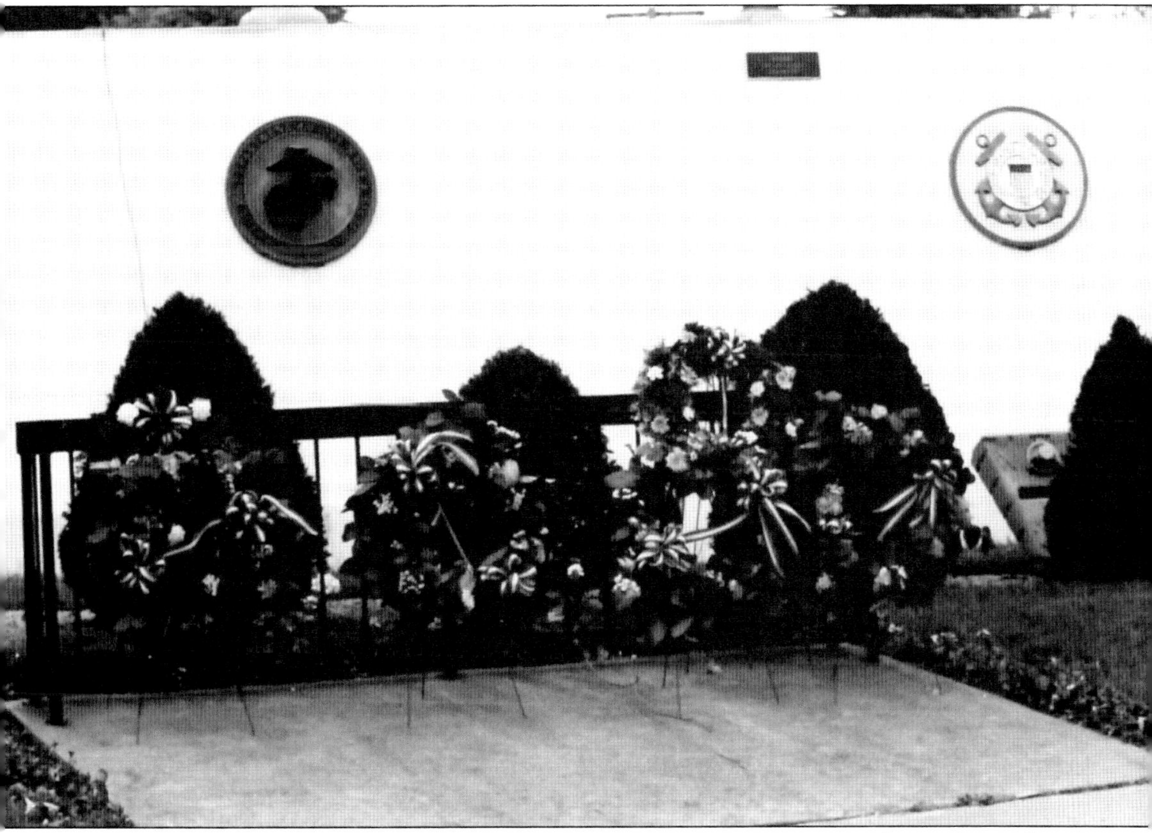

Memorial wreaths are set in front of the Highway of Flags monument as a way to honor those who died in war. The back of the monument pays homage to Mary Lou Kieswetter of Munster, who was instrumental in getting the monument built. The inscription reads, in part: "Her timeless efforts led to the organization of the Indiana Council for the Encouragement of Patriotism in 1968. A founder and director of the council, it has been through her inspirational leadership that this memorial to our flag and all servicemen and women was erected in 1975." Kieswetter died in 2012 at the age of 87.

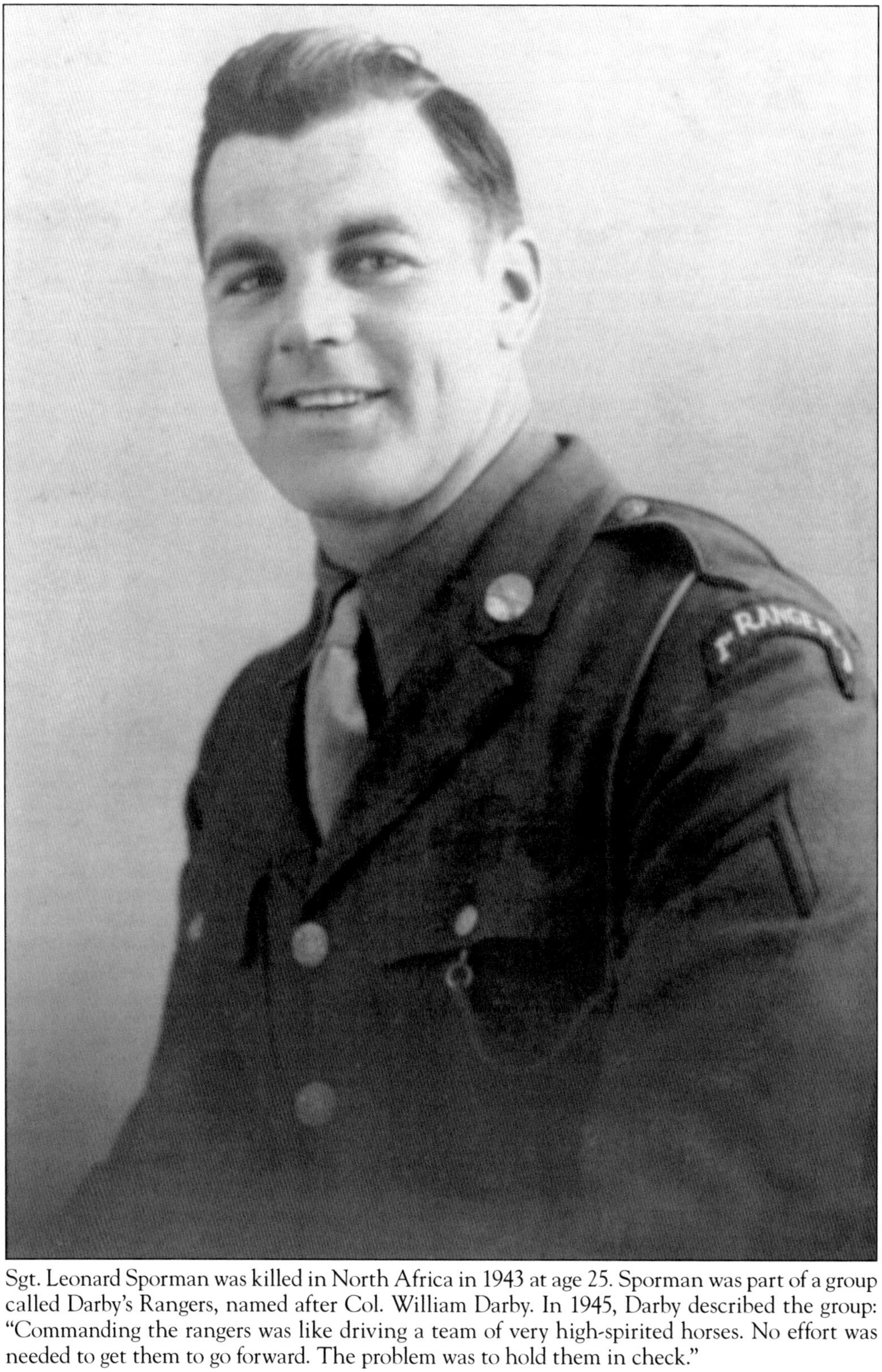

Sgt. Leonard Sporman was killed in North Africa in 1943 at age 25. Sporman was part of a group called Darby's Rangers, named after Col. William Darby. In 1945, Darby described the group: "Commanding the rangers was like driving a team of very high-spirited horses. No effort was needed to get them to go forward. The problem was to hold them in check."

Sgt. William Phillips poses before shipping off to the European front in World War II. This photograph appears to have been taken at his home. He was part of the 10th Infantry Battalion, 4th Armored Division.

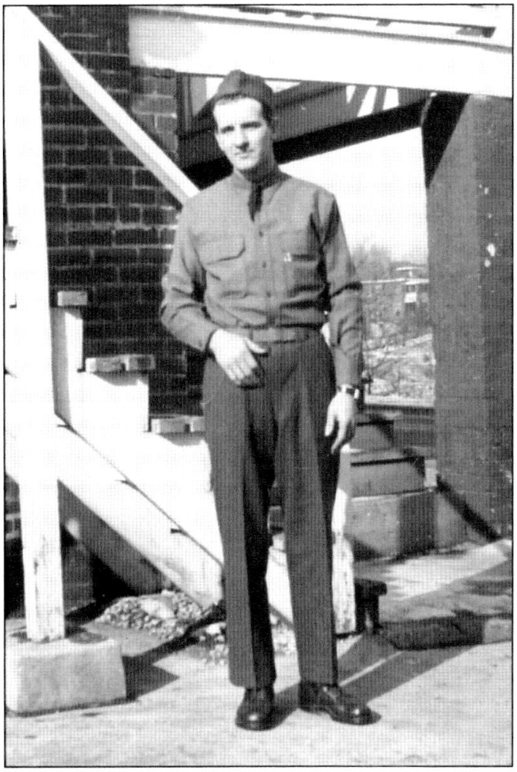

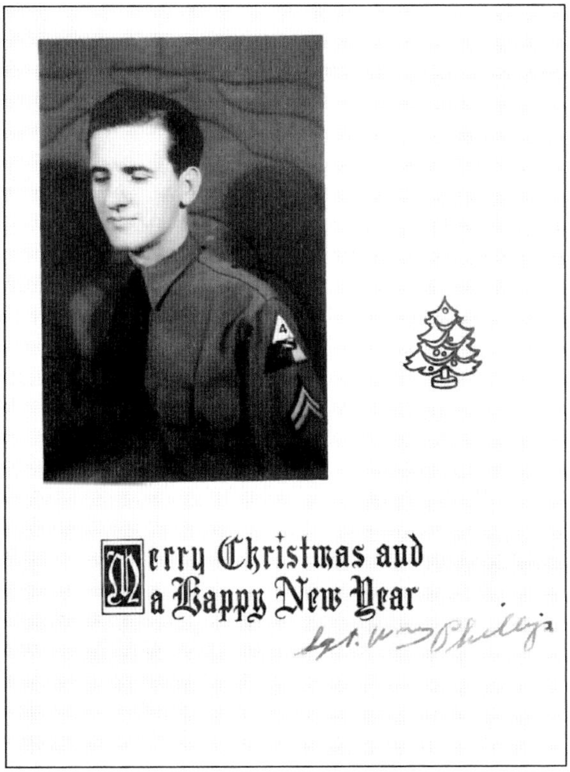

A serious looking Sgt. William Phillips sent these Christmas greetings to his family. Sadly, he was killed in action on Christmas Eve in 1944. He is buried in the American War Cemetery in Luxemburg, where 5,076 Americans, including Gen. George Patton, are interred, many having perished in the Battle of the Bulge (although Patton died in late 1945).

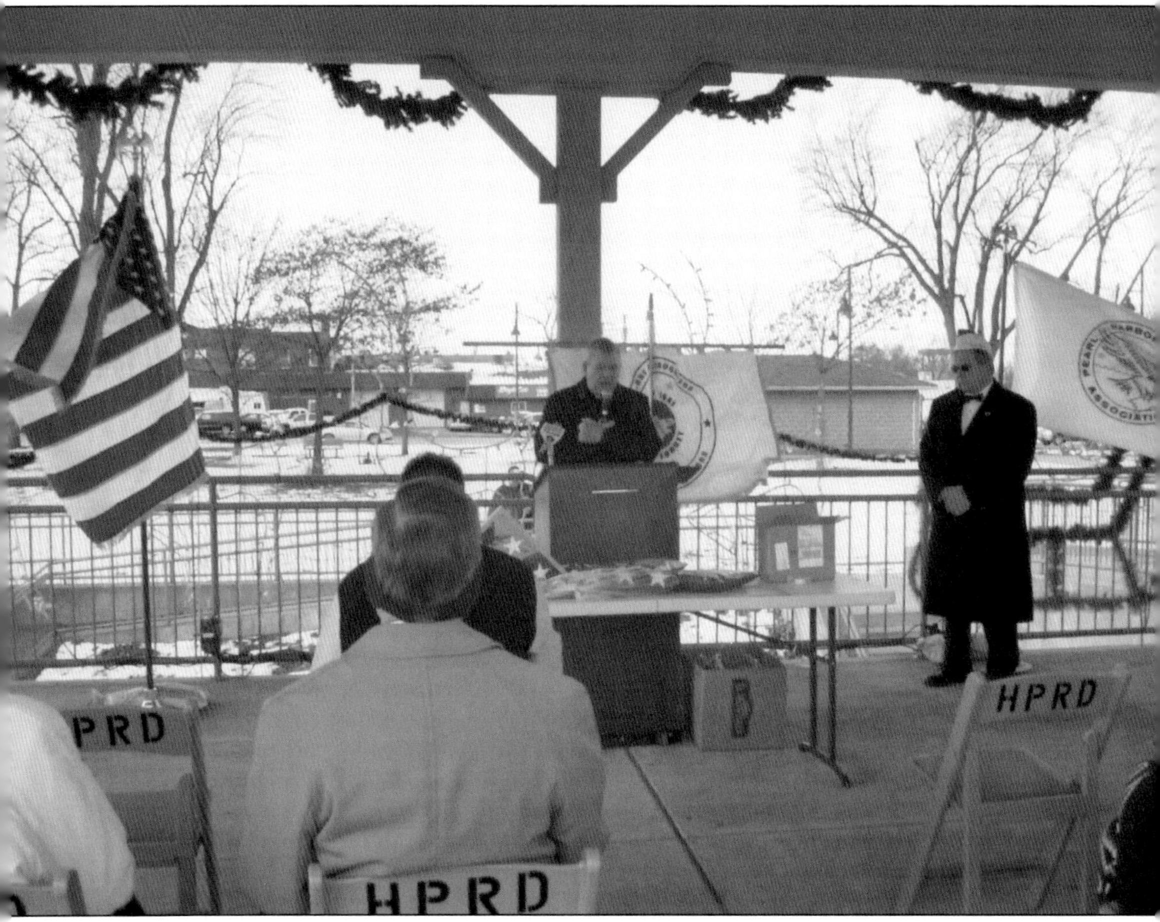

December 7, 2016, was the 75th anniversary of the Japanese surprise attack on Pearl Harbor in 1941. In asking for a declaration of war on Japan, Pres. Franklin D. Roosevelt described the attack as "a date that will live in infamy." On that day, 2,403 Americans were killed. This ceremony in remembrance of the attack was held in the gazebo at Main Square Park. (Photograph by Theresa Pecsek.)

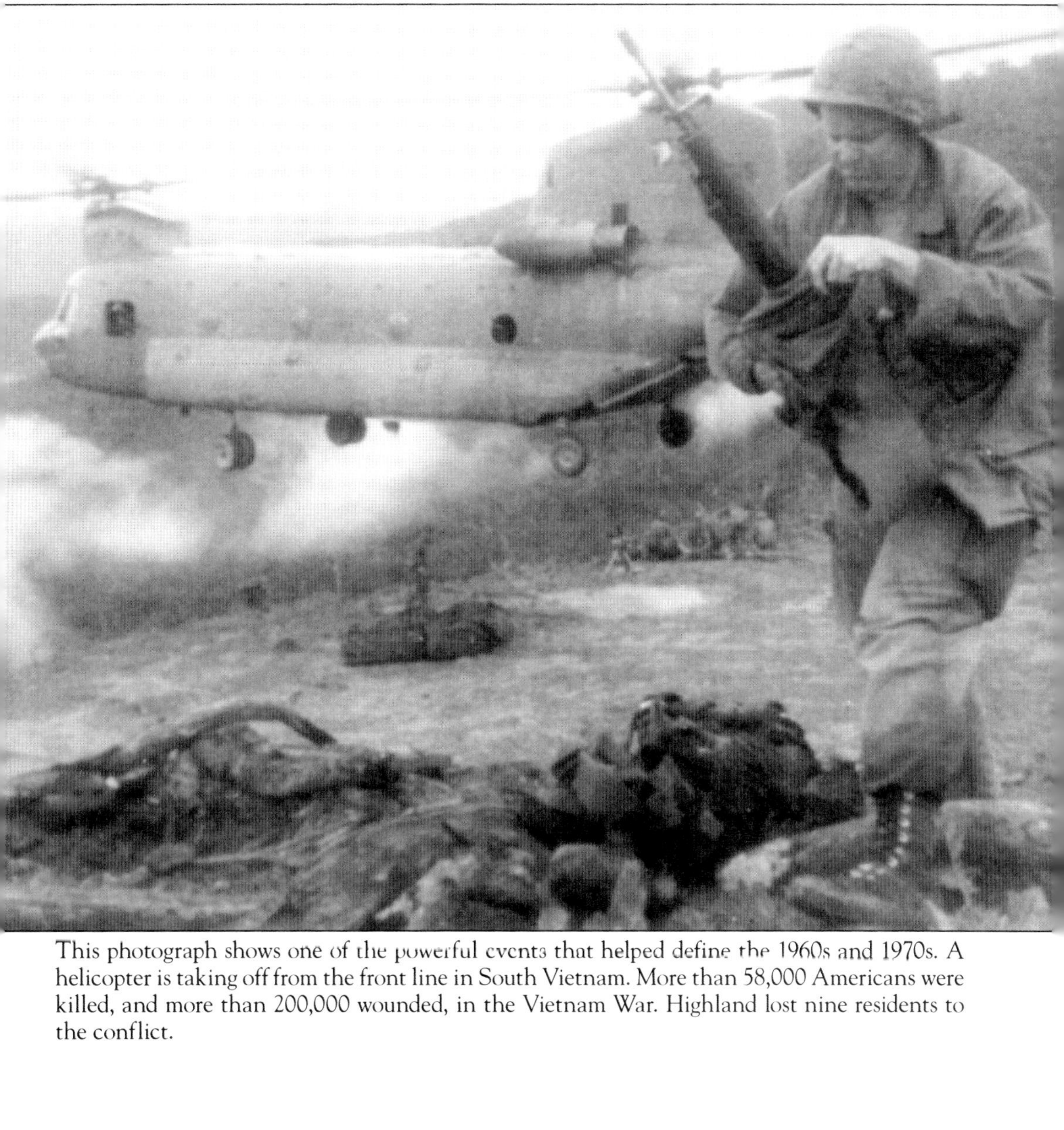

This photograph shows one of the powerful events that helped define the 1960s and 1970s. A helicopter is taking off from the front line in South Vietnam. More than 58,000 Americans were killed, and more than 200,000 wounded, in the Vietnam War. Highland lost nine residents to the conflict.

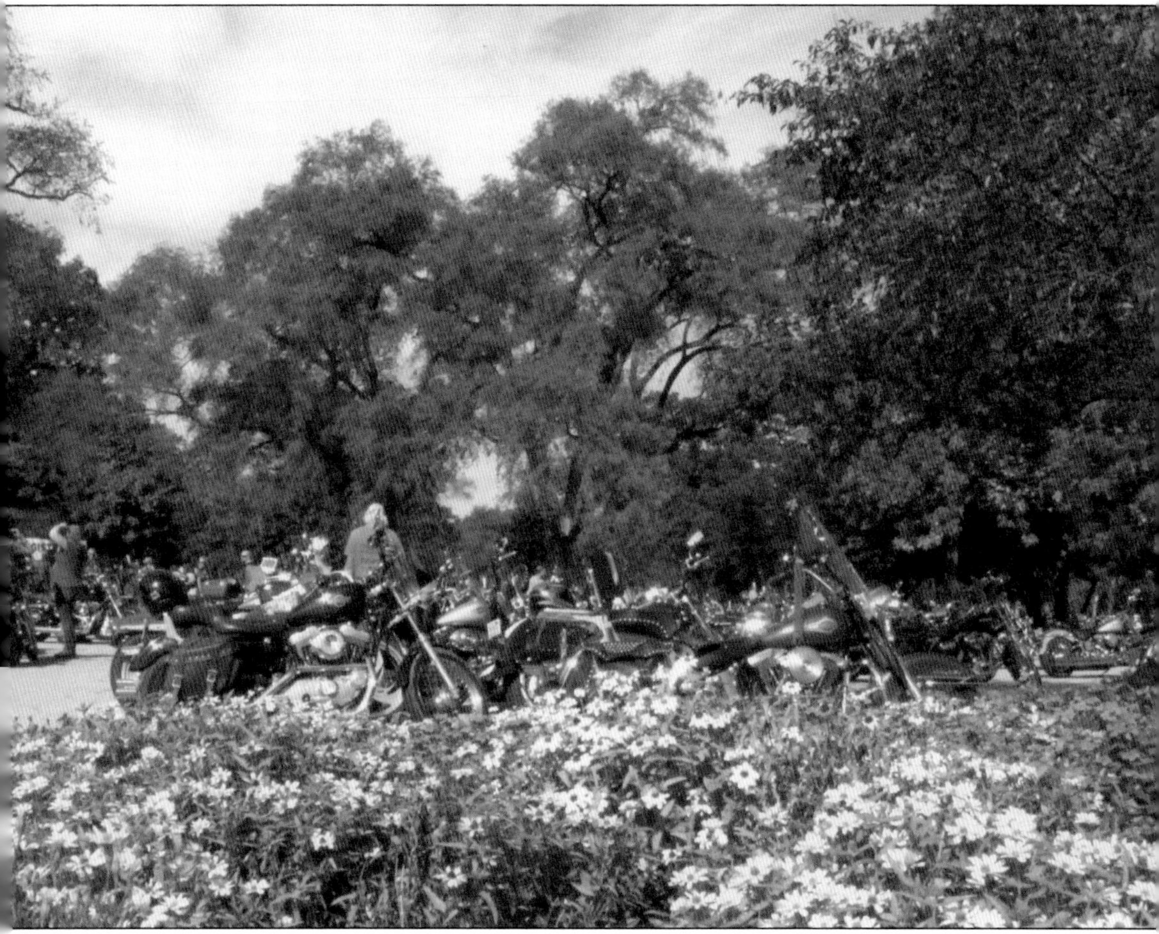

This September 2014 event—the Victory for Veterans Memorial Ride—drew around 2,000 riders. This was the 15th such ride. The event, sponsored by the American Veterans Motorcycle Riders Association, began and ended near Wicker Park. A portion of the proceeds raised by the event was donated to housing services for veterans. (Photograph by Theresa Pecsek.)

Five

Calamities

Highland, like all communities, has not been spared by the forces of nature or calamity. During the second half of the 20th century, the town was deluged by various storms and two massive floods and saw two major businesses ravaged by fire. In 1967, an epic snowstorm descended upon Chicago and Northwest Indiana. The snow did not come down in flakes; it poured down in heavy, white clumps.

The first massive flood roared into Highland and neighboring communities in October 1954, when rainfall was estimated at between six and nine inches in a one-day period. Photographs in the *Hammond Times* showed giant trees uprooted, homes torn apart, residents navigating streets in boats, and heavy equipment plowing through the soggy mess. In 1990, a section of Highland was hit even harder by a late November monsoon 36 years later.

The old cliché "a picture speaks a thousand words" does not apply to the 1990 flood of Wicker Park Manor. The photographs that accompany this section are quite telling, but they only say so much. Wicker Park Manor residents were emotionally devastated.

In late January 1967, the Calumet Region enjoyed some mild weather. After a typical January snowfall, temperatures reached 65 degrees, and by January 25, the snow had turned into mush. Then, early on the afternoon of January 26, the snow started to fall again. This time, it did not stop until over two feet had fallen on the Chicago and Northwest Indiana areas. People did not walk down sidewalks; they plodded through streets and climbed over cars that had been totally covered. Children were thrilled with school closings, but the storm was a serious matter, with one estimate putting the death toll at 77.

On November 29, 1961, Topps, a large discount store, went up in flames. A supermarket called Big D was housed in the same building and was also destroyed. The inferno had started in a storage room and spread rapidly.

Almost 20 years later, another Highland business was lit up by fire when the main building of Highland Lumber and Supply Inc. also went up in flames. Smoke was first detected shortly after midnight by a patrolling police officer. Gusty winds spread the flames. The blaze, which was under control by 6:00 a.m., leapt to the Our Lady of Grace Church rectory to the north on Jewett Avenue. The rectory roof began to burn, but it was controlled and extinguished before any real damage was done.

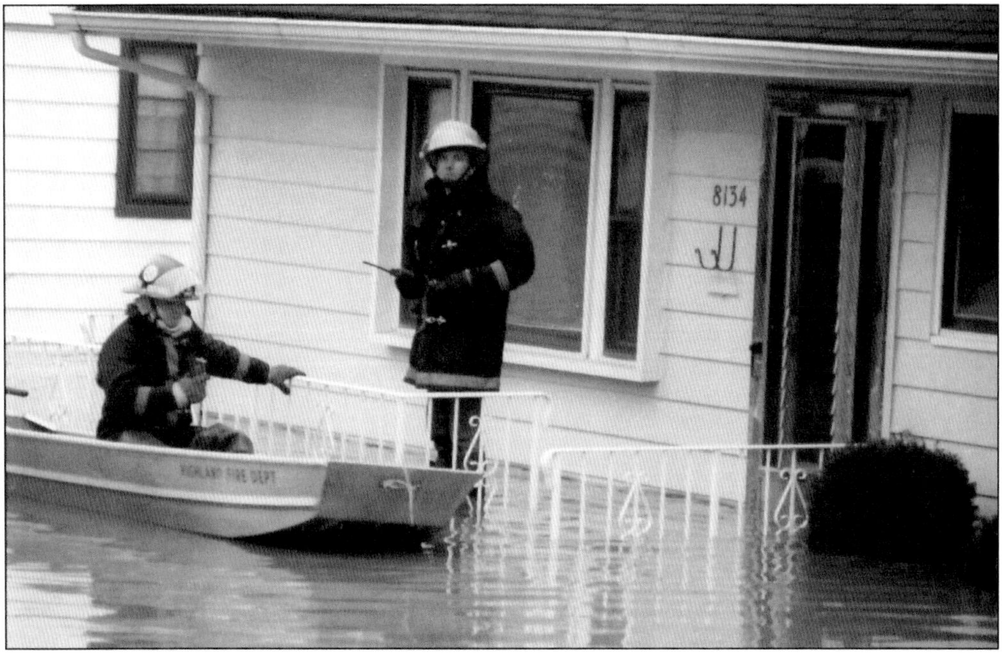

A boat was needed to get to the front door of this home after the torrential rains in late November 1990 saturated Highland and flooded the Wicker Park Manor subdivision. Recent upgrades to the sewer system in Highland are meant to minimize future flooding.

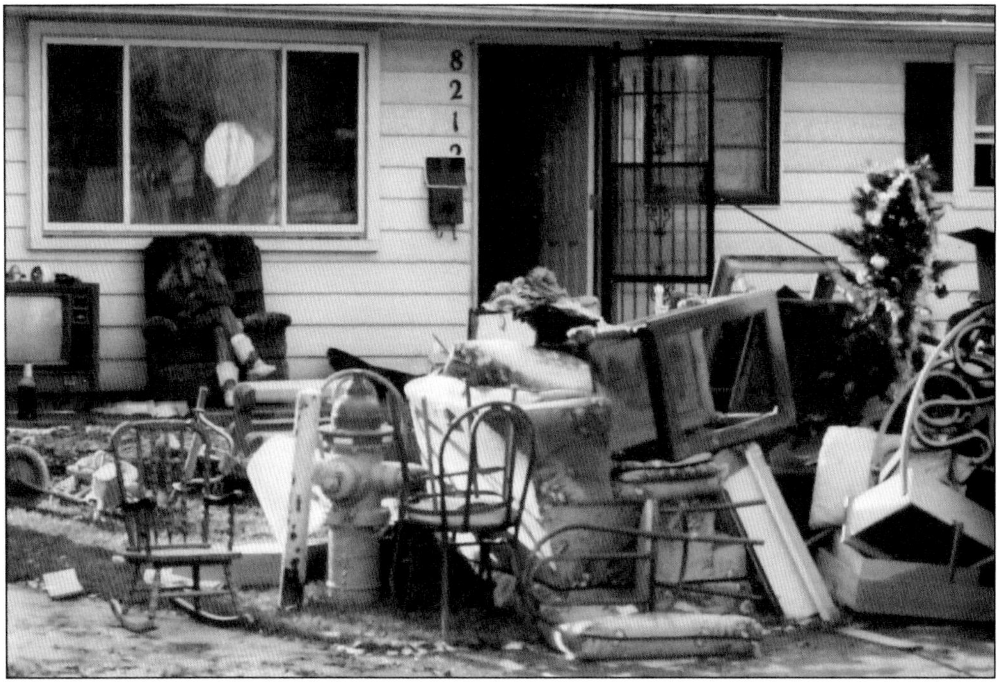

Here, a woman looks at her family's possessions stacked on a now water-free front lawn. Wicker Park Manor resident Nena Kubon told *The Times* newspaper, "When I opened the front door, I cried. I saw everything we worked for the last 12 years torn apart. It was all smashed from the thrust of the water."

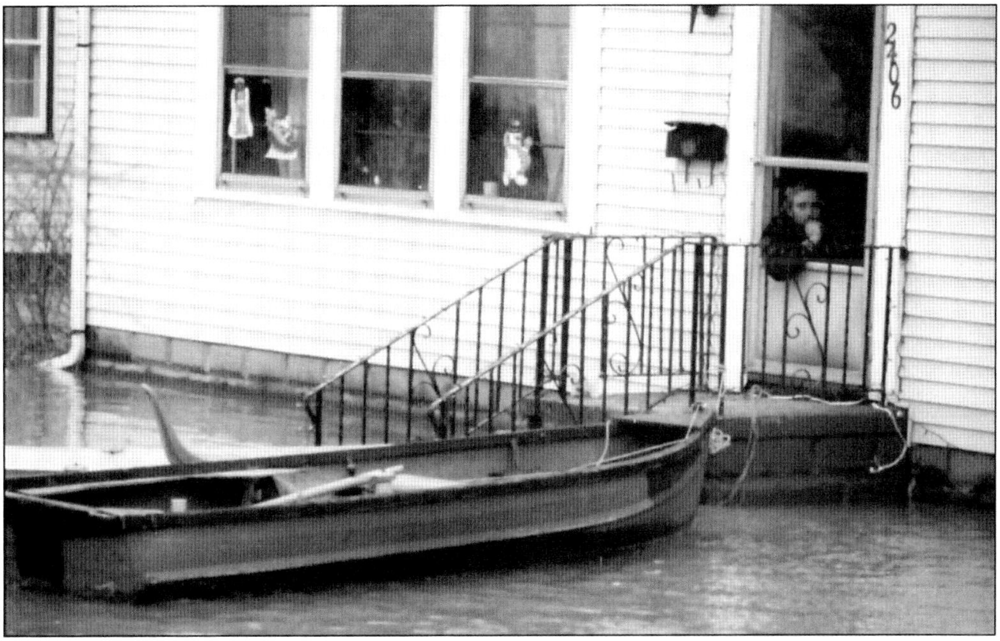

A homeowner looks out his front door as floodwaters turn his home into an island. For a time after the 1990 flood, it was thought that the Wicker Park Manor homes would not be habitable, but many of them were eventually restored.

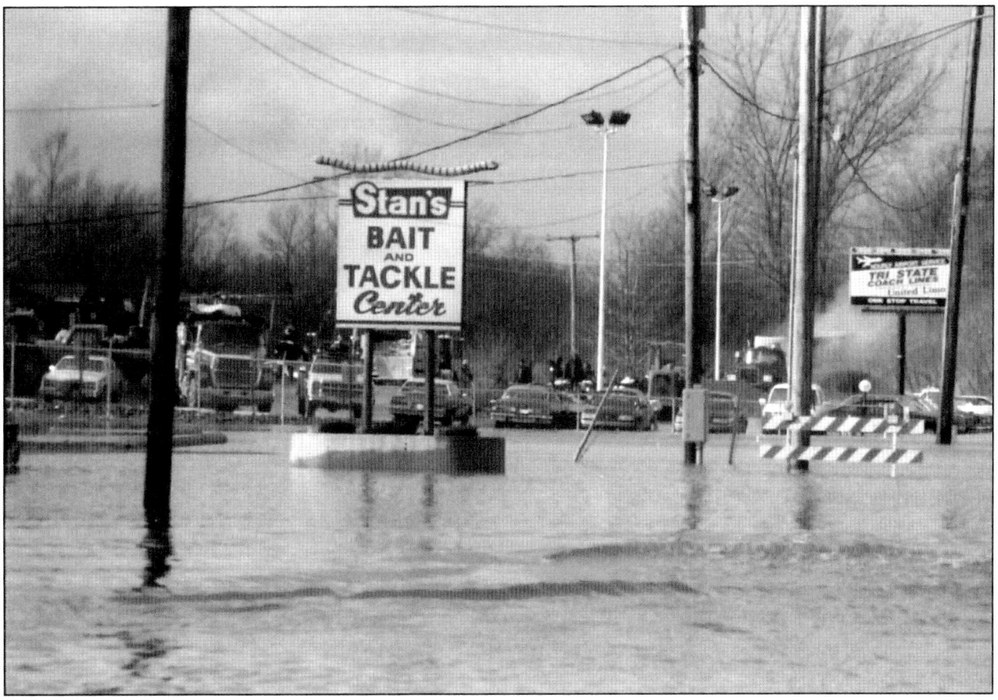

This is the section of Indianapolis Boulevard that runs along the border of Highland and Hammond Avenues during the flood on November 28, 1990. The water had nowhere to go. As bad as this looks, Wicker Park Manor homes fared even worse. One home was described as having a completely flooded basement, with the water rising to almost two feet on the ground floor.

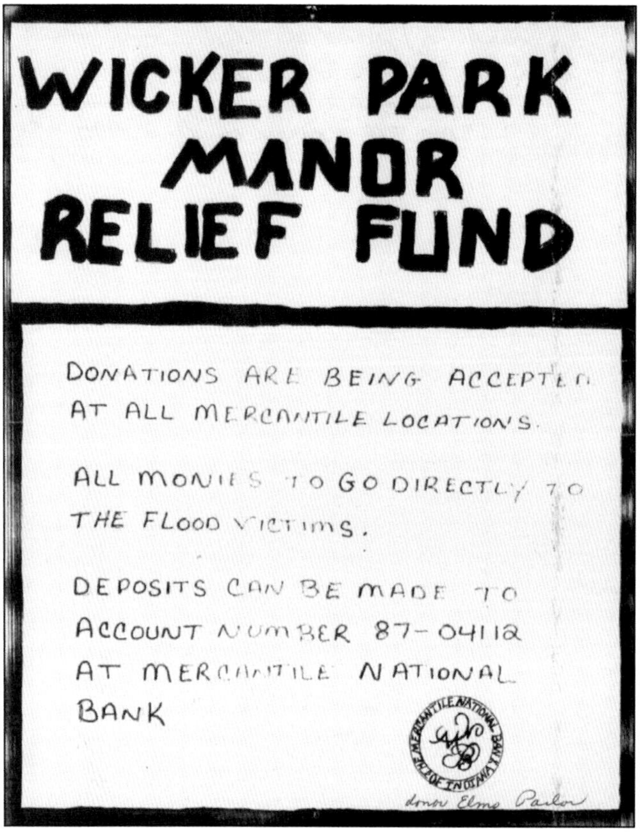

This makeshift sign was created to publicize the need for assistance for the victims of the 1990 flood. Even the sign appears to be waterlogged.

Highland also had water runoff problems. This little flood was due to a Christmas season rainstorm that pummeled the area with about six inches of rain. The Highlander Food Store was located next to Mama Puntillo's restaurant on the 3300 block of Forty-Fifth Street.

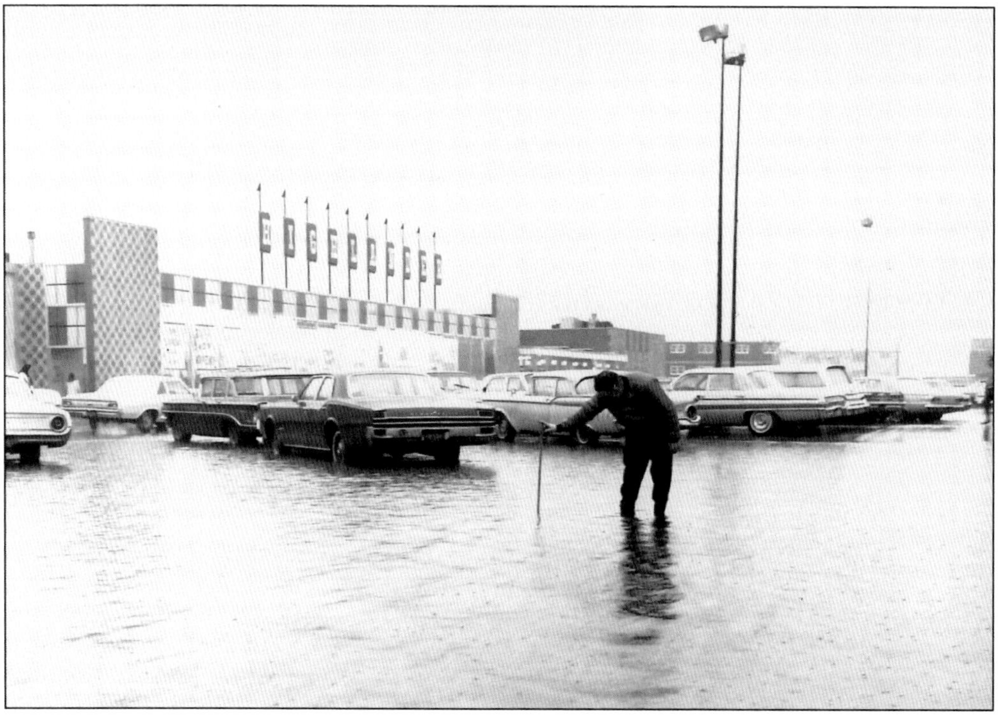

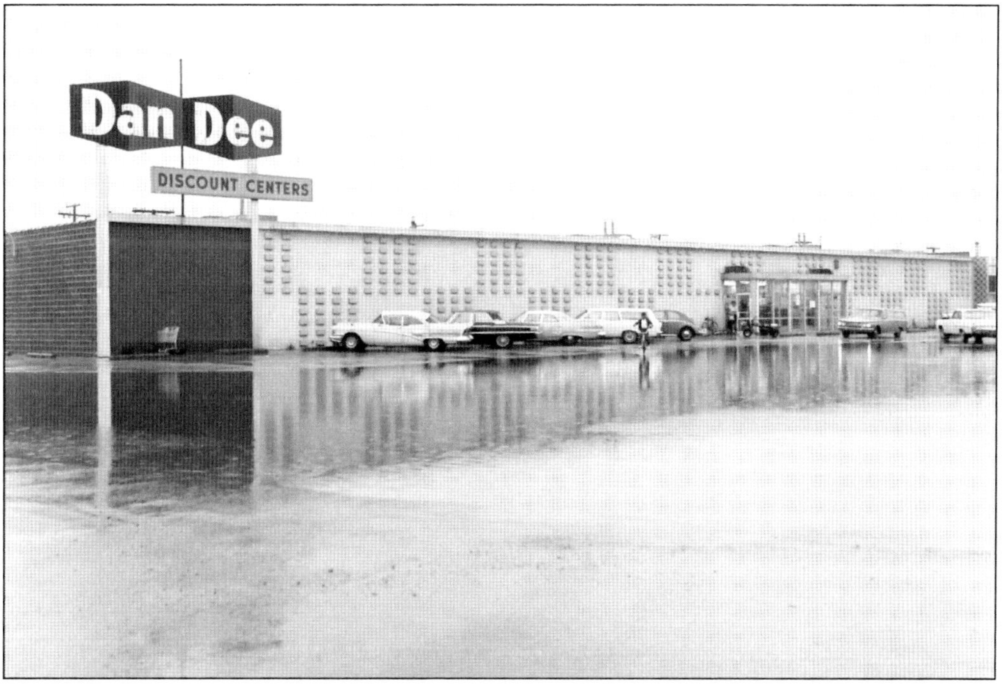

Wading boots were needed to get to the entrance of this store. DanDee, a variety store that sat in a small mall on Forty-Fifth Street, closed in 1976. This business area was called Ellendale Plaza and also included Mama Puntillo's restaurant.

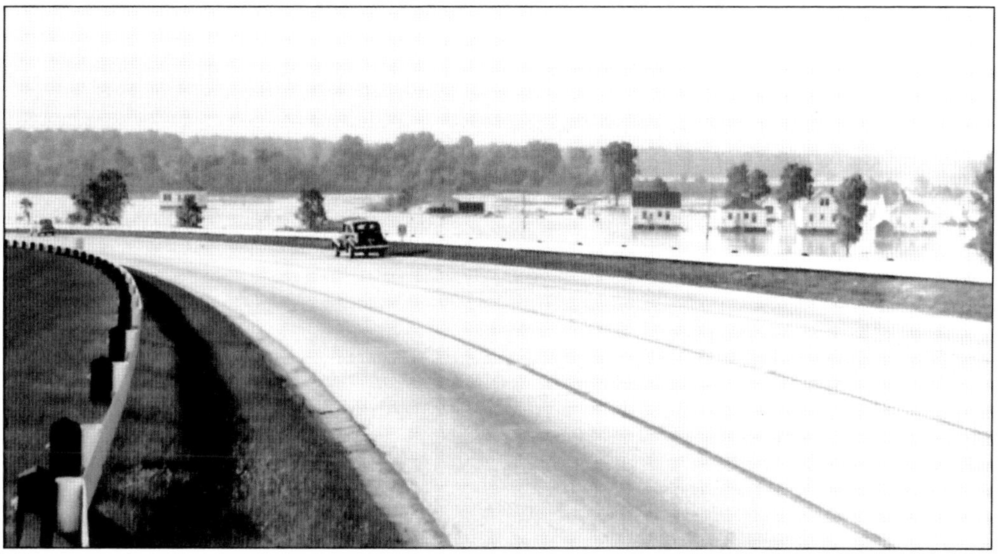
This 1941 photograph shows more flooding—perhaps a harbinger of things to come. Two lonely cars make their way down Indianapolis Boulevard as the homes in the background are surrounded by water. This is the viaduct over US Route 41 that was flanked by Wicker Park to the west.

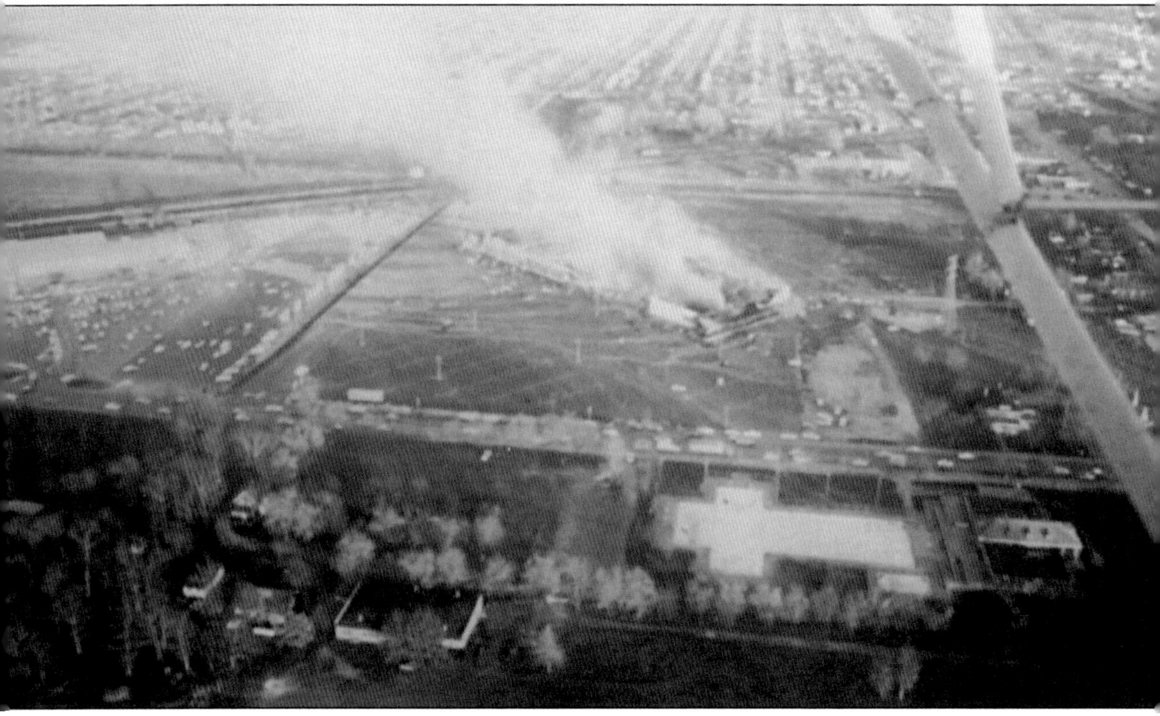

An aerial photograph of the November 1961 fire at the Topps variety store shows the billowing smoke stretching out over the horizon. Employees of Topps and the adjoining Big D supermarket stood outside watching the blaze and lamented the loss of their jobs right before the Christmas holidays. The store had just had its grand opening a month before.

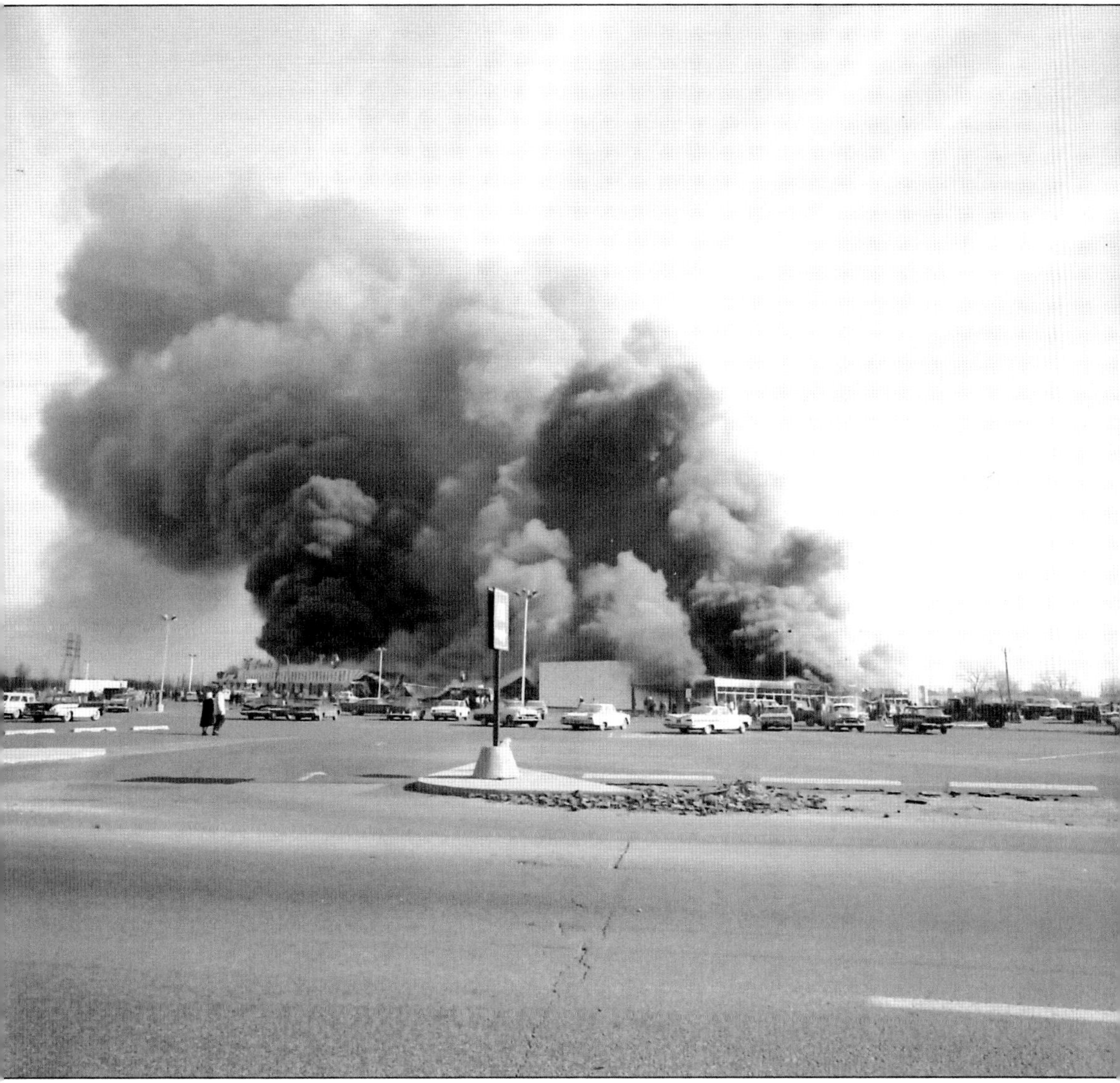

This is a view from across Indianapolis Boulevard of the 1961 Topps fire. The blaze looks like something out of a war zone. A home video posted on YouTube shows relentless flames, blinding smoke, and a building collapsing under the intense heat.

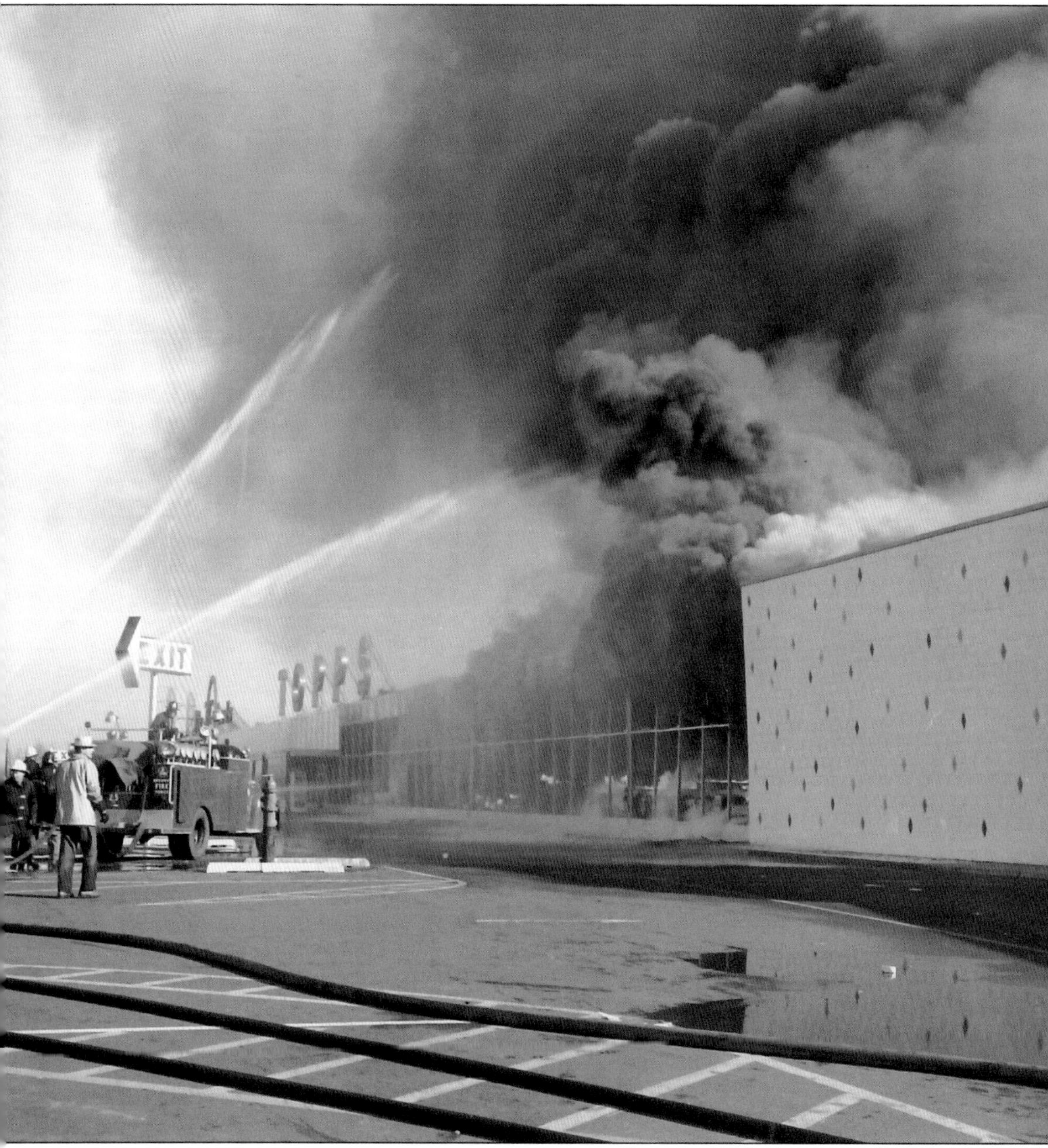

Fire hoses were stretched out as local fire departments battled the 1961 Topps blaze. The store did not have a sprinkler system, and damages were estimated at $2 million. Amazingly, there were no personal injuries due to the blaze, but newly hired Topps employees lamented as they watched their jobs go up in smoke.

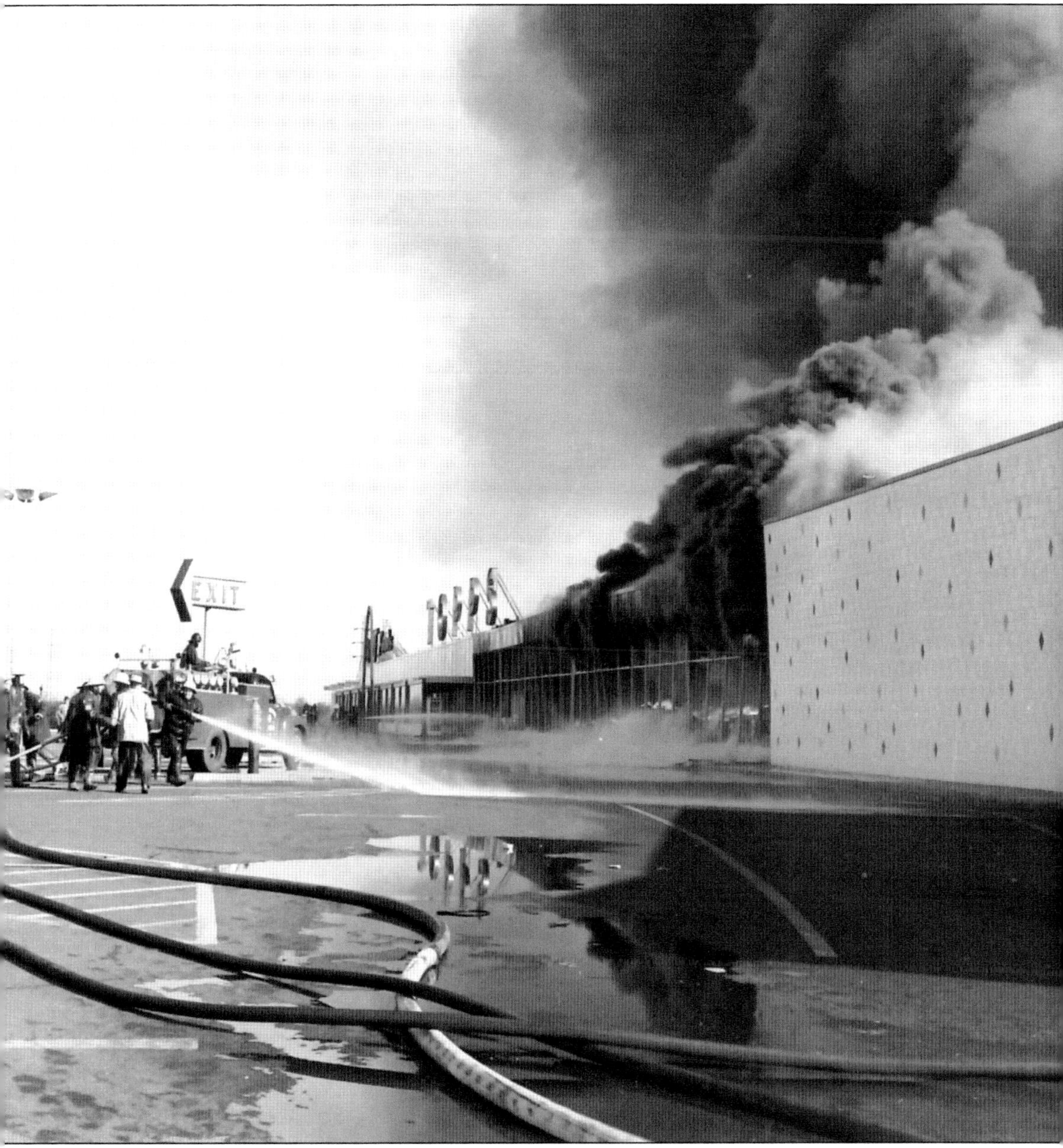

Fire departments from Highland, Griffith, and Munster worked in a dedicated but futile attempt to save the Topps store. The fire was discovered at 8:00 a.m., and the firewall collapsed two and a half hours later.

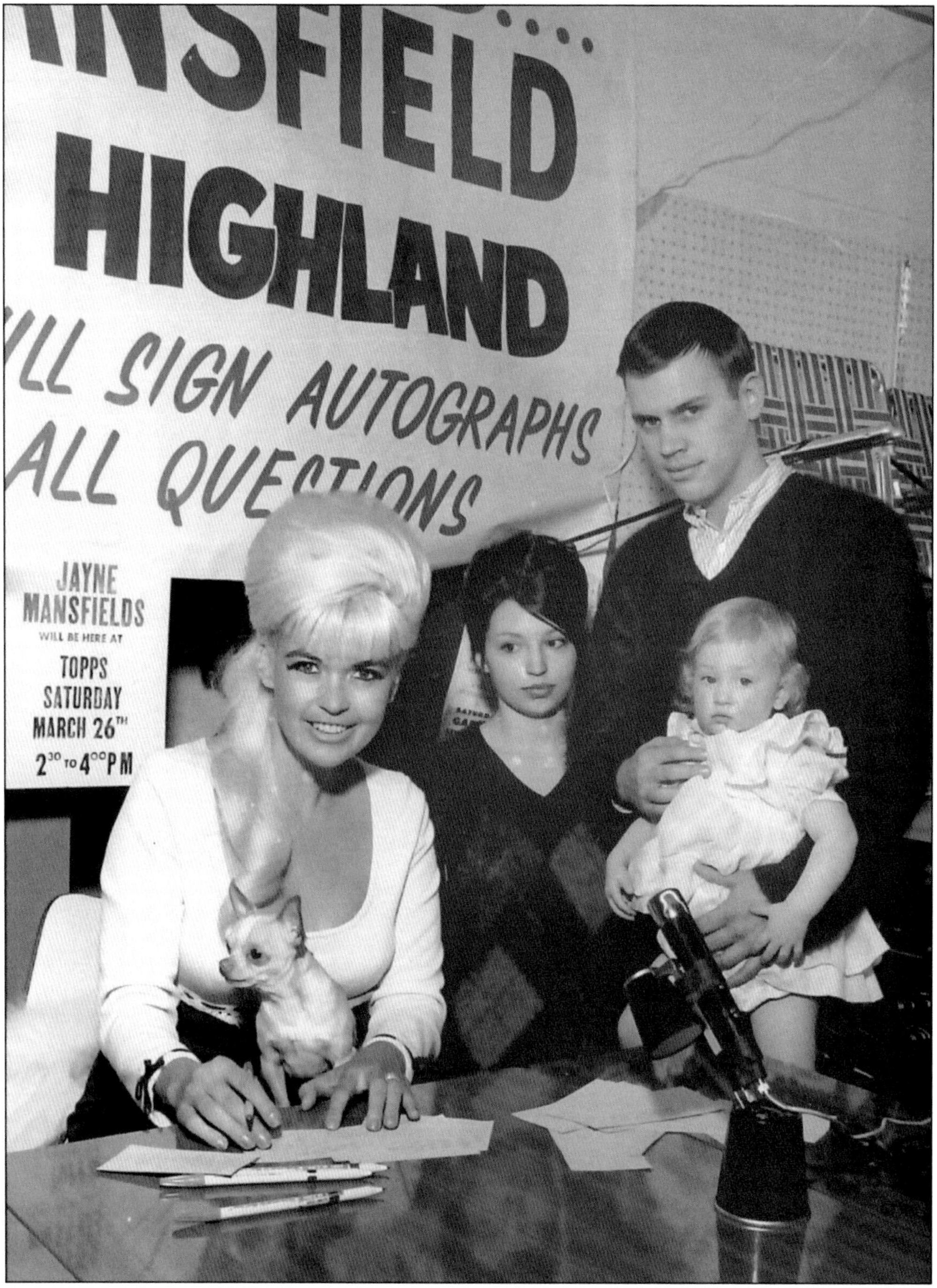

Actress Jayne Mansfield made a public appearance at the hard-luck Topps store in March 1966. A little over a year later, she tragically died in a car accident on her way to New Orleans to appear on a midday radio program. Mansfield's autograph was distinctive in that her first and last names were looped together. Mansfield's daughter, Mariska Hargitay, has gained fame for her role as Detective Olivia Benson on NBC's *Law & Order: Special Victims Unit*. Hargitay's autograph looks similar to her mother's.

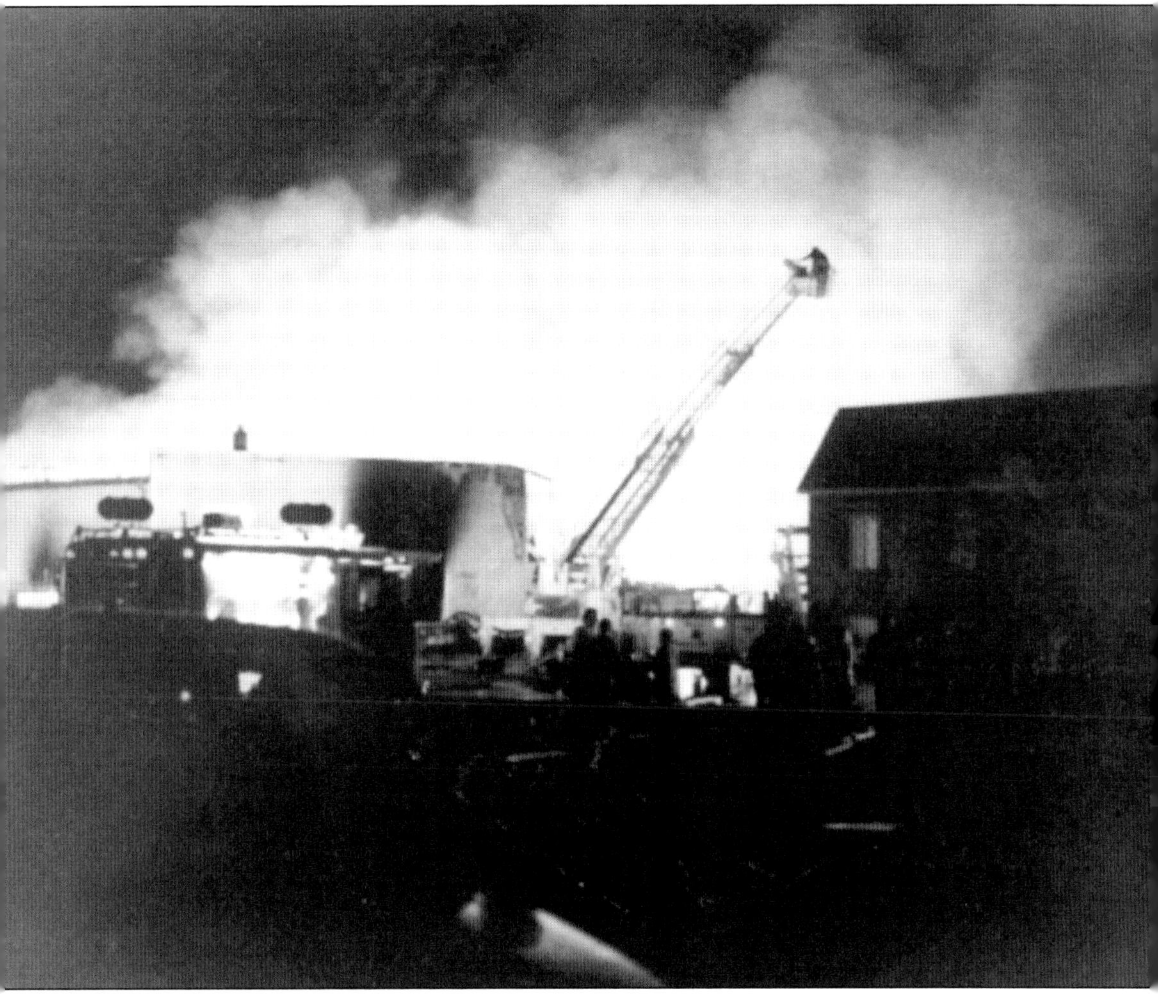

This photograph shows a large section of Highland Lumber in flames in the spring of 1981. Damages were estimated to be over $1 million. Downtown businesses suffered a power outage for slightly less than two hours due to the fire. A townhouse development now stands in this location. There were no serious injuries as a result of the fire.

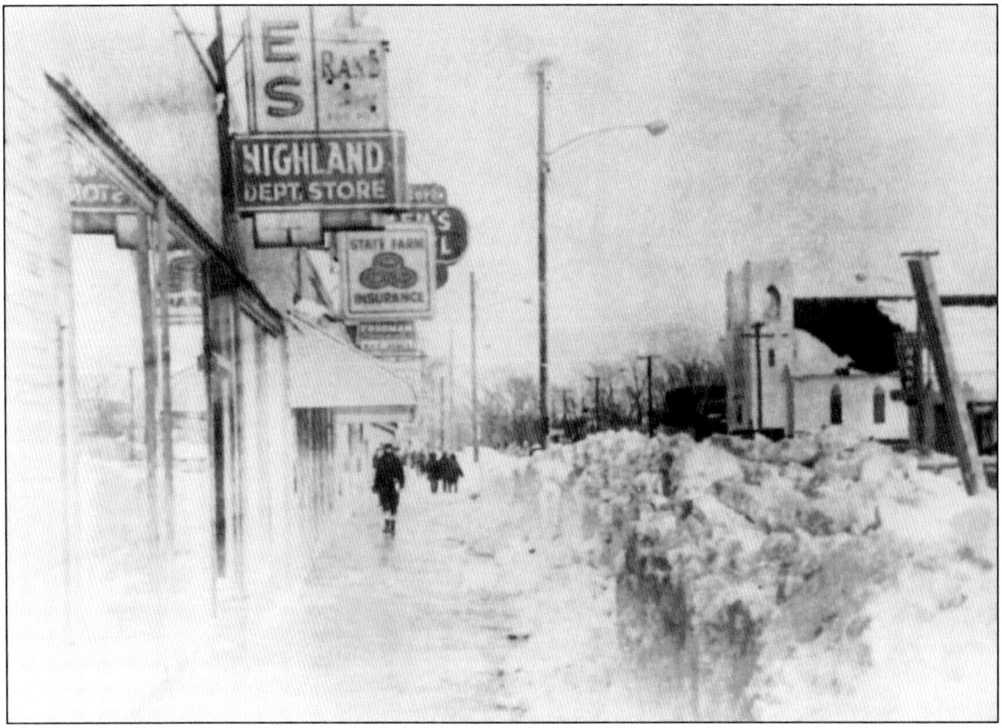

This was almost a miracle; the sidewalks were actually cleared in downtown Highland during the immediate aftermath of the 1967 snow deluge. The local response to the storm, at least as shown here, was good.

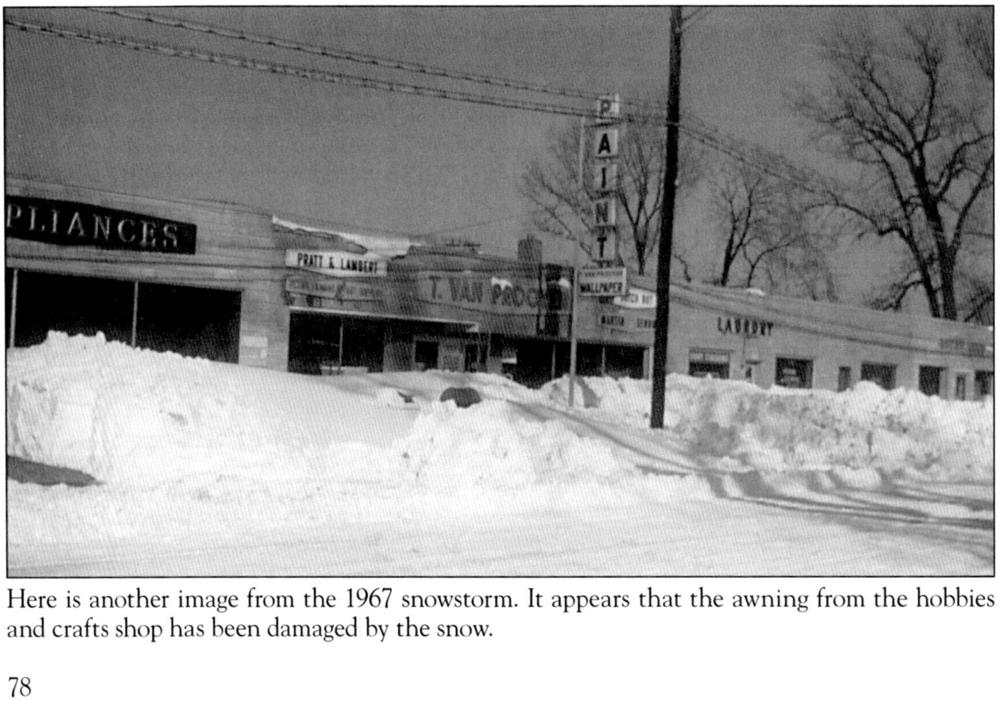

Here is another image from the 1967 snowstorm. It appears that the awning from the hobbies and crafts shop has been damaged by the snow.

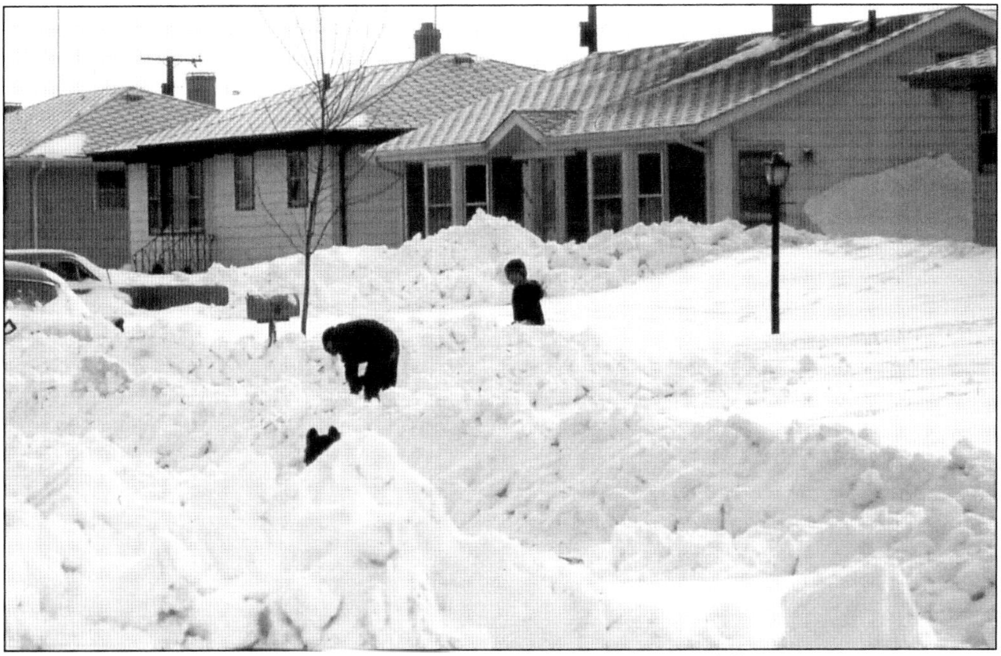

This photograph shows Ninety-Eighth Street right after the snow fell in 1967. Even the most powerful snowblower would have a hard time with these drifts. When shoveling, one had to take the snow off in layers. Many times, it took three layers to get down to the sidewalk. (Photograph by Andy Finick.)

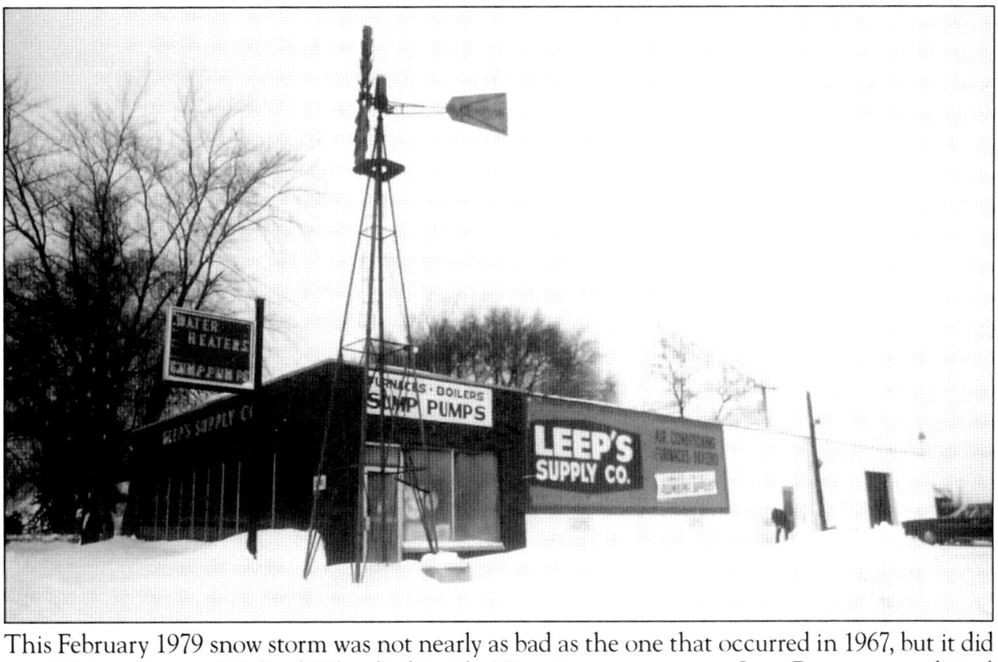

This February 1979 snow storm was not nearly as bad as the one that occurred in 1967, but it did cost Chicago mayor Michael Bilandic his job. His primary opponent, Jane Byrne, ran political commercials with snow falling all around her. She then dumped on Bilandic's snow-clearing efforts and was elected as Chicago's first female mayor. There was no such political fallout in Highland.

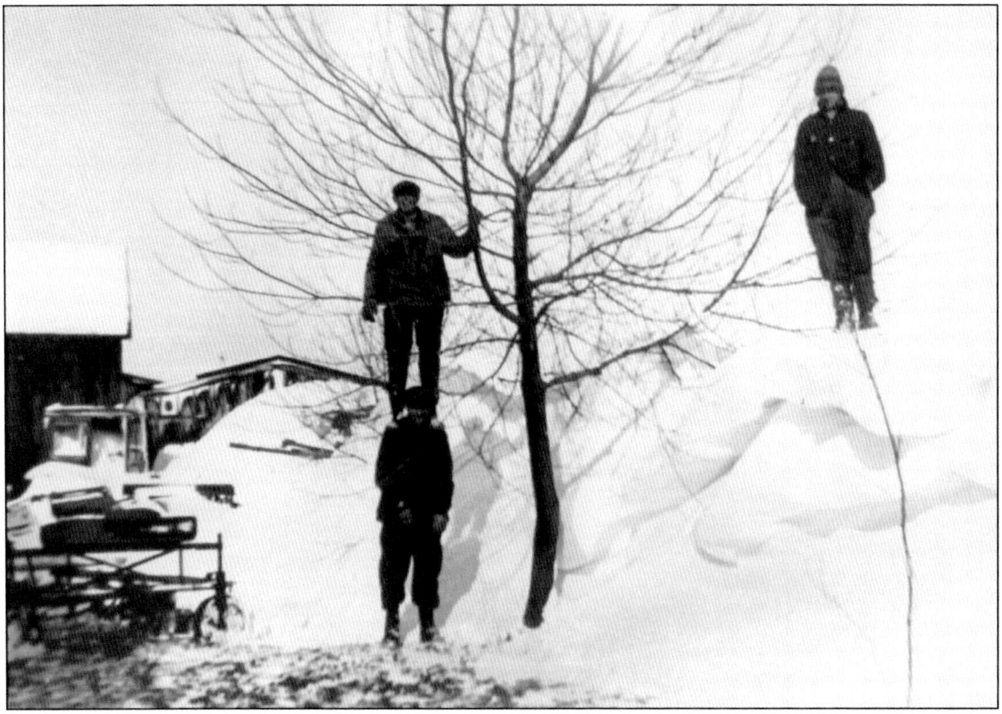

This solid snow drift would have made a good fort and was the result of a spring weather front. This storm happened in 1929 just at a time when warm weather was anticipated.

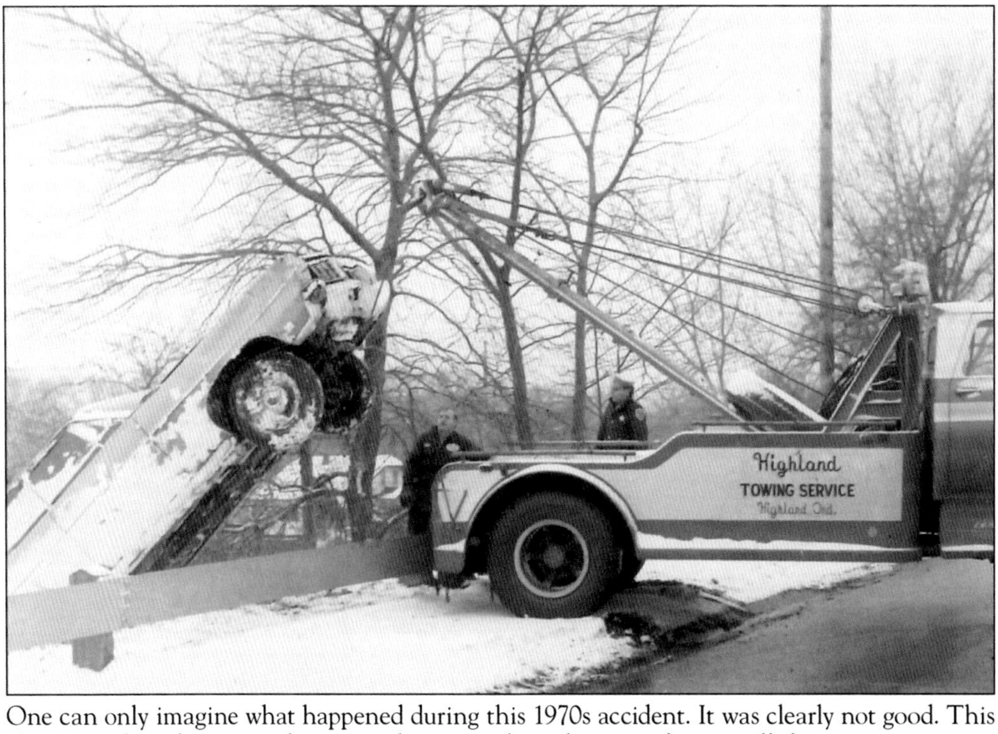

One can only imagine what happened during this 1970s accident. It was clearly not good. This chapter ends with a true calamity, and it certainly took quite a feat to pull this car out.

Six

Wicker Park

This section represents a phase of life which is typically American. A few short years ago, it was an uninhabited area of sand and plain. Today it is a great industrial metropolis. The people of this region have been creating the most fascinating epics.

—Opening remarks made by President Calvin Coolidge at the dedication of Wicker Park on June 14, 1927

On June 14, 1927, Wicker Park, which was formerly regarded as a pasture, was dedicated as a memorial to World War I veterans. Pres. Calvin Coolidge spoke of Wicker Park not only as a war memorial but as a symbol of a region that had quickly grown as a business center. In his address, he referred to the oil refinery in Whiting, the steel mills along Lake Michigan, and the developing communities and cities bordering Highland

In addition, the 30th president also put things in historical perspective. He said that in ancient times, parks were built and developed for the elite ruling class. Coolidge believed that modern places like Wicker Park had a different origin and a better common purpose:

> The present century has seen a tremendously vital development in the opening up of small parks in congested centers, the laying out of playgrounds for children, the building of community centers to minister to the normal social life of the young folks, and the establishment of athletic and recreation fields for the general public.

A future president visited Wicker Park 81 years later. On October 31, 2008, Sen. Barack Obama made a campaign appearance for a late evening speech just days before he was elected as the first African American president of the United States. There was an elevated feeling of excitement that night, as presidential candidates do not usually visit Northwest Indiana. There was also an almost-unseen but chilling presence of the Secret Service as agents scanned the crowd for threats. An estimated 40,000 people attended Senator Obama's campaign appearance.

Although Wicker Park was a key factor in the development of Highland, the facility has been a main spot for recreation for those in the surrounding communities as well. As President Coolidge said during its dedication, it is a park that is to be accessible to all—not just to the elite.

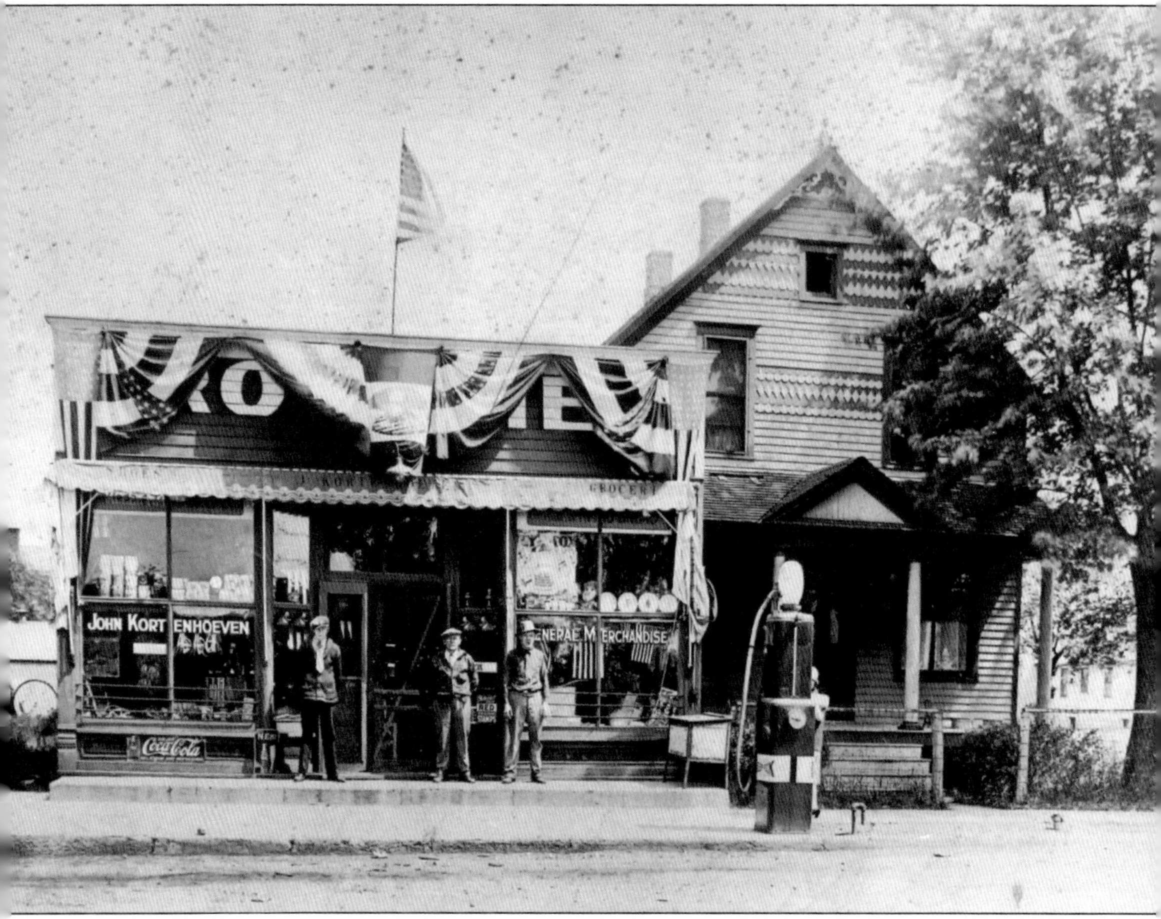

Korthaven's was an example of the prototypical general store—it sold many things, including gasoline. Here, the store was decorated in anticipation of President Coolidge's June 14, 1927, visit to Highland to dedicate Wicker Park.

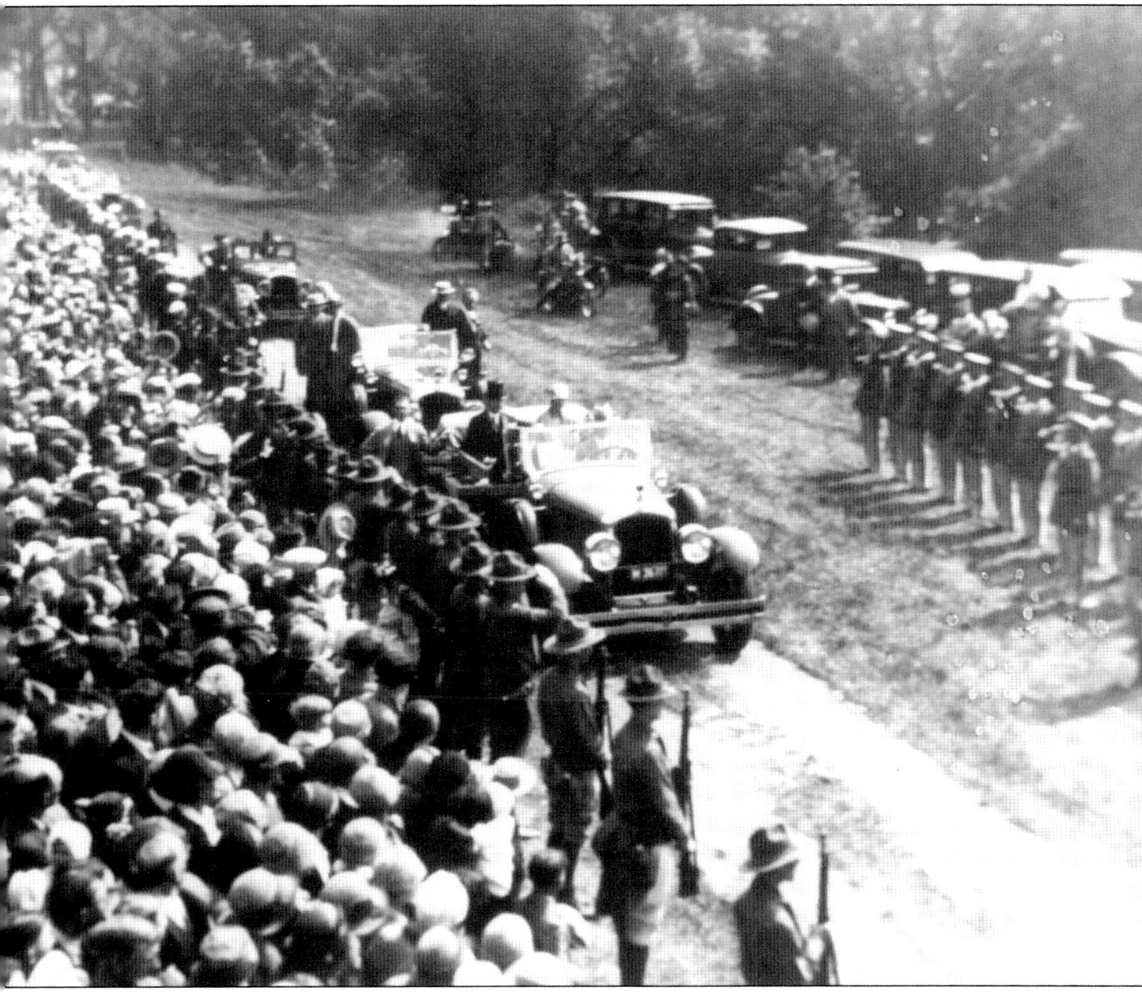

A large crowd encompasses President Coolidge's motorcade. An estimated 40,000 people attended presidential candidate Barack Obama's Wicker Park campaign stop on October 31, 2008. At one point, someone in the crowd passed out in front of Obama. He tossed a bottle of water into the crowd and instructed people to be calm. "She's just been standing too long," he said.

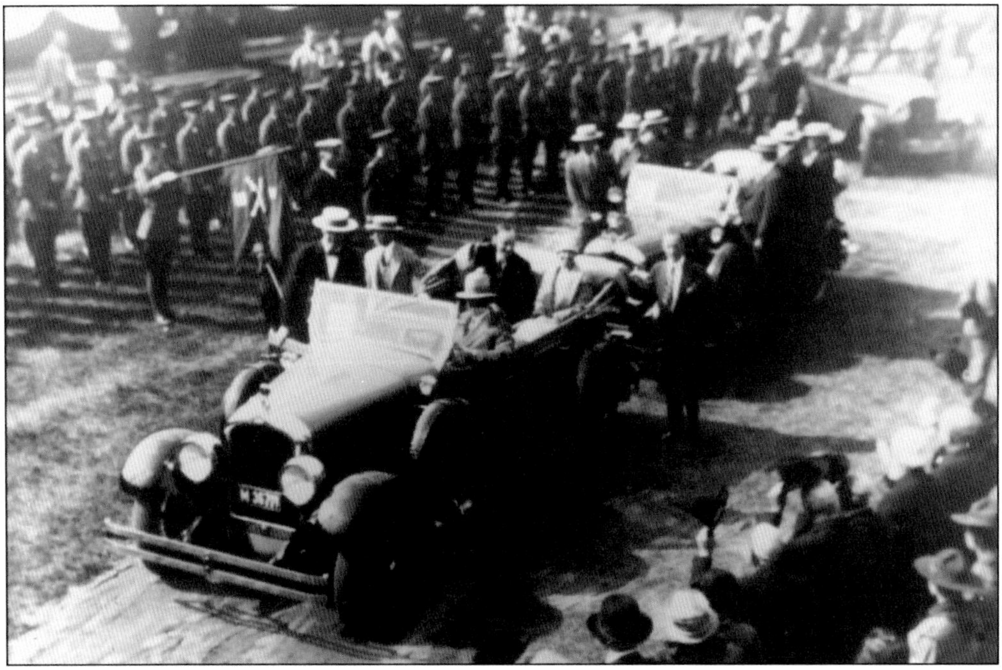

Here, the presidential motorcade is entering Wicker Park on June 14, 1927. Because of security concerns, motorcades are rare these days. In this image, it appears that onlookers got an intimate view of Coolidge; note that he is riding in an open-air vehicle.

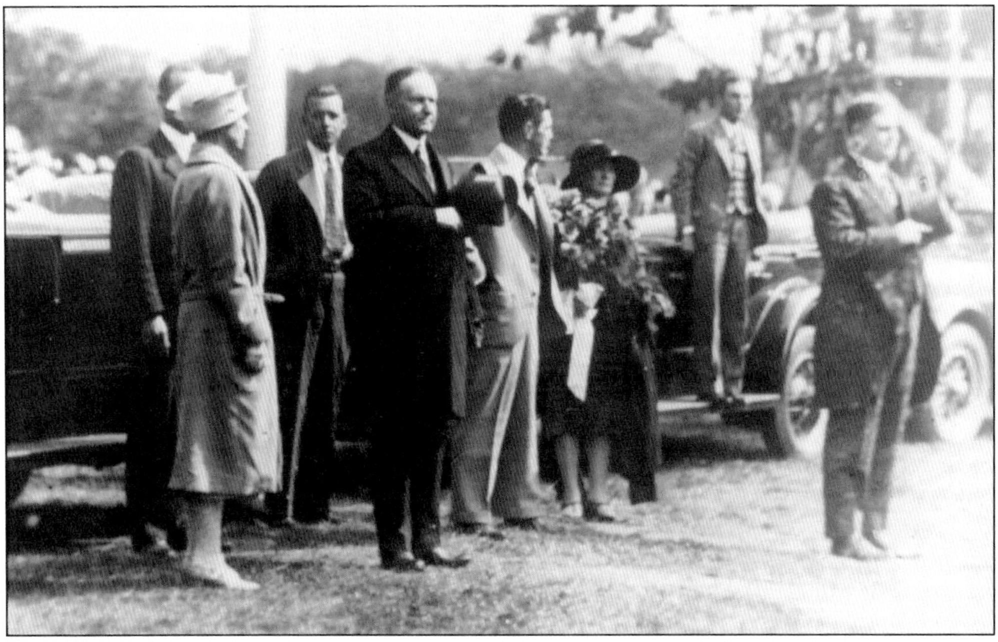

President Coolidge looks solemn as he stands with his entourage at the Wicker Park dedication in 1927. His hat looks distinguished. Certain historians maintain that the prim and proper Coolidge restored dignity to the White House after the incompetent and scandal-ridden Warren Harding administration. The main purpose of the Wicker Park dedication was to honor the fallen heroes of World War I.

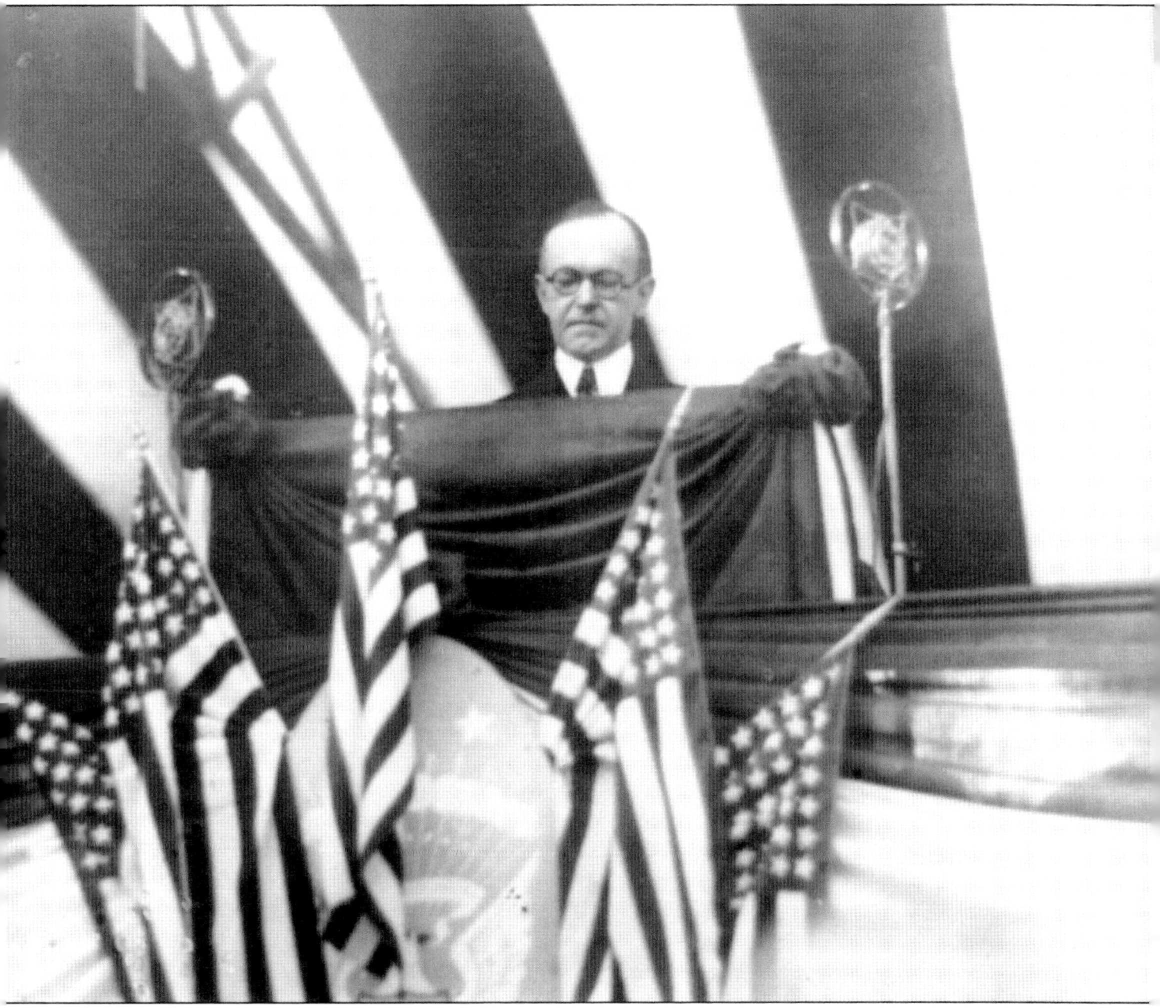

President Coolidge is shown speaking at the Wicker Park dedication on June 14, 1927. Coolidge not only dedicated the new park, he praised Highland and its surrounding communities for their progressive thinking, solid education system, and economic growth.

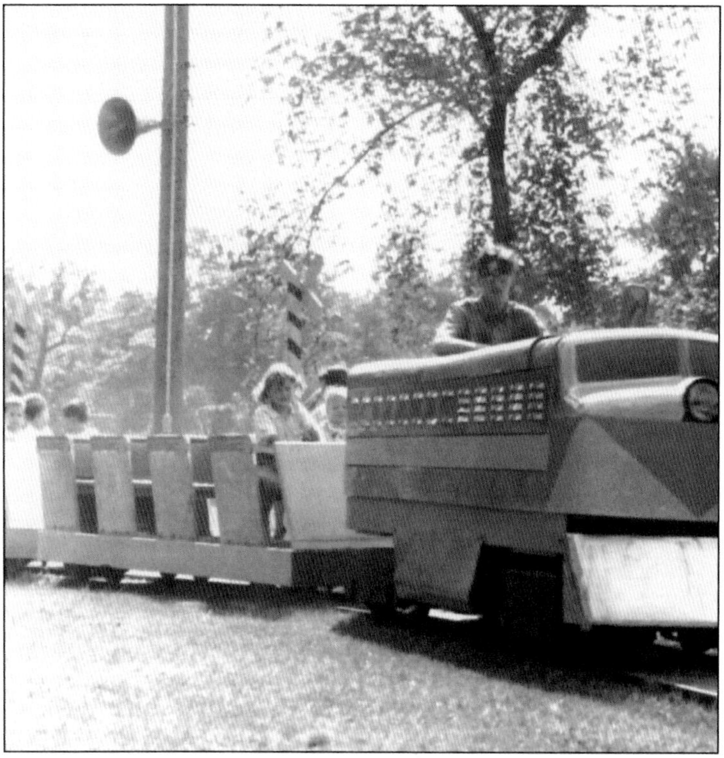

This photograph shows a children's ride in Wicker Park in the 1960s. Rides like this, and other attractions, drew frequent field trips from grade schools outside of Highland to Wicker Park.

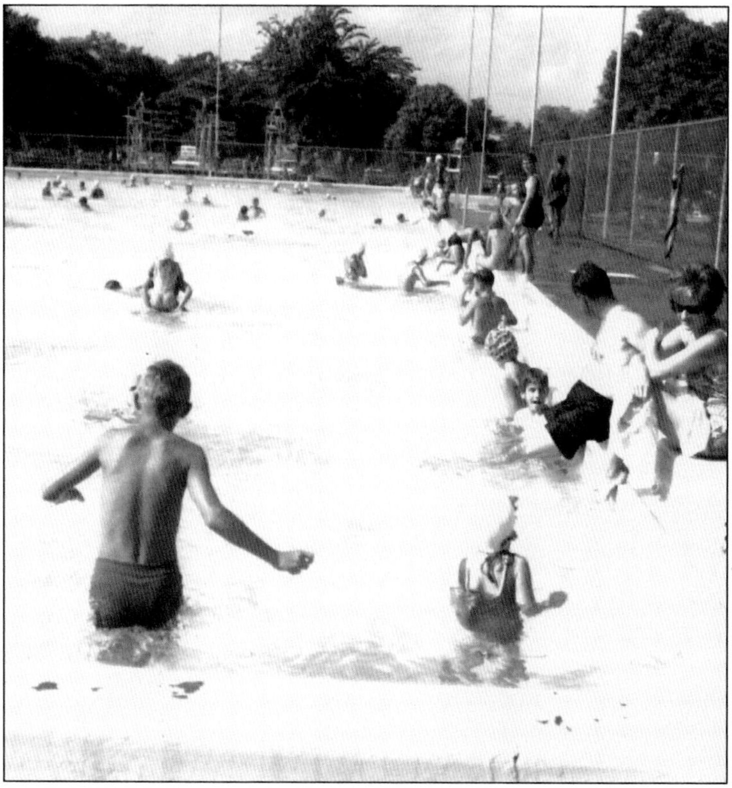

Locals once cooled off at public pools like this one at Wicker Park. This pool closed in 1989 after a 50-year run and was razed in 1999. Many communities in Northwest Indiana still like the idea of having pools for residents but cite the financial burden as a reason to not construct or maintain them. Wicker Park now has a "splash pad" for kids to enjoy.

Hank Huizenga (second from right) served as the picnic constable for the annual Christian School Picnic on July 4. This event for the Highland and Munster Christian schools was held at Wicker Park.

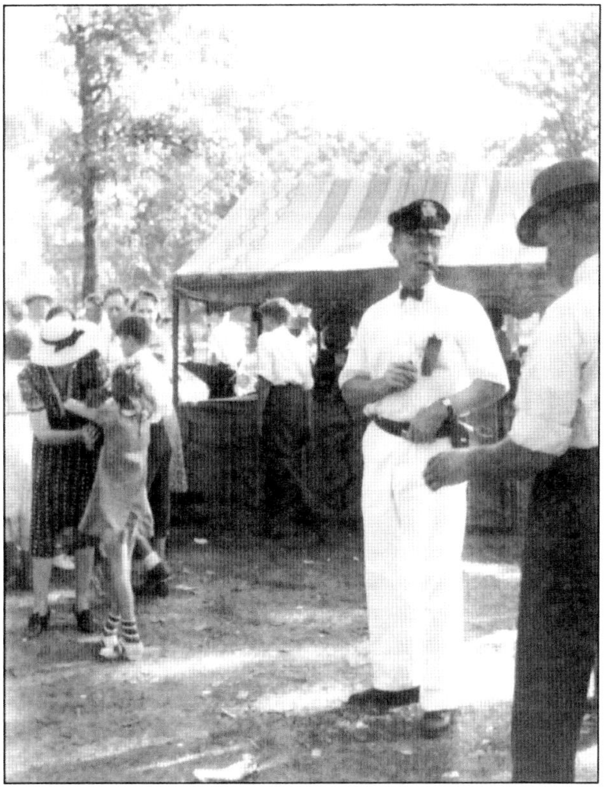

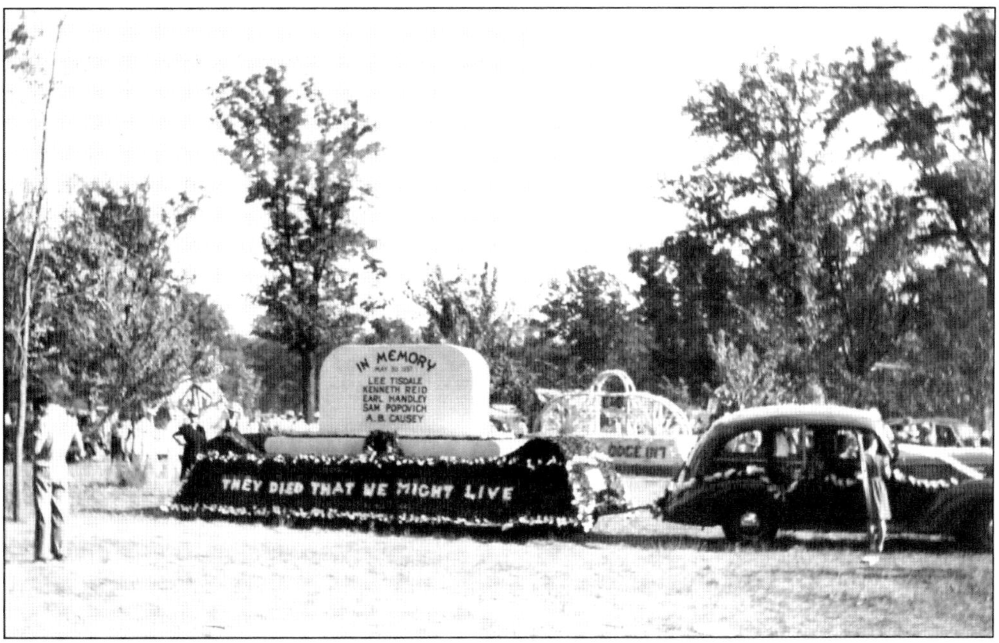

This is a different type of memorial. The five people listed on this large "gravestone" were killed by the Chicago police on May 30, 1937, when members of the Steelworkers organization committee marched toward a Republic Steel plant on Chicago's south side. It is believed that this float made its way through Wicker Park.

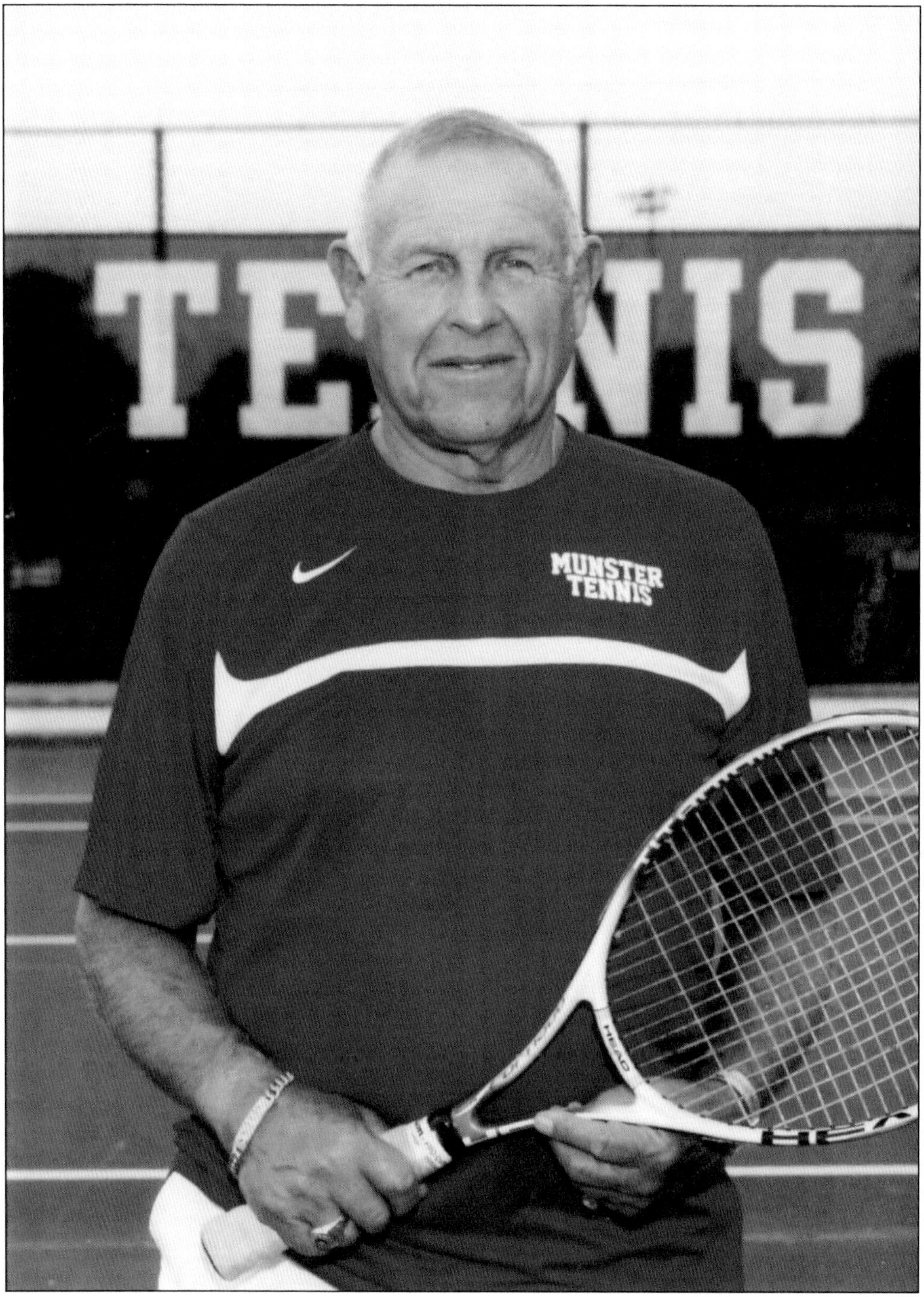

Sid Rothstein is known locally as "Mr. Tennis." Rothstein ran a summer camp at Wicker Park for kids from four to eighteen. Through the decades, it is estimated that he coached more than 10,000 youngsters. Rothstein is still a coach at the nearby Munster High School. (Sid Rothstein.)

Seven

Town Theatre

Going to the movies has been a part of American culture for more than a century. For many people, a simple trip to the theater was a rite of passage. Whether it is a grade-school child seeking independence from a parent, a teenager going on a date, or an adult taking a night out, a trip to the movies can provide a lasting memory.

The Town Theatre, Highland's only theater (for the most part) since 1946, did not have a balcony like other theaters of its day, and seated less than 400. On top of its triangular marquee were the capital letters "TOWN." The small ticket office protruded slightly out into the sidewalk.

Going to "the Town" was like traveling through time to the past. Movies were interrupted by an intermission, during which coffee and cake were served. During warm weather, moviegoers would step out into the street with their refreshments and unwind before watching the second half of the film. It was a simple pleasure, and it appealed to the more mature customer.

Moviegoers enjoyed the Town's old-time atmosphere. The red seats were not so roomy, but they had charm, and there was something about how the thick curtain pulled away from the screen as the movie started.

However, with time, it became obvious that the Town was facing challenges. Some of the seats were in disrepair. The carpet began to fade and had thinned out in spots. The building was simply old and, as with any aging structure, needed rehabilitation. The question became, did the owners (or any prospective new owners) have the resources to keep the theater afloat?

The Town closed in 2008. In 2012, the Town of Highland assumed ownership due to nonpayment of back taxes. In early 2017, The Highland Town Council voted down a plan to refurbish and reopen the Town due to concerns of the economic viability of such a project.

As of this writing, Highlanders must drive to a neighboring city to see a movie, since there is no other theater in town. Theaters like the Town are scarce in the Calumet Region—and in the country in general.

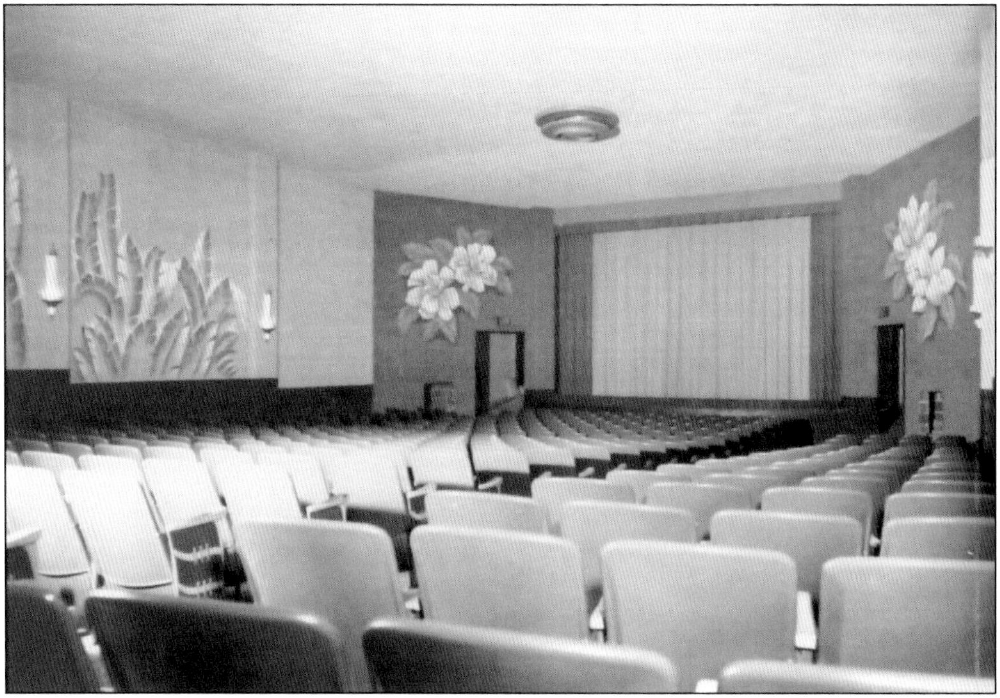

This cozy photograph of the Town Theatre was taken shortly after it opened in 1946. The flowers on each side of the screen were eventually replaced by suits of armor. The opening of the velvet curtain served as a dramatic precursor to the featured movie of the week.

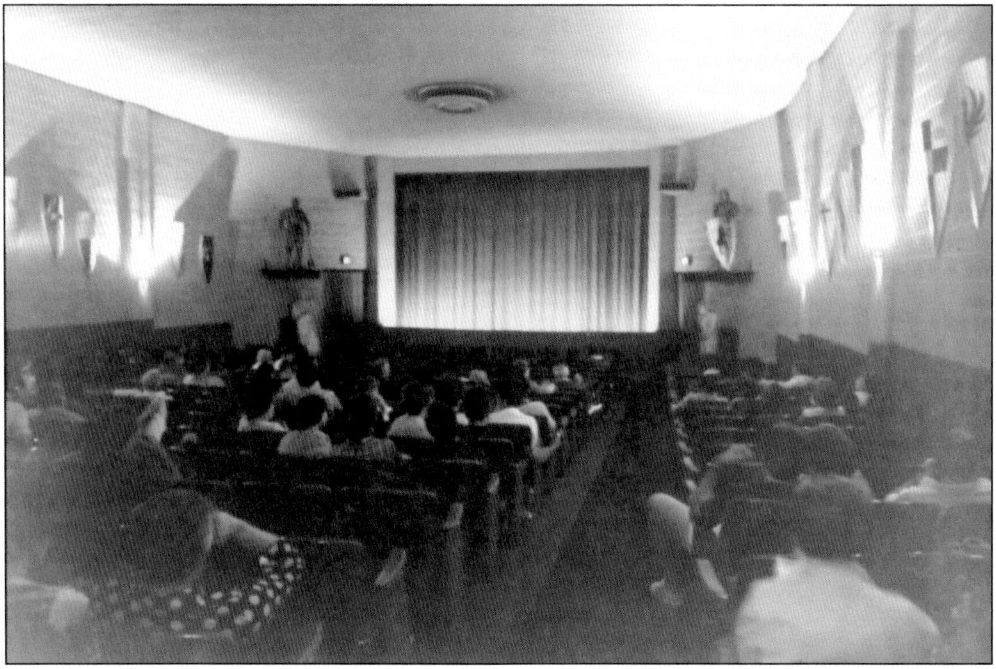

In this September 1977 picture, the suits of armor and other medieval decor had been put in place. This image shows the distinct atmosphere of the Town Theatre. The armor has been preserved and is being stored by the town.

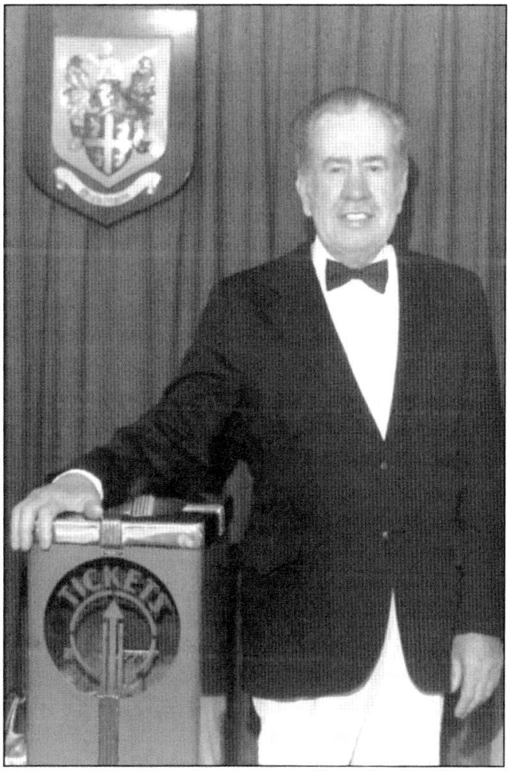

Town Theatre owner Ken Dickinson awaits moviegoing patrons in 1977. The Town was one of the last theaters of its kind—a locally owned, independent theater. In later years, a person could call the theater and get a recorded summary of what was playing that day. The Town remained in business for 62 years.

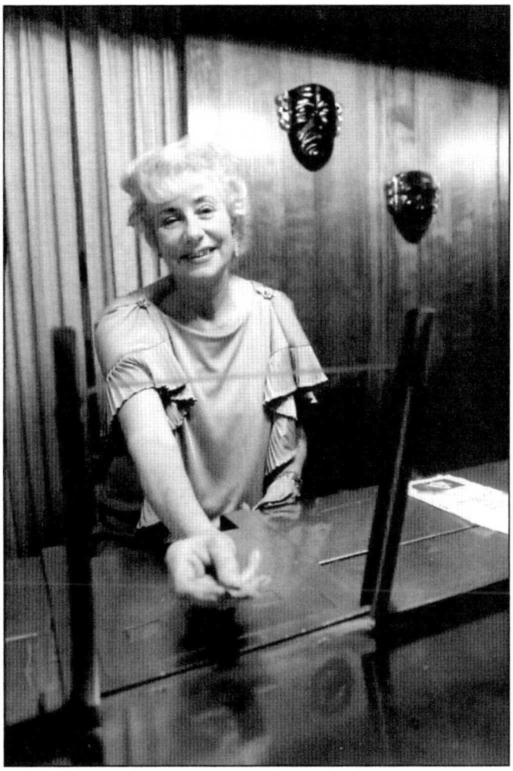

On September 3, 1977, Irene Dickinson, wife and business partner of Ken Dickinson, is handing over a small admission ticket. The feature playing on this date was *The Last Tycoon*, which starred Robert De Niro, Tony Curtis, Robert Mitchum, and Jack Nicholson. The showings were at 8:00 and 10:15 p.m. Other 1977 releases included *Star Wars*, *Smokey and the Bandit*, and *Exorcist II: The Heretic*.

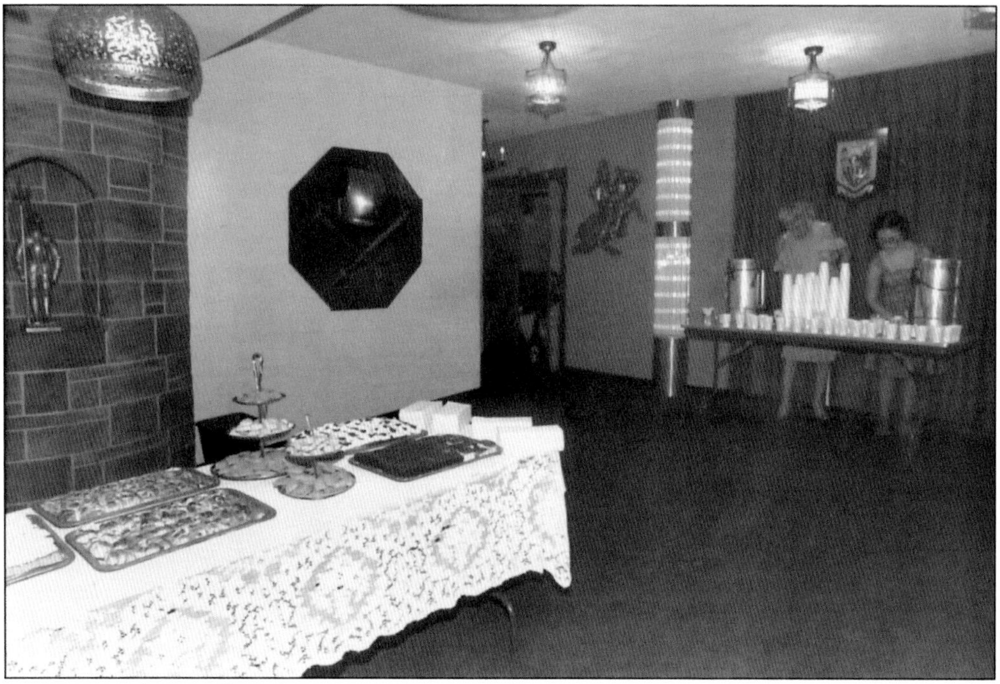

Sometimes the smallest things are the most pleasurable. Here, free coffee and cakes await moviegoers during an intermission at the Town Theatre. One would be hard-pressed to find a present-day movie theater that does this.

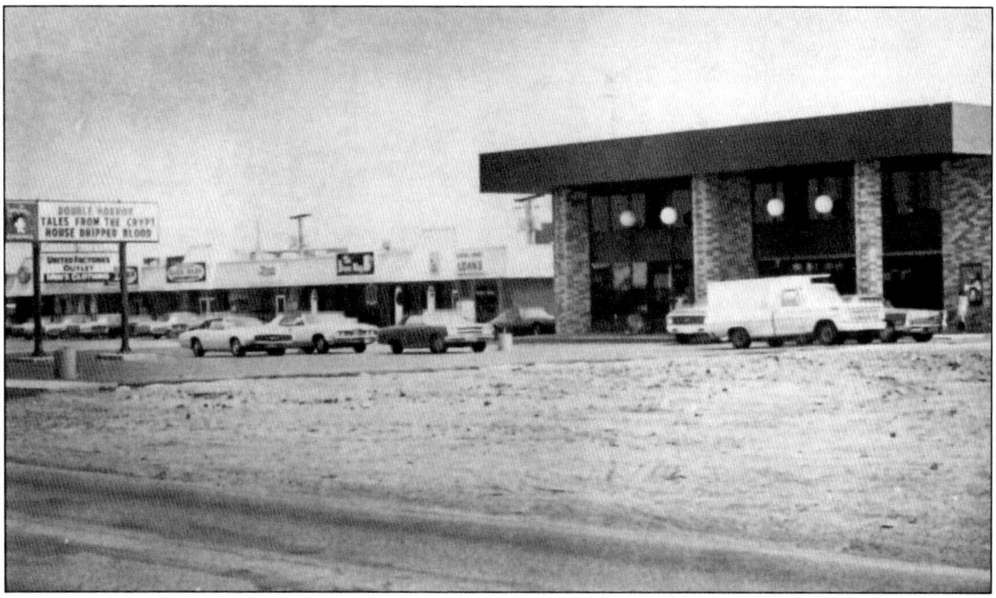

For a brief time during the 1970s, Highland had two movie theaters. This building housed a theater that was part of a national chain owned by movie star Jerry Lewis. The venture failed, driving many to economic ruin, including Lewis himself. In the end, the Lewis theater posed little threat to the Town, and it is barely remembered—if it is remembered at all.

Eight

Memories through the Years

As this short history demonstrates, Highland has grown, changed, and evolved since its incorporation in 1910. Highland began as a sparsely populated agrarian area, then adapted as the Calumet Region developed into a heavily industrialized economy. The town's population spiked during the post–World War II baby boom. Its landscape was altered due to necessity and inevitable change.

Highland has had to cope with natural and manmade disasters. Residents have had to deal with loss and trauma, and had their share of mourning. While seemingly far away from jarring world events, Highlanders had to be concerned with hot wars, cold wars, and terrorism. Men and women went off to fight and die in wars that were thousands of miles from the boundaries of the town. They are still doing that, and women have now taken a more active role in frontline action. There is little doubt that Highland will face different types of adversity in the future, whether by design or accident.

Meanwhile, the town has carved out a strong sense of identity. People have a good idea of what it means to live in Highland. Activities are organized to bring the community together, local traditions are observed, and a quality standard of living is maintained. Highland is no utopia, because no such place exists. However, the town has flourished and provides a stable and diverse living environment for its residents.

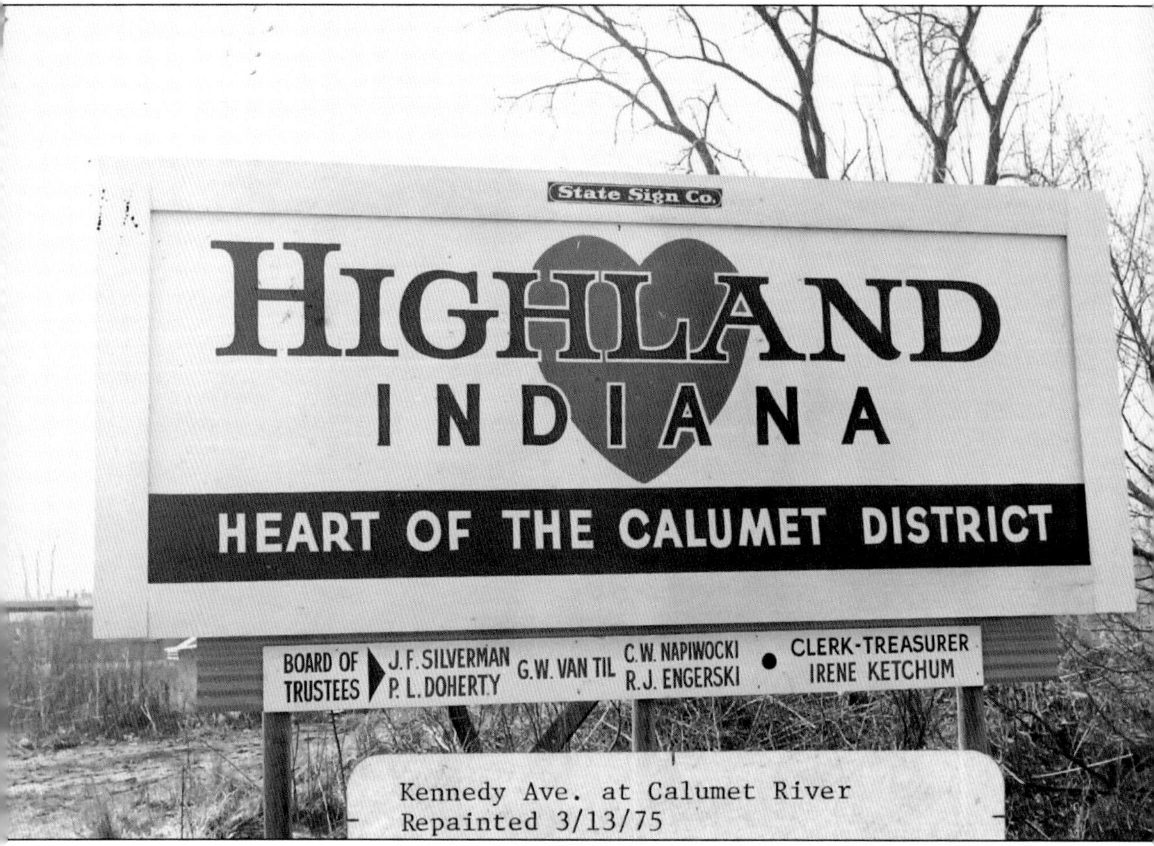

This Highland town sign welcomed visitors in 1975. Irene Ketchum served as clerk-treasurer for 23 years. Current clerk-treasurer Michael Griffin has now surpassed her record, as he is in his 25th year in the position. Paul Doherty held the job for 11 years between Ketchum and Griffin.

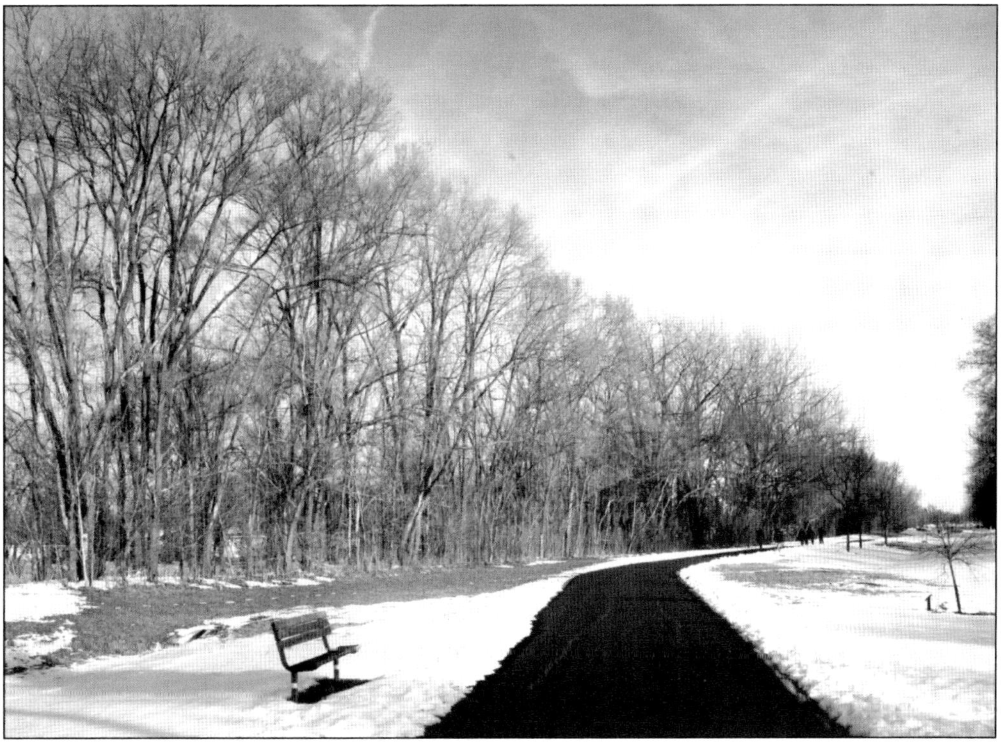

Although this might have been a little cold for bicycling, some are taking a casual stroll down one of the bike paths in Highland. The path is maintained by the Highland Parks Department. (Photograph by Gordon Wilder.)

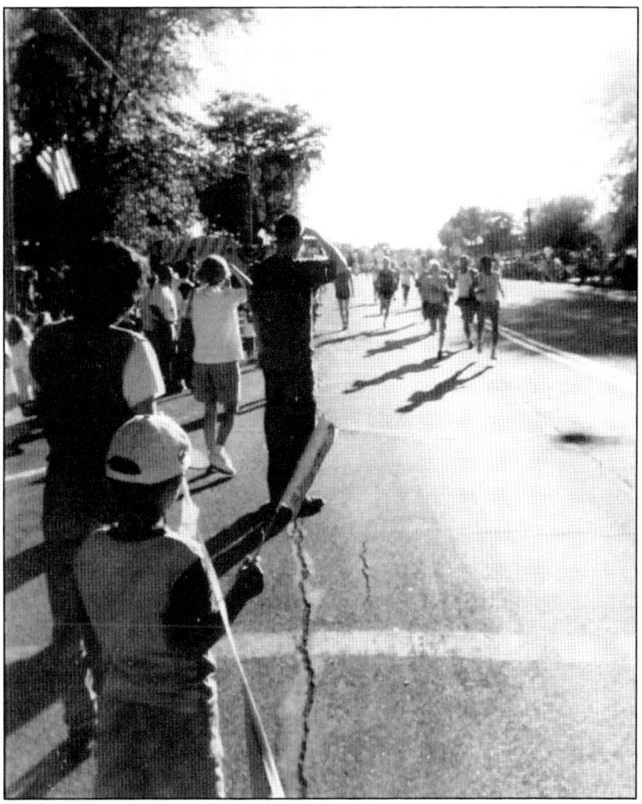

Participants are shown running in the Citizens Financial Mile, one of the holiday events sponsored by the town. Highland puts on and/or sponsors events including parades, concerts, and races like this one. The Citizens Financial Mile is held annually before the Fourth of July parade.

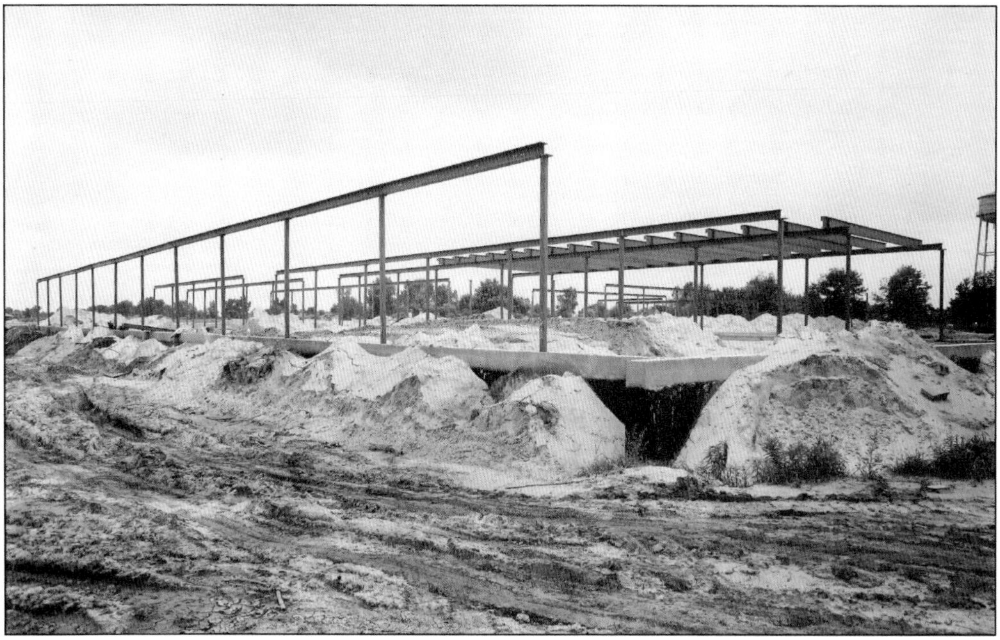

This August 2, 1956, photograph shows the beginning of construction of Highland High School. The baby boom after World War II made it necessary for the town to expand its school system. Before Highland High School opened in 1958, local high schoolers attended Griffith High School.

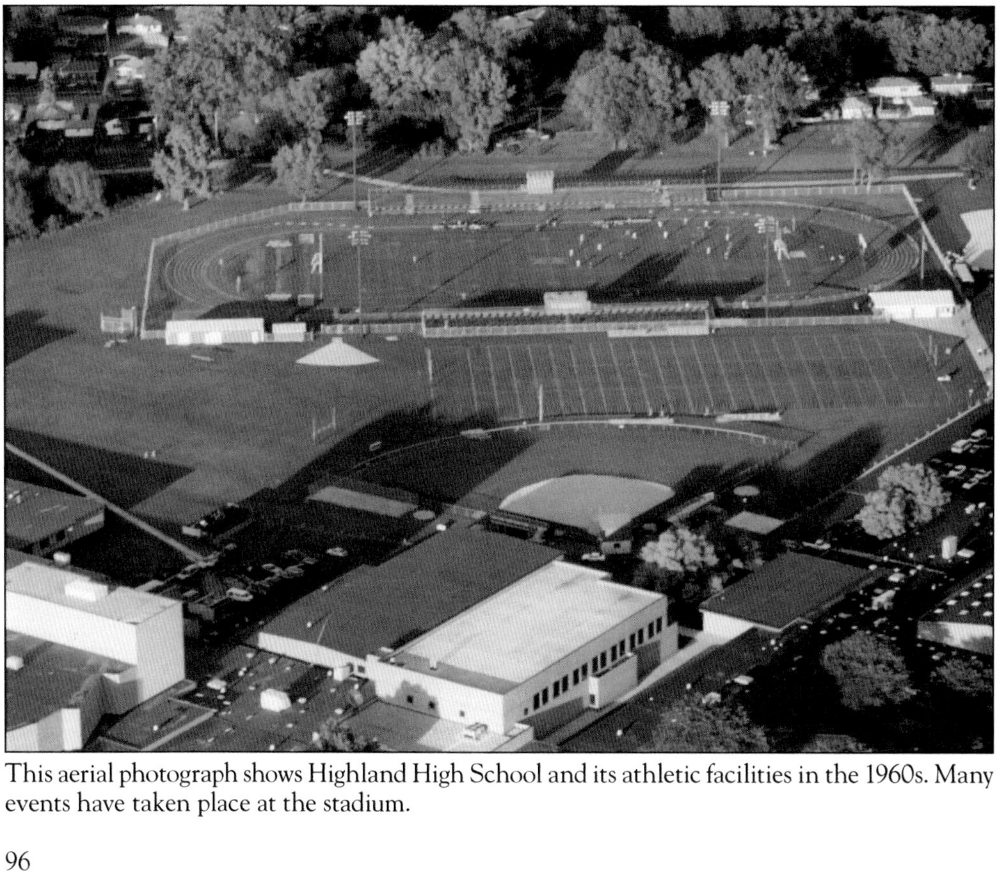

This aerial photograph shows Highland High School and its athletic facilities in the 1960s. Many events have taken place at the stadium.

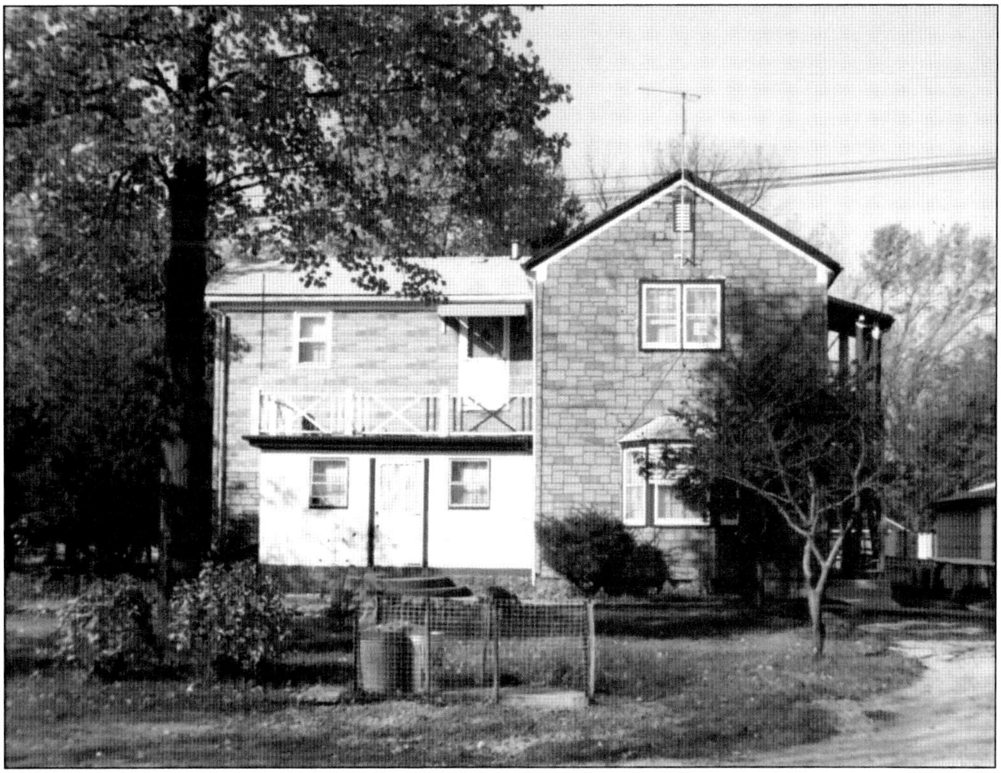

It appears that these Highland homeowners needed to protect their garbage from wild predators. Raccoons, deer, skunks, and even an occasional coyote still roam the town.

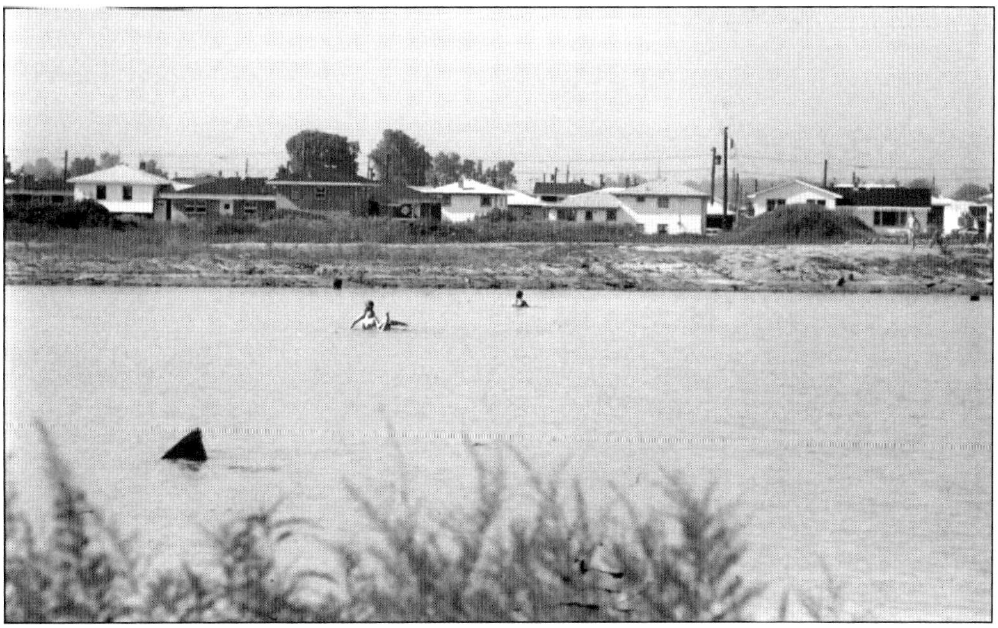

This small lake sits in the subdivision appropriately called Lake Side. In this 1968 photograph, something looking like a shark fin is jutting out of the otherwise calm water. There has been no history of shark attacks in Highland at Lake Side or anywhere else nearby. (Andy Finick.)

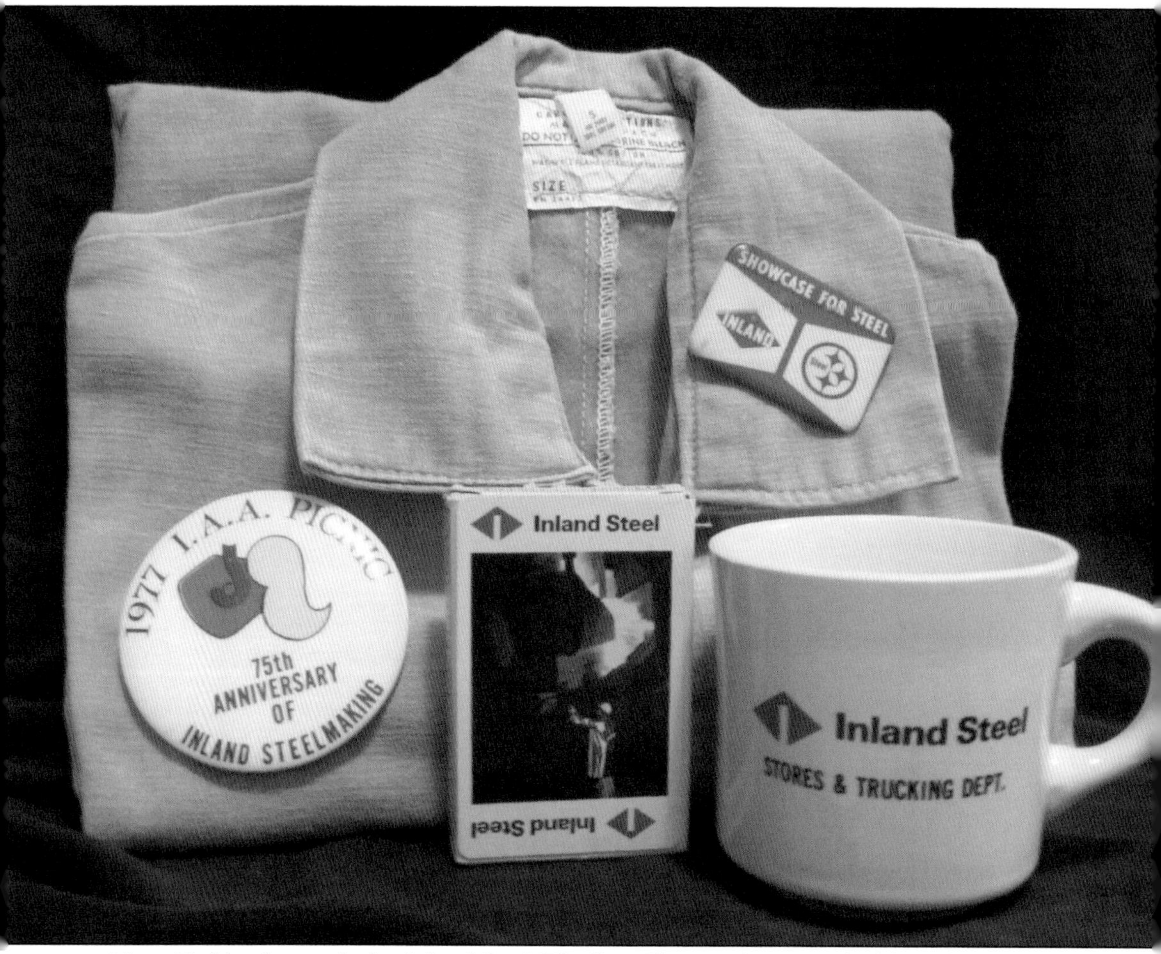

Many Highlanders worked at Inland Steel. The East Chicago plant stretched for miles on the Lake Michigan shore. In 1977, when the company celebrated its 75th anniversary, Inland boasted a payroll of over 24,000. Twenty years later, Inland was purchased by Ispat International, and those assets are now part of Arcelor Mittal. It is a profitable facility, but its employment numbers are much lower than in 1977. This green jacket is made of a flame-retardant material that shields workers from steel that is sometimes heated to thousands of degrees. (Photograph by Theresa Pecsek.)

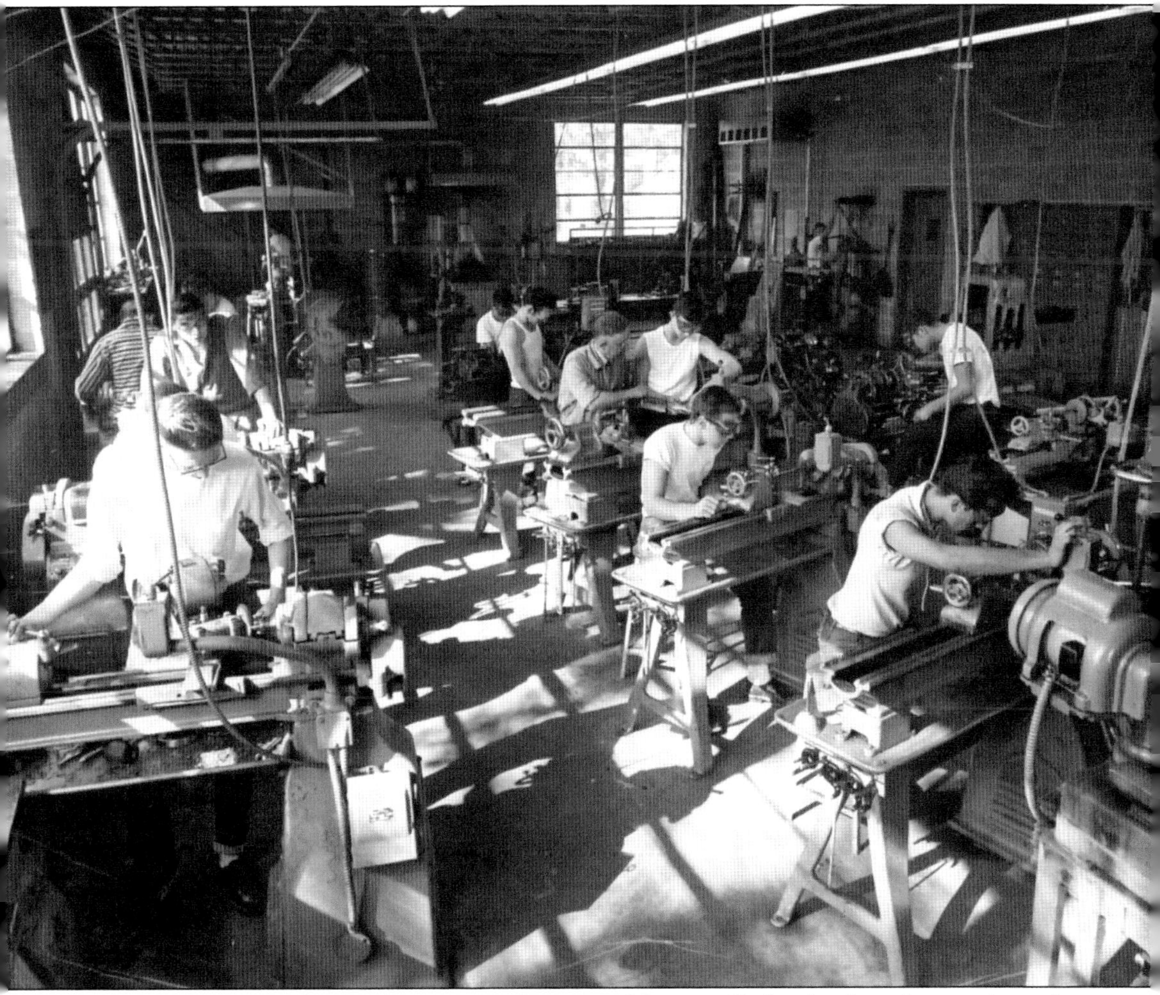

This 1955 Griffith High School image is truly a relic of the past. High school machine and metal shops provided early training for young men to work in local steel mills and other manufacturing concerns. The mills still operate but are not employment intensive, relatively speaking, which is an indication of the industrial downturn in the United States. In 1955, Highland students attended Griffith High School, and Highland resident Andy Finick was in this class. (Andy Finick.)

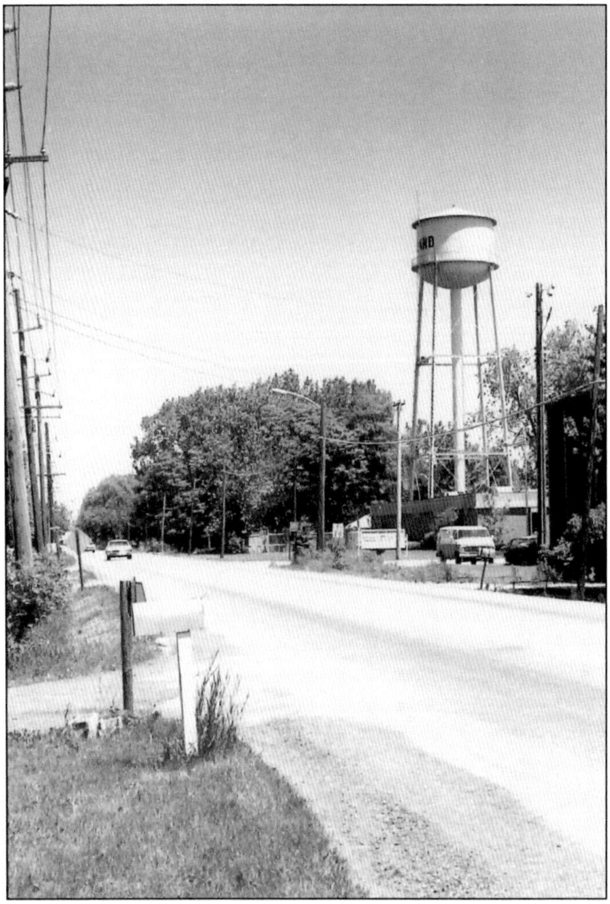

This northward view shows Kennedy Avenue during the 1970s, just before the road was expanded. The town water tower and school administration building are to the right. Note the rural mailbox and the lack of curbs. The water tower no longer exists. (Andy Finick.)

The beginnings of St. James the Less Catholic Church are pictured here during the early 1970s. St. James is now a sprawling facility and a major part of Highland's religious community. This image looks west on Forty-Fifth Street and Kennedy Avenue. In the background is Fire Station No. 2. (Andy Finick.)

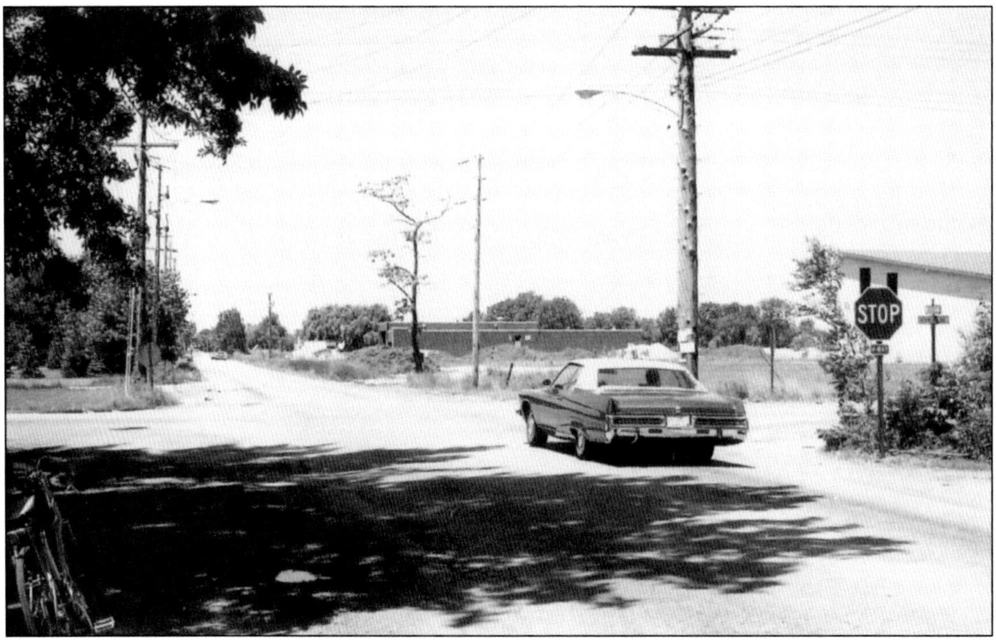

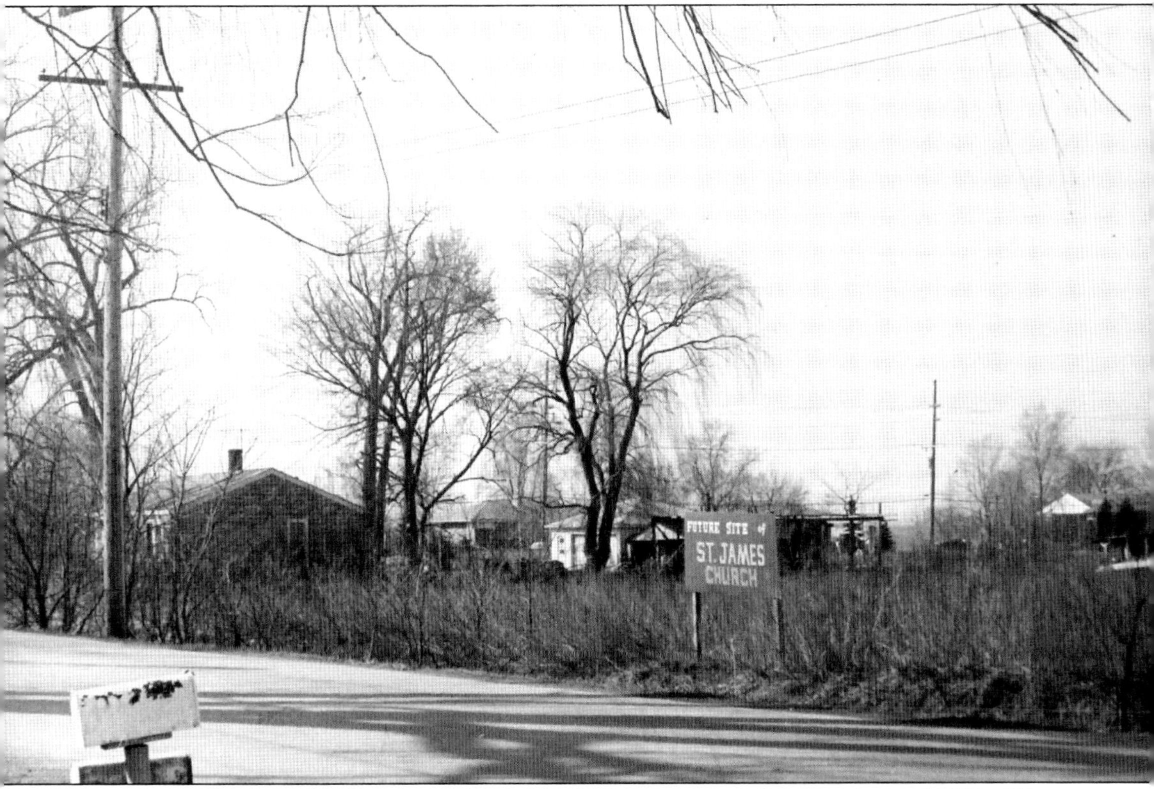

The corner of Forty-Fifth Street and Kennedy Avenue is shown here in the mid-1970s. This intersection is now quite a bit busier. In addition to the St. James the Less Catholic Church, it is now occupied by First Financial Bank, Wendy's, and a Speedway gas station. (Andy Finick.)

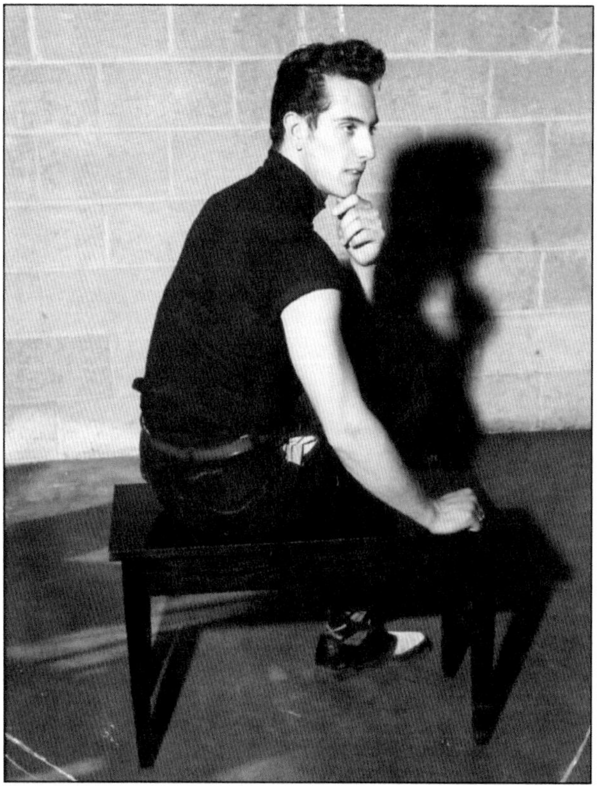

A pensive Andy Finick is pictured during his high school years getting ready to rehearse for a school play. He jokingly told the authors that his acting career ended after high school, and the decision seemed to be made for him. (Andy Finick.)

This is the first-grade class picture taken at Lincoln School in 1961.

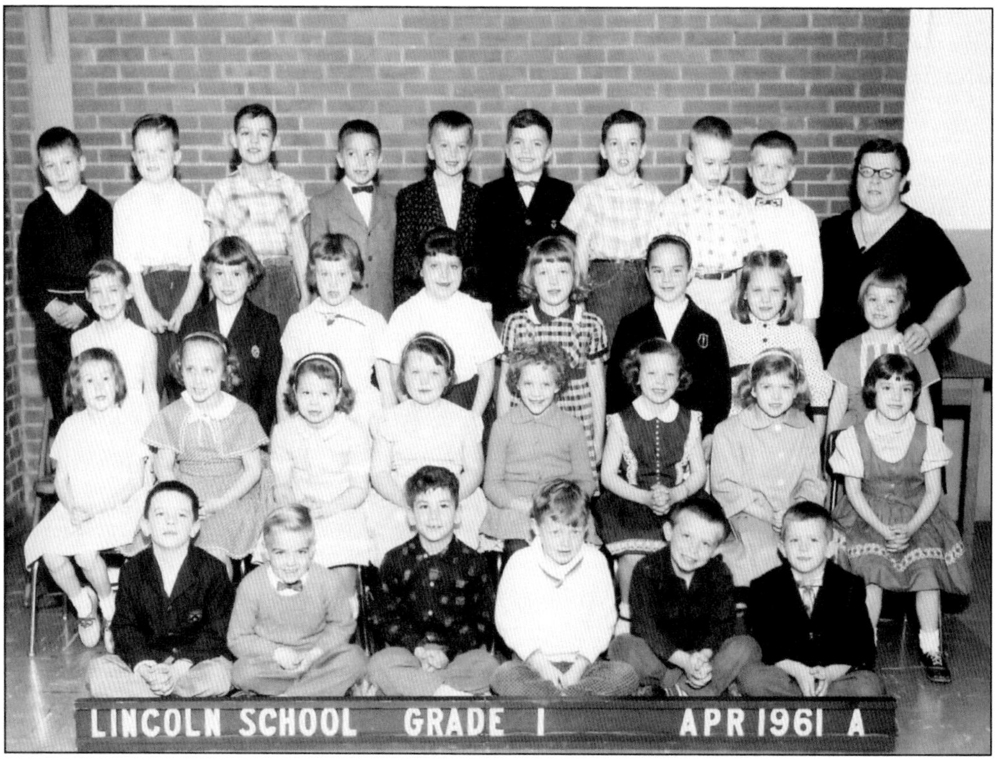

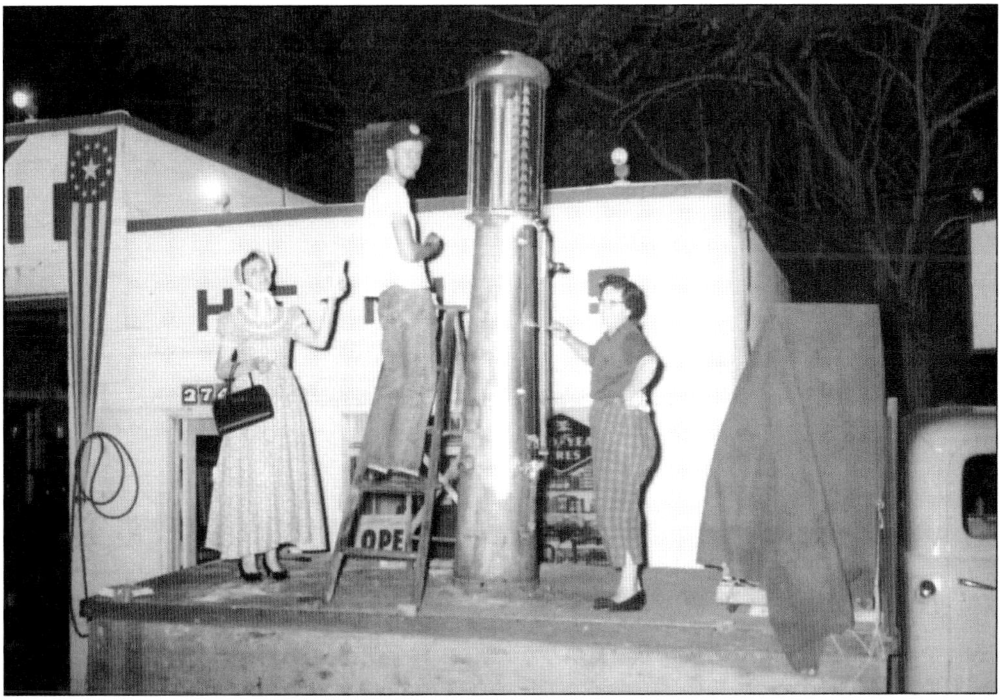

The activity of decorating the bed of a truck for a Fourth of July parade has become a timeless tradition in the United States. The woman on the left was perhaps dressed to act in a play.

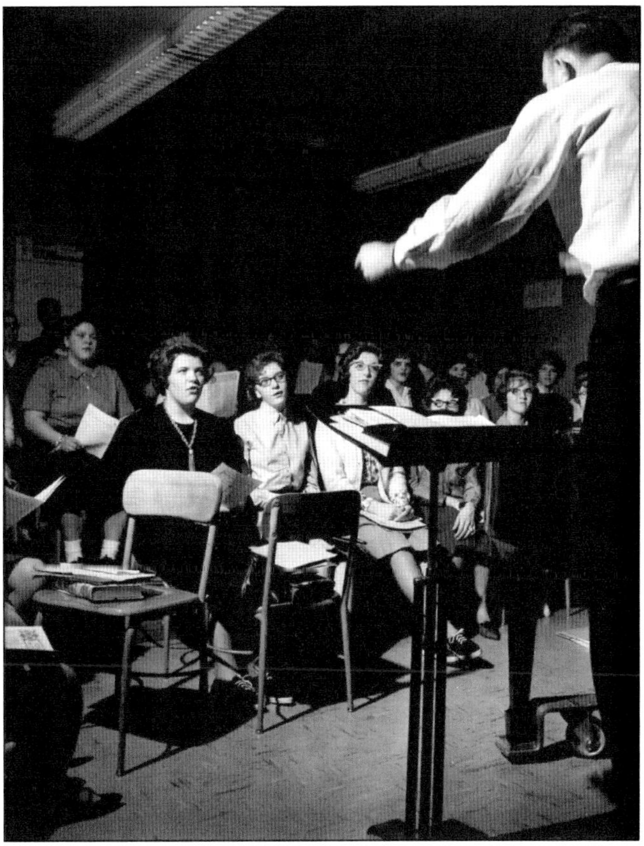

Highland High School teacher Gordon Wilder is leading the choir. Wilder taught for nearly 30 years in the Highland school system and also helped produce high school musicals.

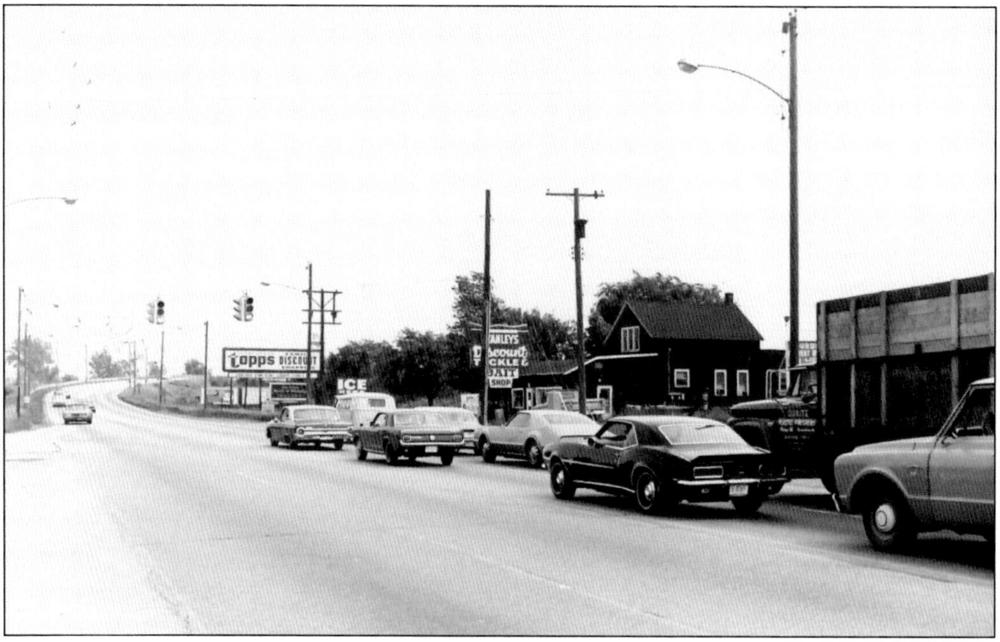

This is a stretch of Indianapolis Boulevard during the early to mid-1960s. This part of US Route 41 has changed several times since then and now looks little like this.

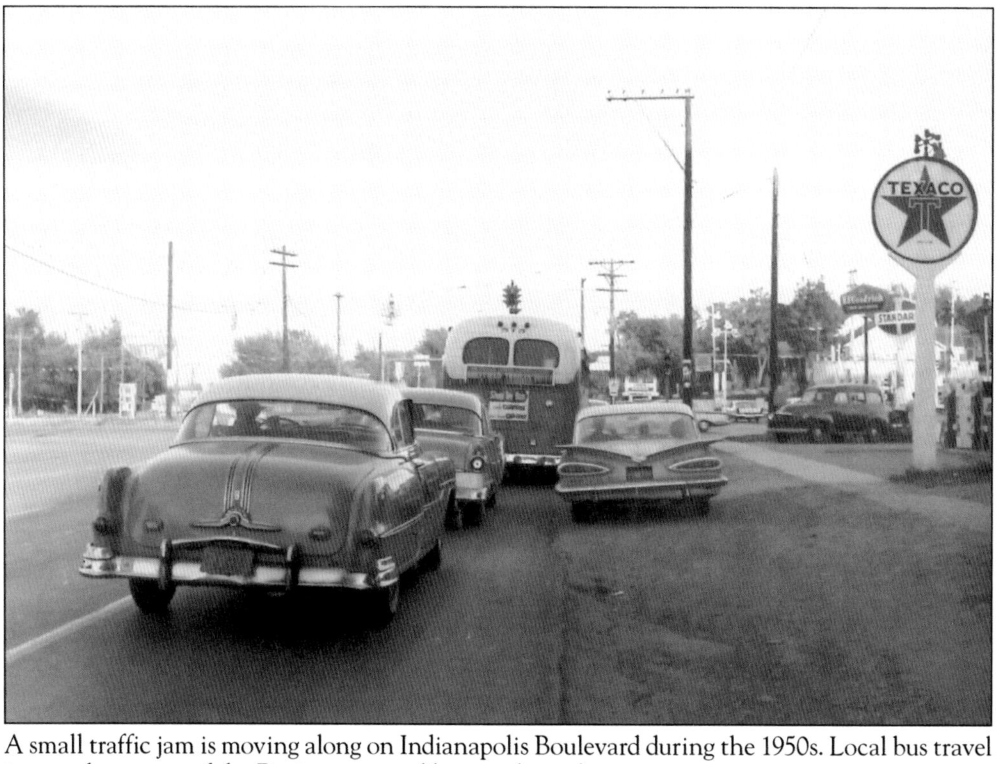

A small traffic jam is moving along on Indianapolis Boulevard during the 1950s. Local bus travel is not a large part of the Region now and has not been for some time.

This 1960s picture features the old press box at the Highland High School football field. The sign shows the team's schedule for about half of the season. Edison and Emerson no longer exist. Dyer became the present-day Lake Central High School.

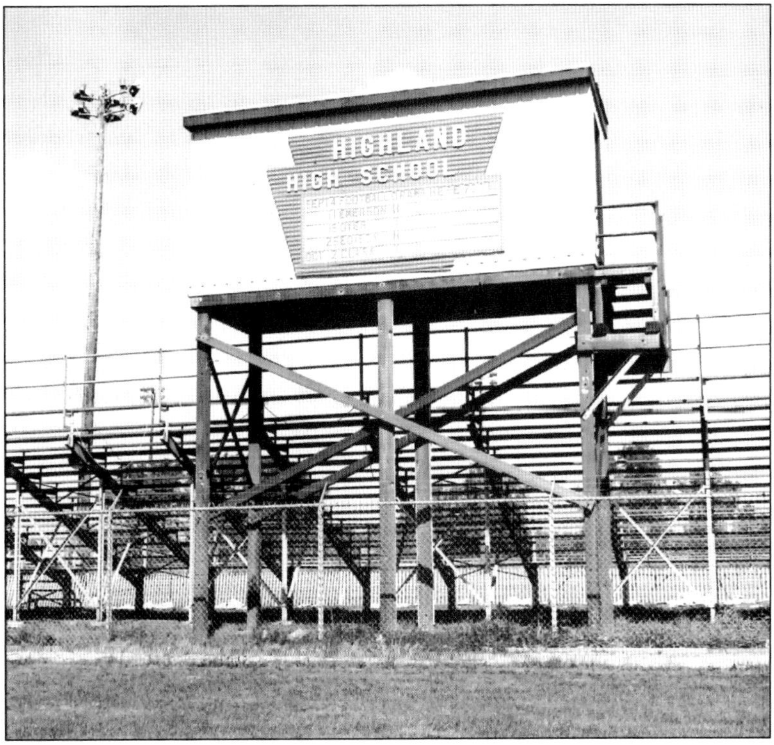

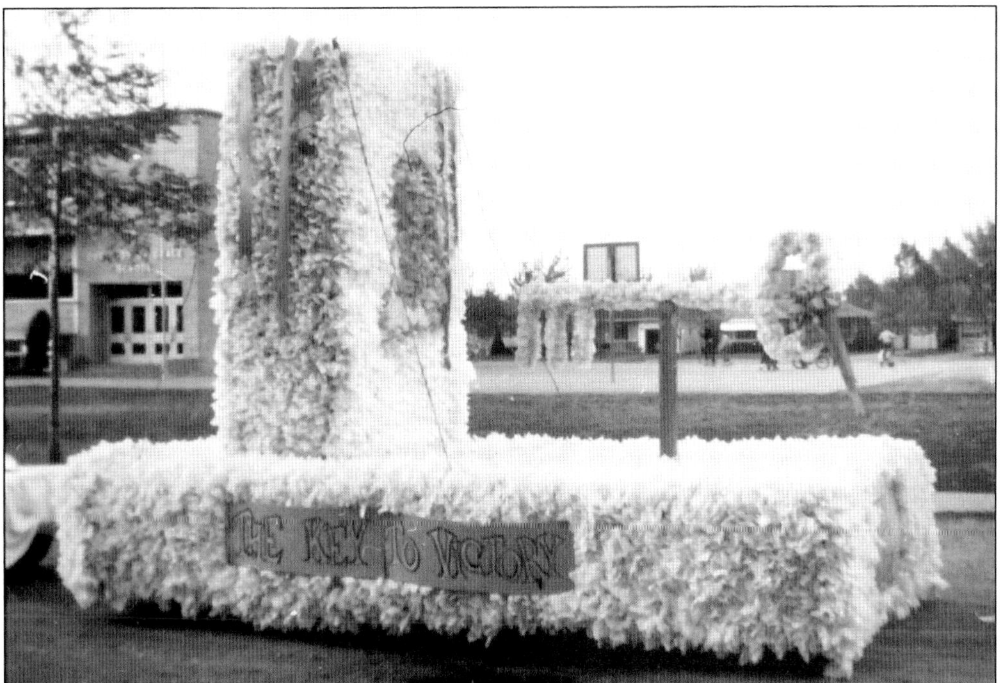

This is a float encouraging the Highland High School football team to victory. Our Lady of Grace Catholic Grade School is in the background as the float is making its way down Highway Avenue. Our Lady of Grace Church was not built until 1967.

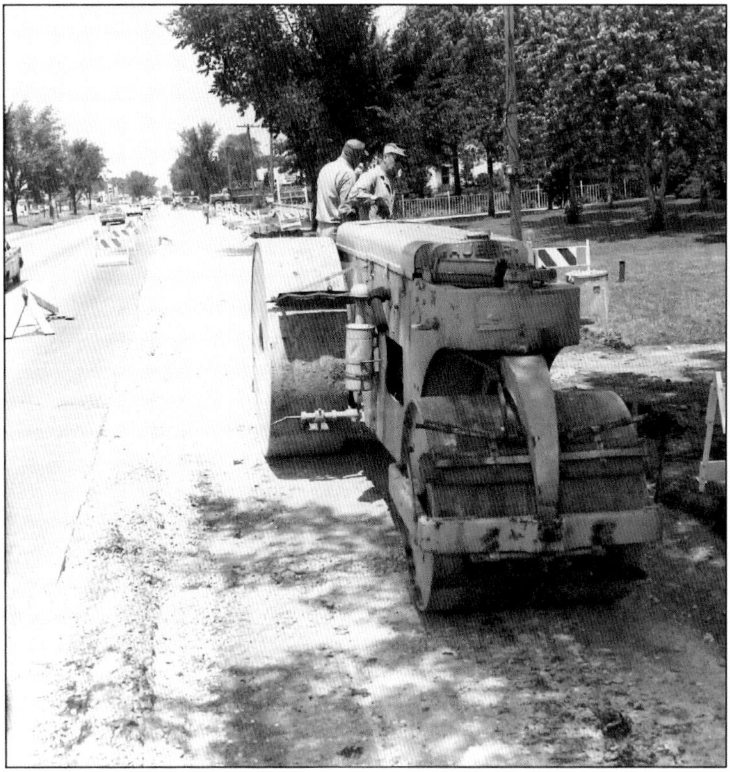

These construction workers are helping with the ambitious widening of Kennedy Avenue during the mid-1970s. Curbs and lanes were added to form a four-lane road. In 2016, a major water line project was completed and the road was resurfaced from Highway and Kennedy Avenues to Forty-Fifth Street.

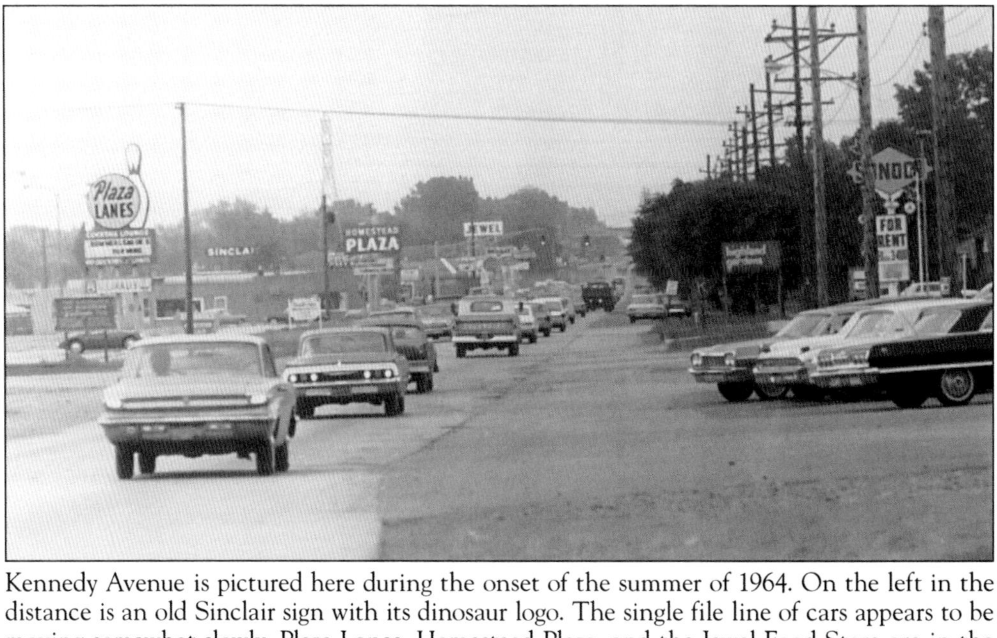

Kennedy Avenue is pictured here during the onset of the summer of 1964. On the left in the distance is an old Sinclair sign with its dinosaur logo. The single file line of cars appears to be moving somewhat slowly. Plaza Lanes, Homestead Plaza, and the Jewel Food Store are in the background. This view looks south on Kennedy Avenue.

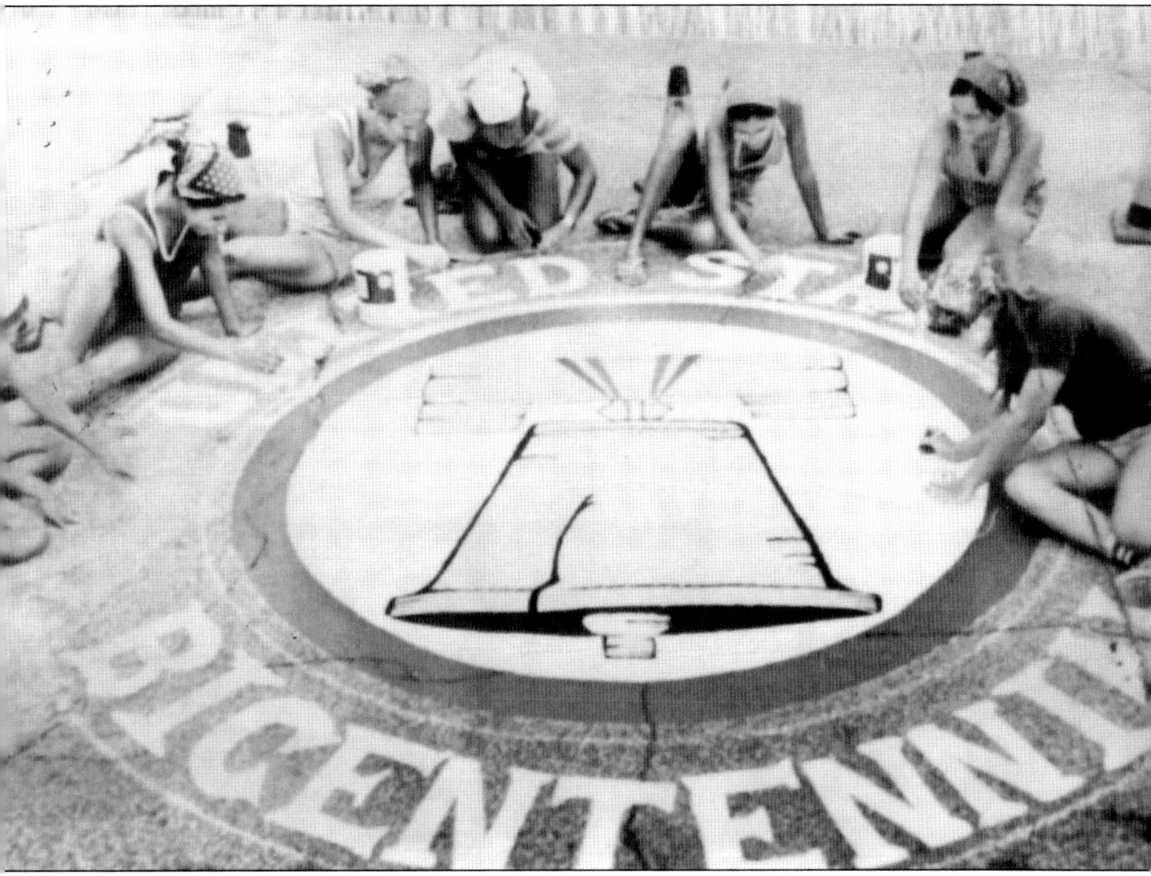

High school students are shown working on a seal observing the nation's bicentennial in 1976. The celebration was a needed diversion after the traumas of the Vietnam War and the Watergate scandal. Many Americans made it a point to travel to historical sites that summer. In Highland, the smoke from the fireworks show in town hung in the air during the warm July 4 summer night.

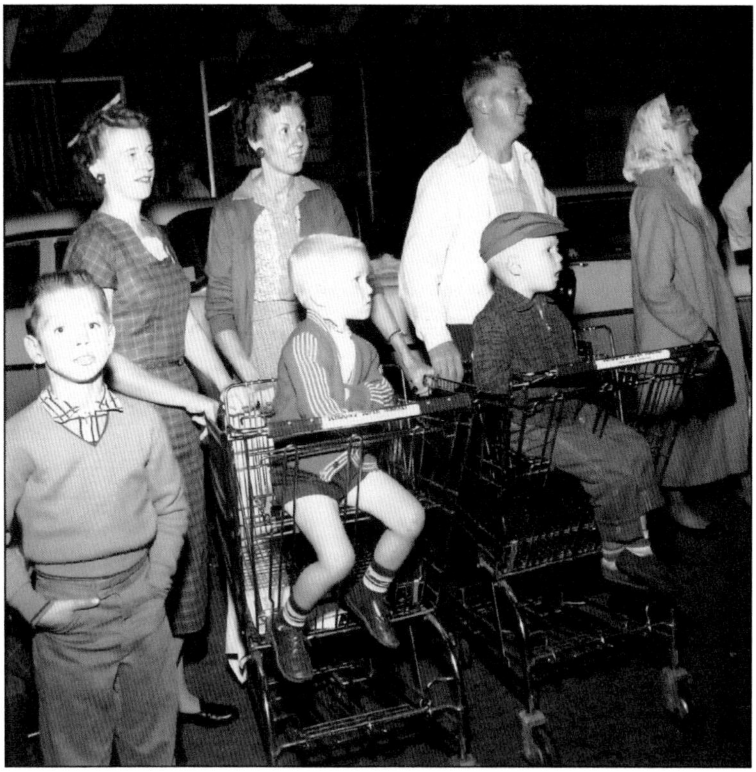

In this image from the 1950s, several families are waiting for the Fourth of July parade to come to downtown Highland. Traditionally, the parade is held on the evening before the Fourth.

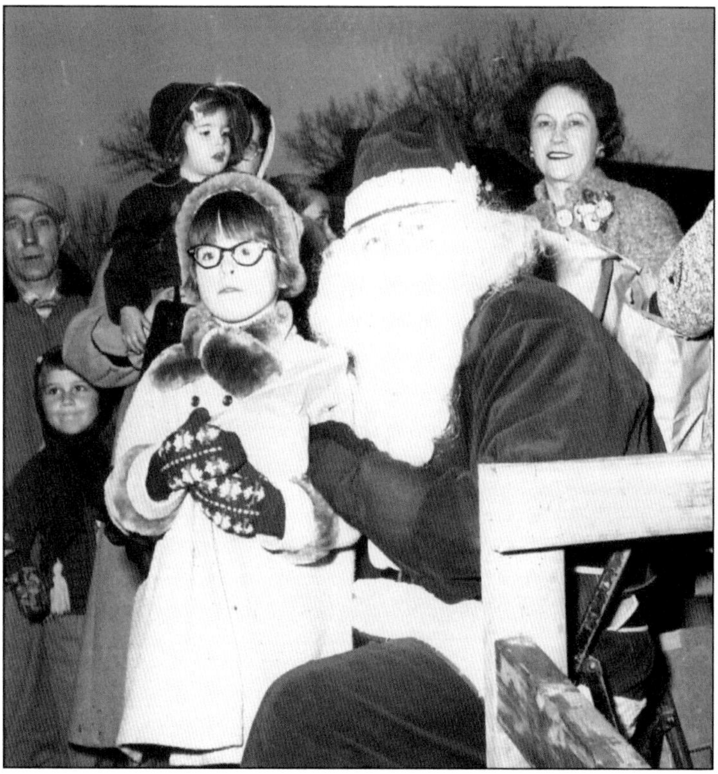

Santa Claus has always been a visitor in downtown Highland at the end of the holiday parade. This picture is from December 1956. Longtime city councilman John Farmer, who served during the 1950s, played the role of Santa Claus on many occasions. Farmer, who was also a prominent Highland businessman, died in 1974.

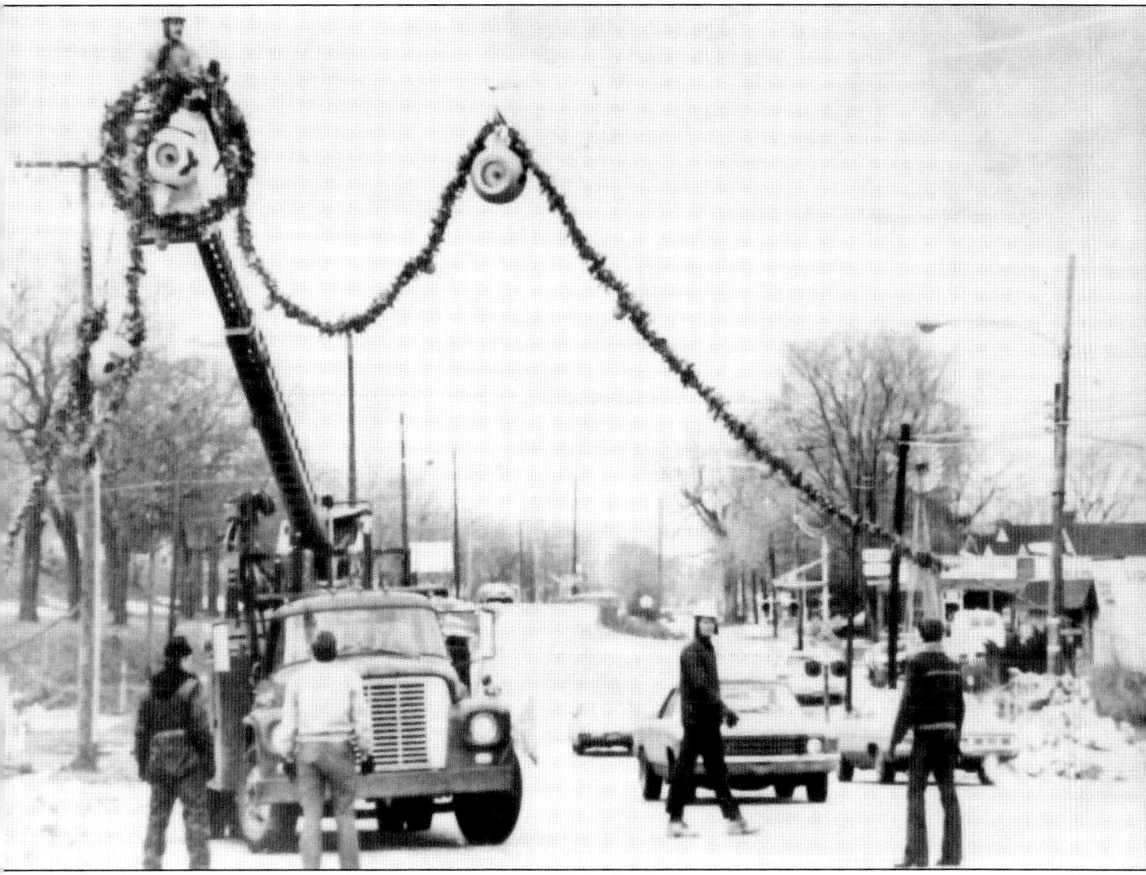

In this 1974 photograph, Highland town workers are putting up decorations during the early part of the holiday season. Holiday decorating remains a Highland custom.

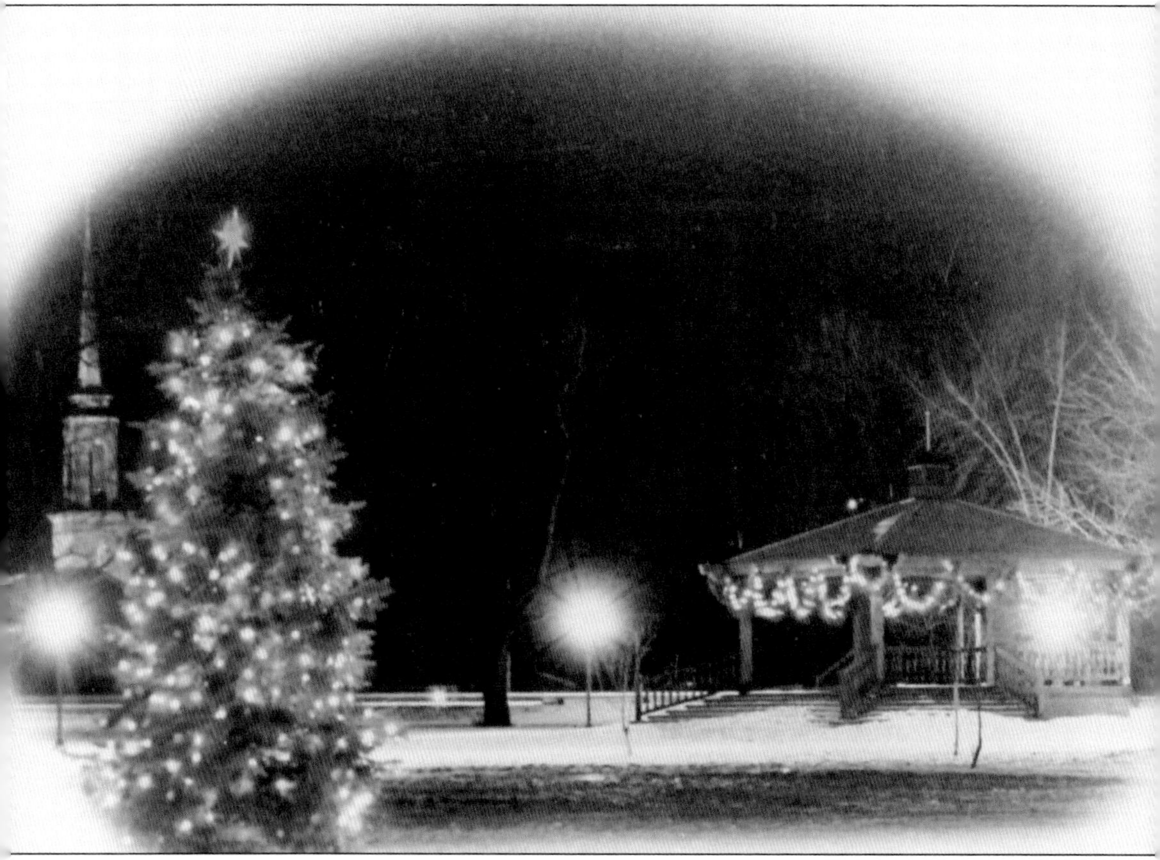

This Christmas card–type image shows the Highland Main Square in the 1980s. The Main Square gazebo provides a nice backdrop for the picture.

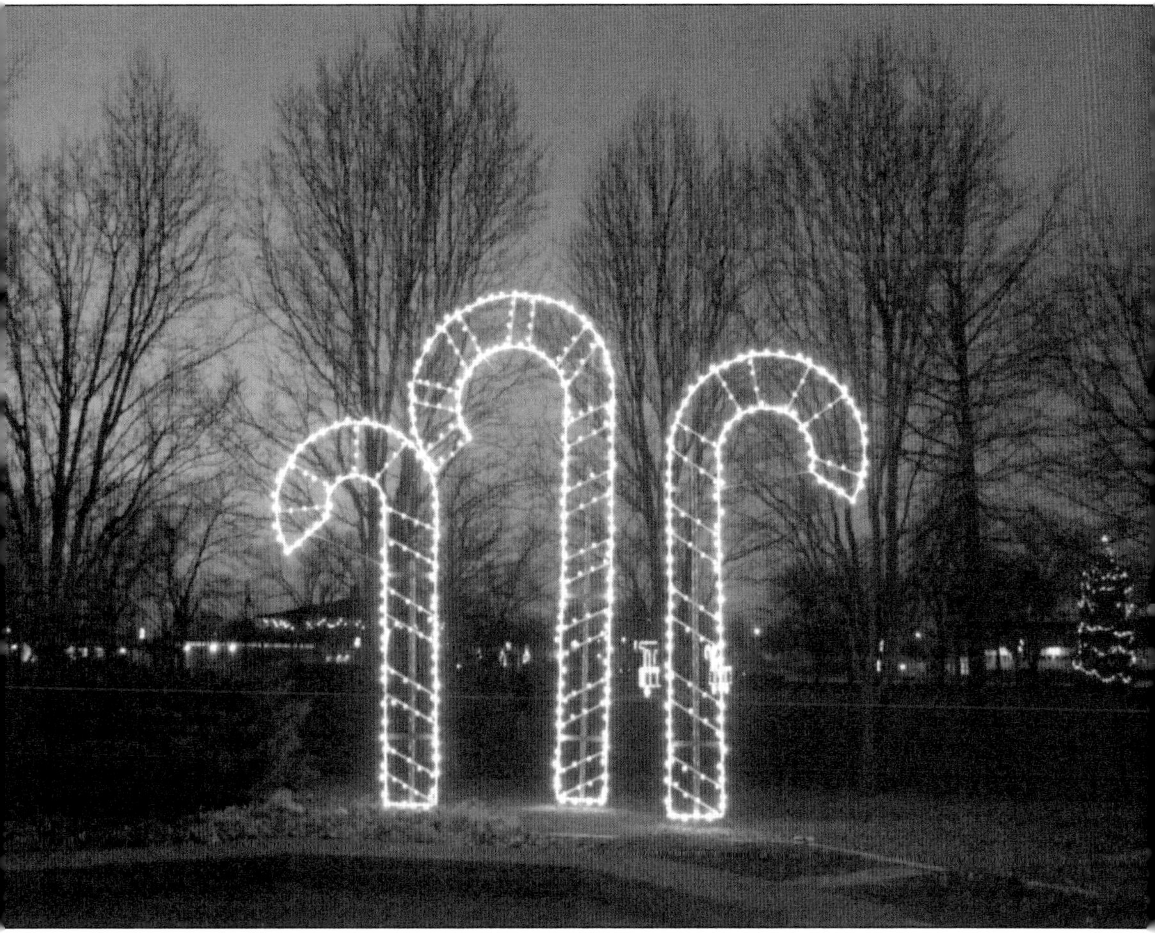

Main Square Park is the center of decorating in the town. On December 6, a switch is thrown, and the square is illuminated with lights of various shapes and sizes. Here, candy canes shine in the direction of Highway Avenue, and the perimeter of the park is also decorated. (Photograph by Theresa Pecsek.)

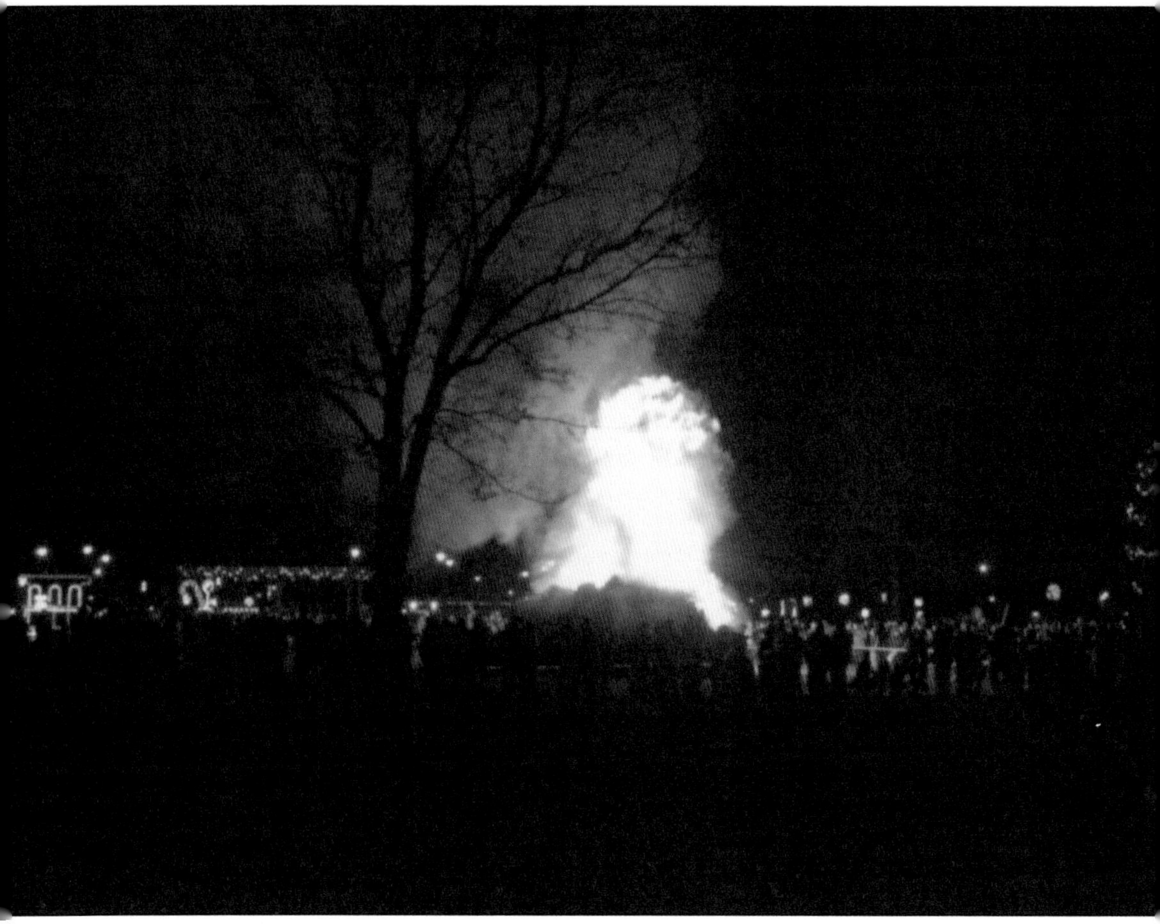

Highland residents celebrate the 12th night of Christmas by burning live Christmas trees. This bonfire lights up the area near the backdrop of the Main Square seasonal lighting. The fire is always supervised by the Highland Fire Department. (Photograph by Theresa Pecsek.)

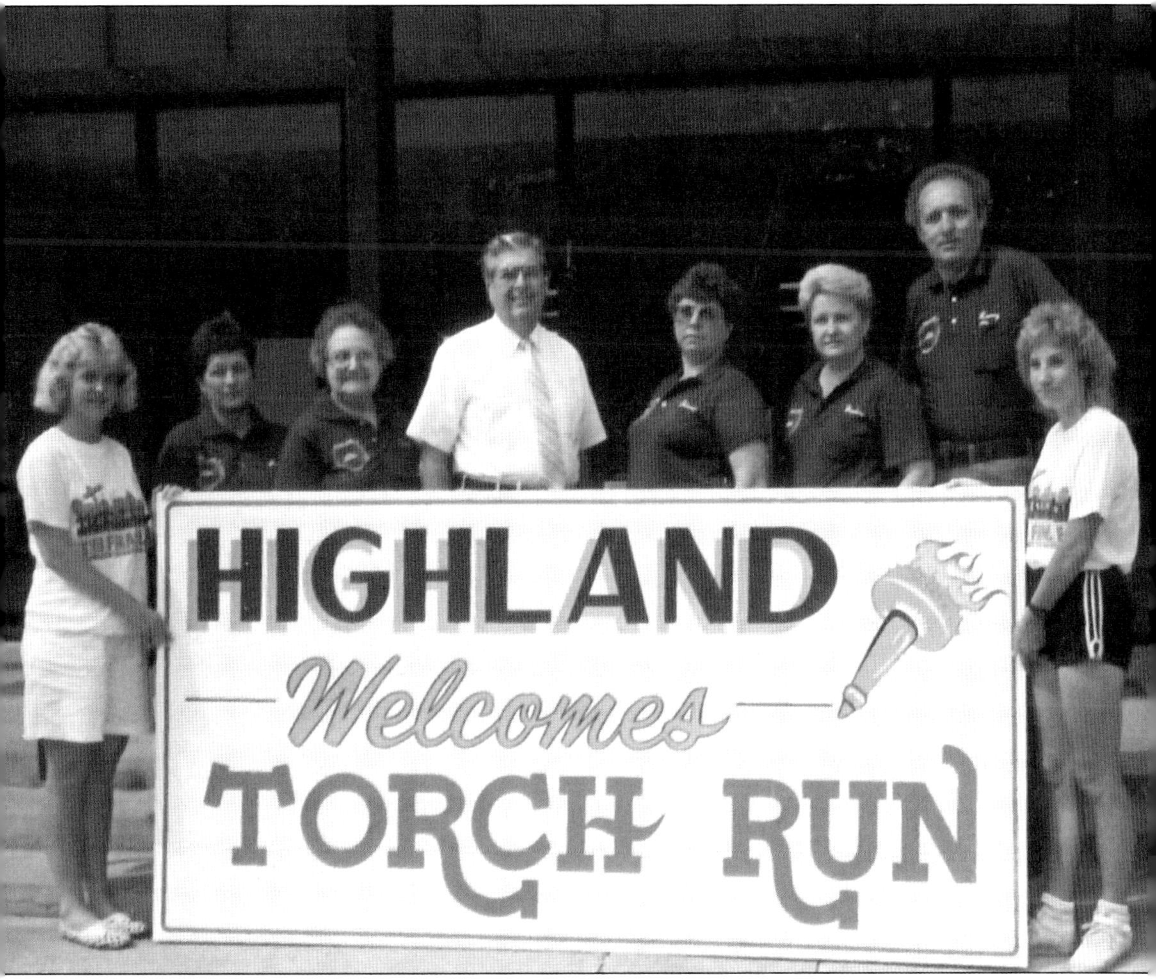

Paul Doherty is in the center of this image. Doherty served as both a town councilman and clerk-treasurer. He moved to Highland from Illinois during the 1960s. For a large part of his career, Doherty worked for AT&T. During the mid- and late 1960s, he handled communications when Pres. Lyndon Johnson visited the area. Doherty found himself standing next to Johnson several times but never spoke to the president. Doherty was an interesting political figure in his own right.

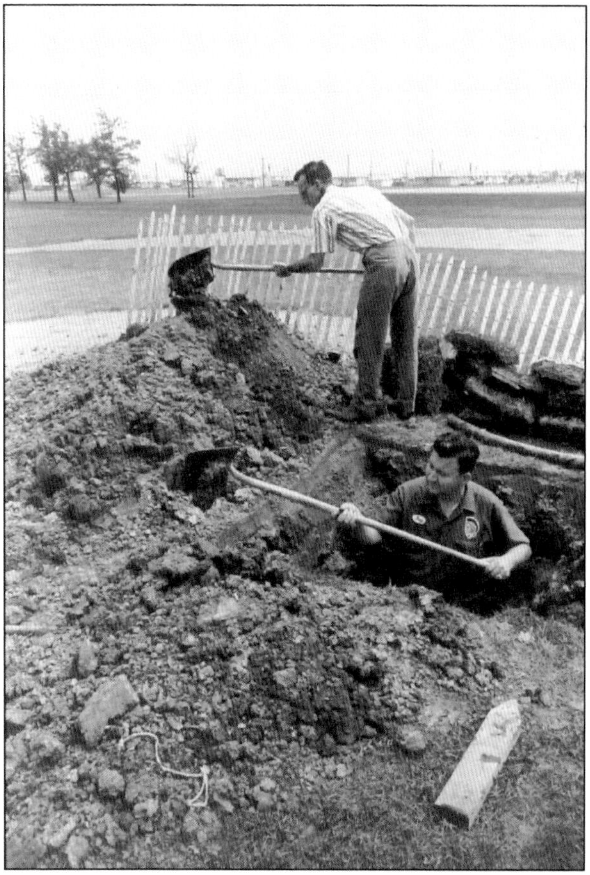

In this 1960s image, town employees look like they are digging for gold—although they are most likely making some kind of repair.

This is a recent photograph of Niko's restaurant on Highway Avenue. It was in business until 2016. The location is now an Italian/Peruvian restaurant called Jose's Family Restaurant. Hoosier Highlander has been in business since 1946. Independent and local businesses are still the backbone of downtown Highland.

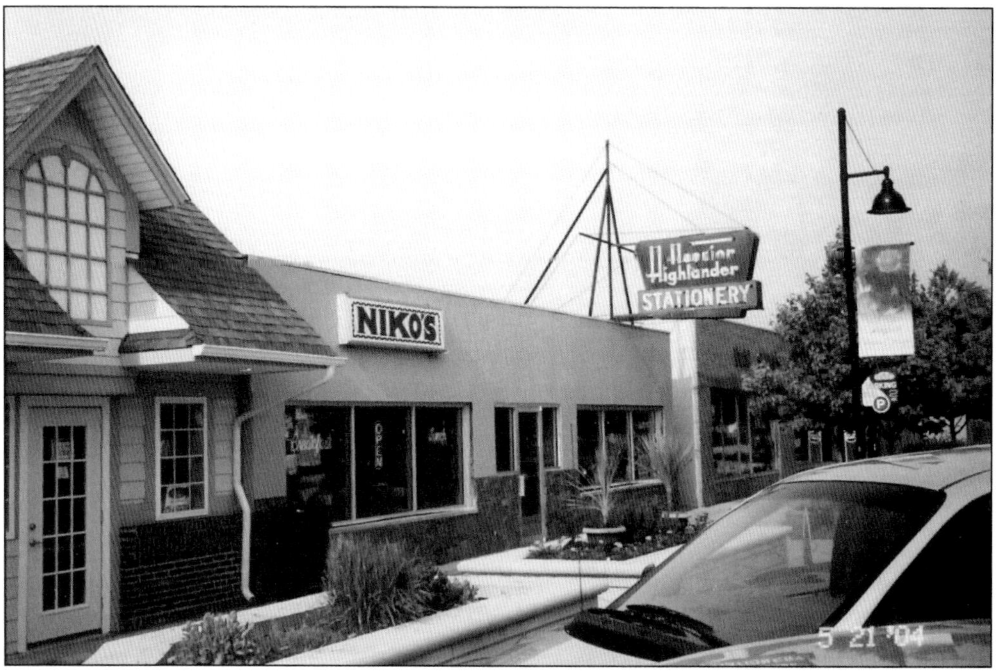

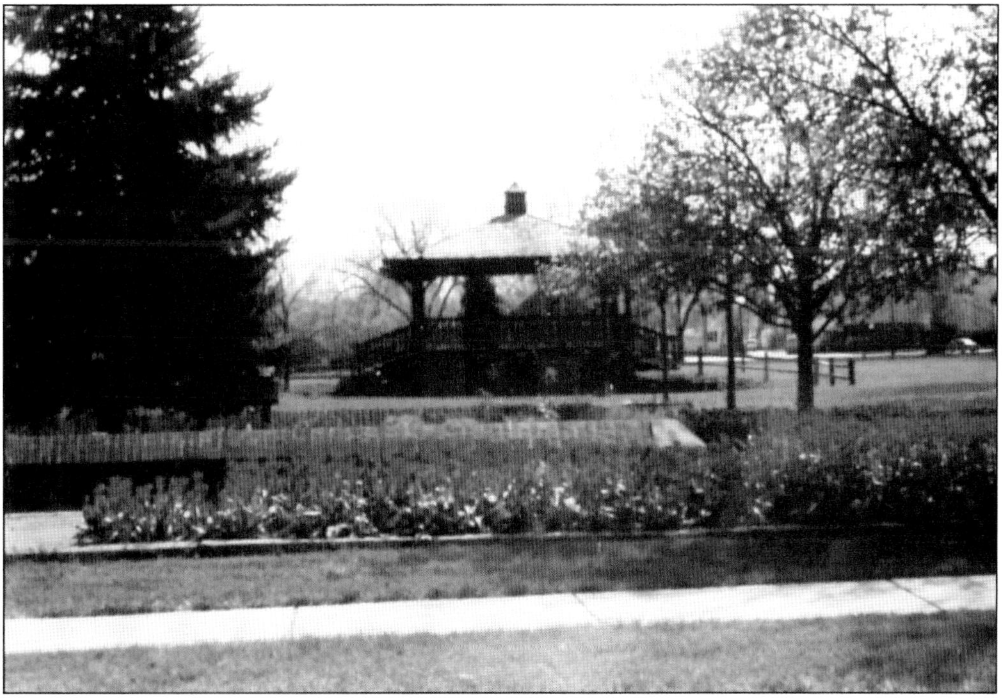

This is the Main Square Gazebo. This, the original version of the iconic Highland structure, was built in 1981. The newer version was built in the 1990s, and the town assured it would be accessible to people with disabilities in accordance with the Americans with Disabilities Act. Concerts and plays are performed at the gazebo in warm-weather months. The gazebo was a major addition to the town, provides a strong image, and is a center for many town activities.

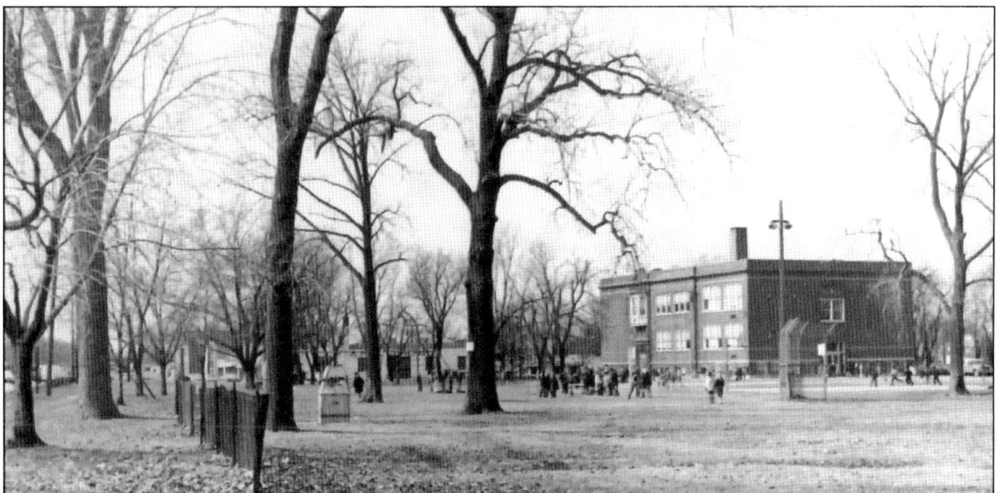

These children are playing in front of Main School in the middle of a bright fall day. The school system has grown and expanded significantly in the past few decades. The school operated from 1915 to 1972, and was razed in 1977. Main Square Park and the gazebo now reside in this location.

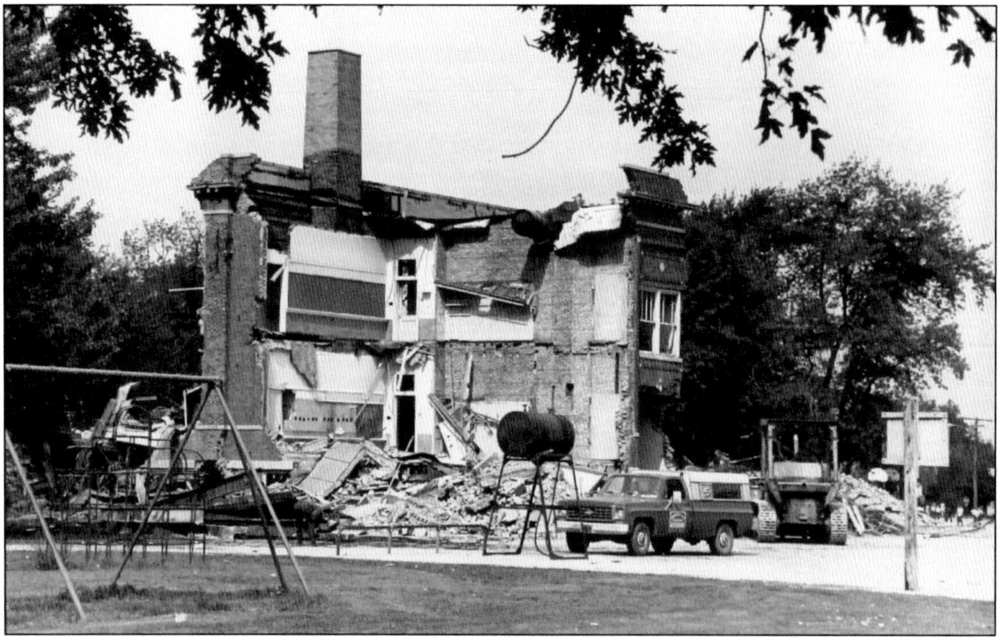

This image shows the demolition of Main School in 1977. The razing made way for the creation of Main Square Park. Note the vintage bulldozing and playground equipment.

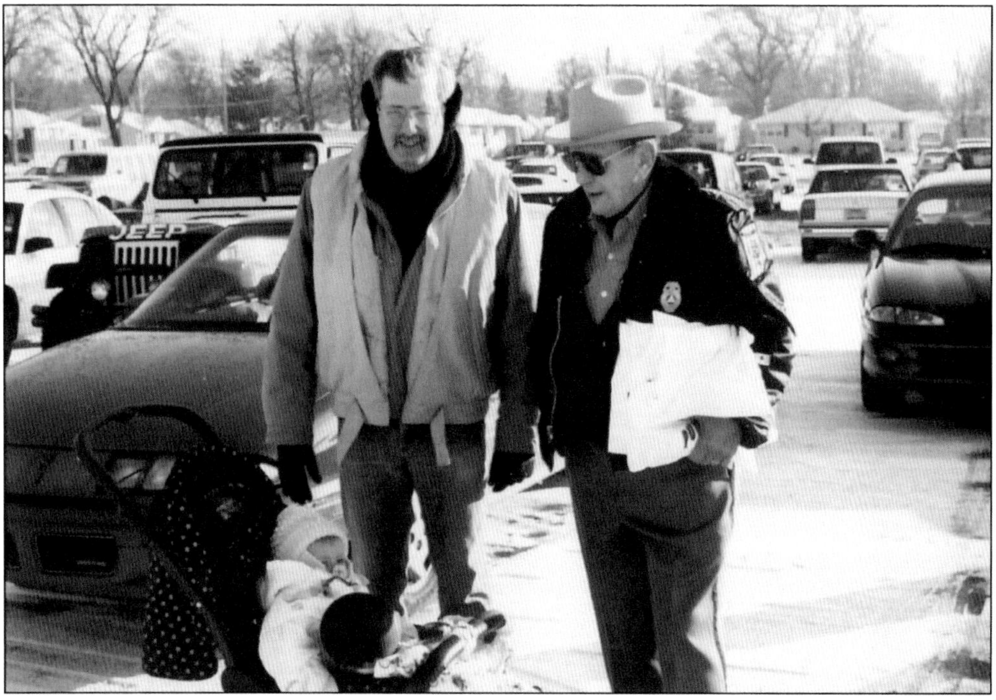

Every Thanksgiving Day morning, the town of Highland sponsors an event called the Pumpkin Plod. Residents can either walk or run on a designated and supervised route. Author Dan Helpingstine is on the left in this photograph. His daughter Leah is bundled up in the stroller. Leah was six months old at the time of her first Pumpkin Plod in 1996. Joe Szendrey, head of Highland Civil Defense, is on the right.

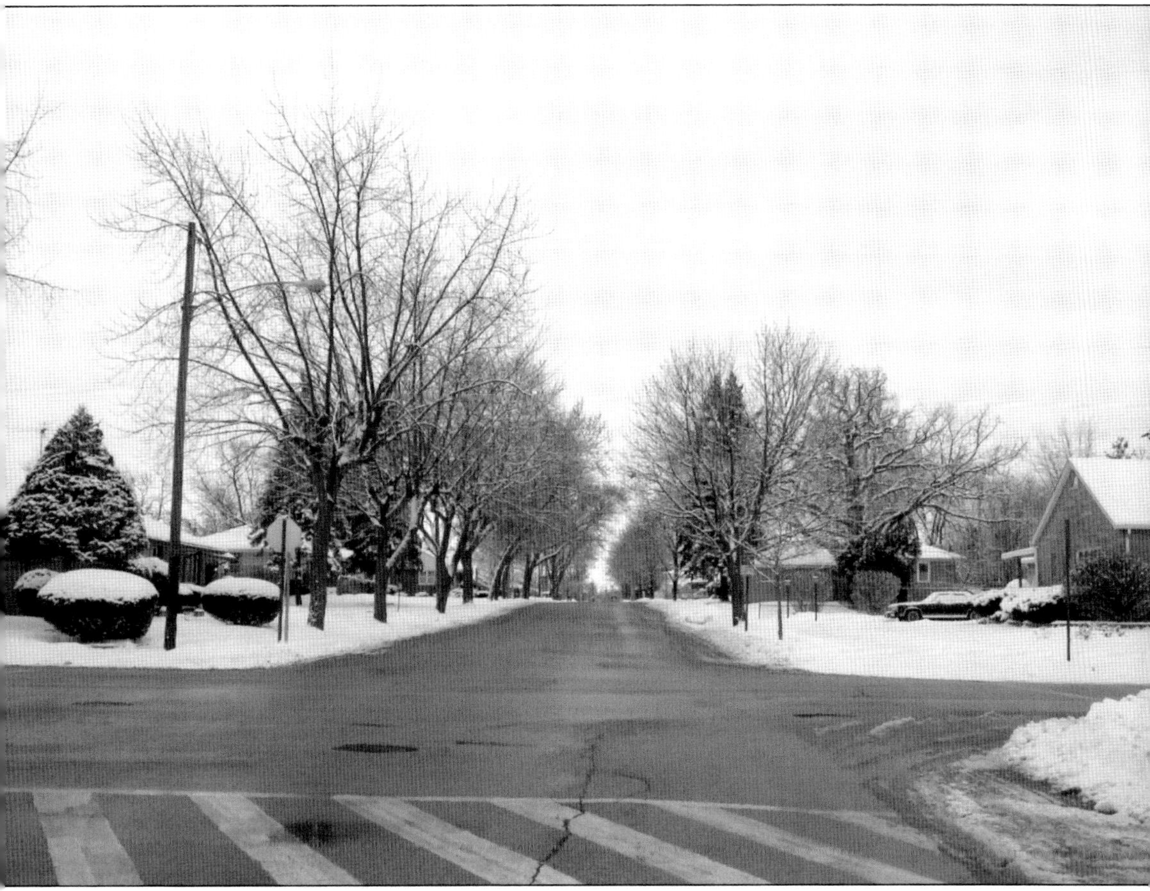

This wintry scene on a southern stretch of Fifth Avenue may calm the senses. A major portion of Fifth Avenue starts at the high school and then runs to the Lake Side subdivision. This stretch, which is about a mile long, is lined with churches, businesses, and homes. (Photograph by Theresa Pecsek.)

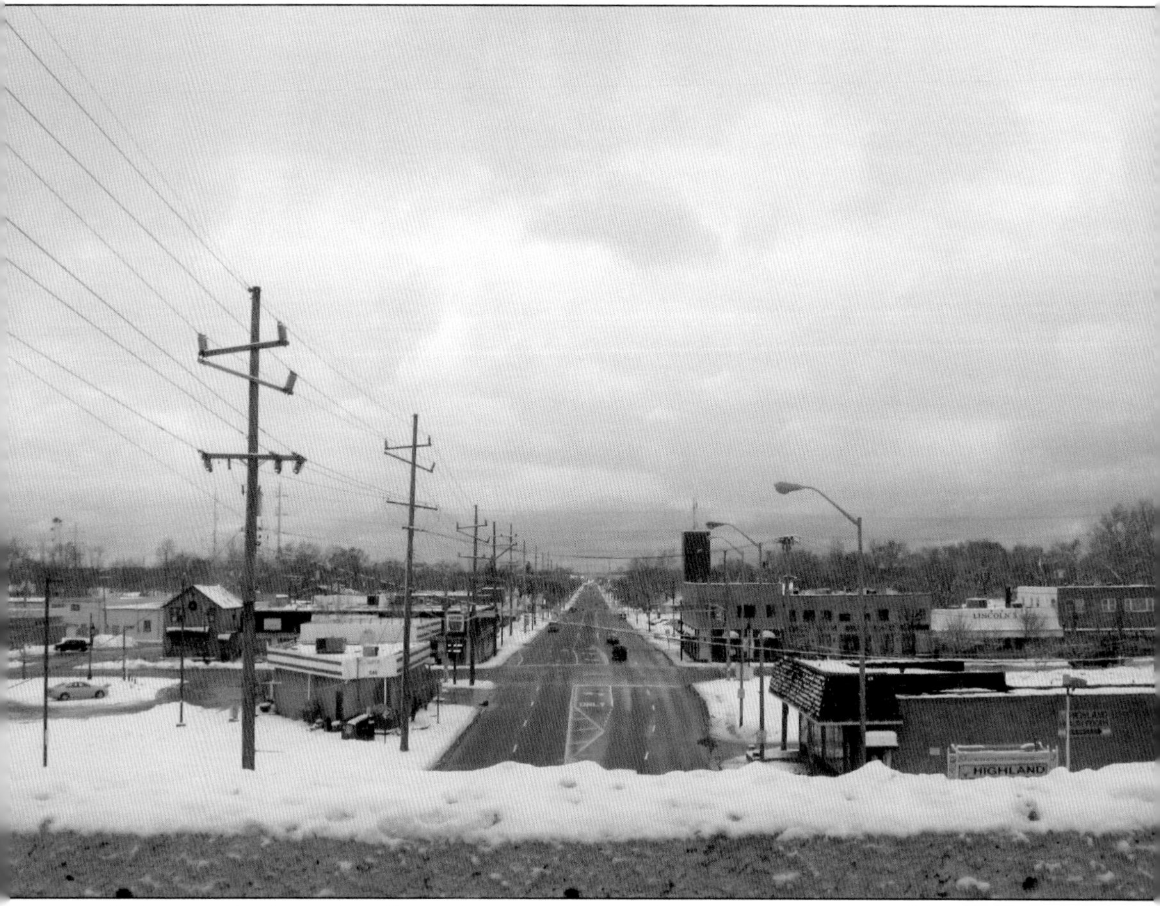

This picture looks north on Kennedy Avenue during what appears to be a peaceful winter morning. The sign for Lincoln's sandwich shop is visible at right. Lincoln's now occupies the site that was once home to the Highland Department Store. (Photograph by Theresa Pecsek.)

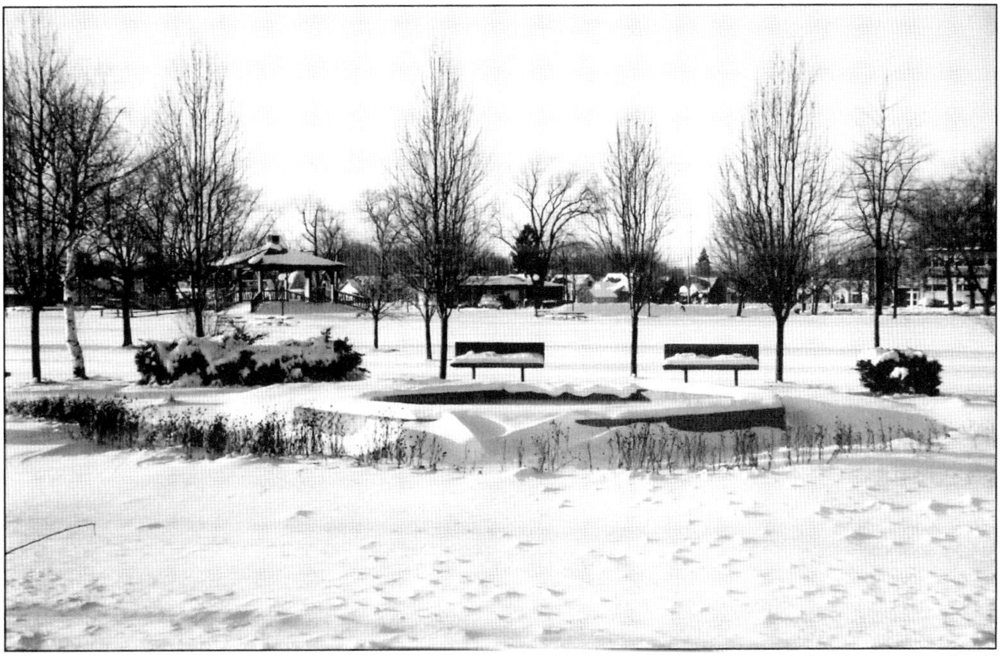

This is a recent and quiet wintry view of the fountain at the Main Square Park. The fountain, which is located at the southeast corner of the park, looks appealing even when it is not in operation.

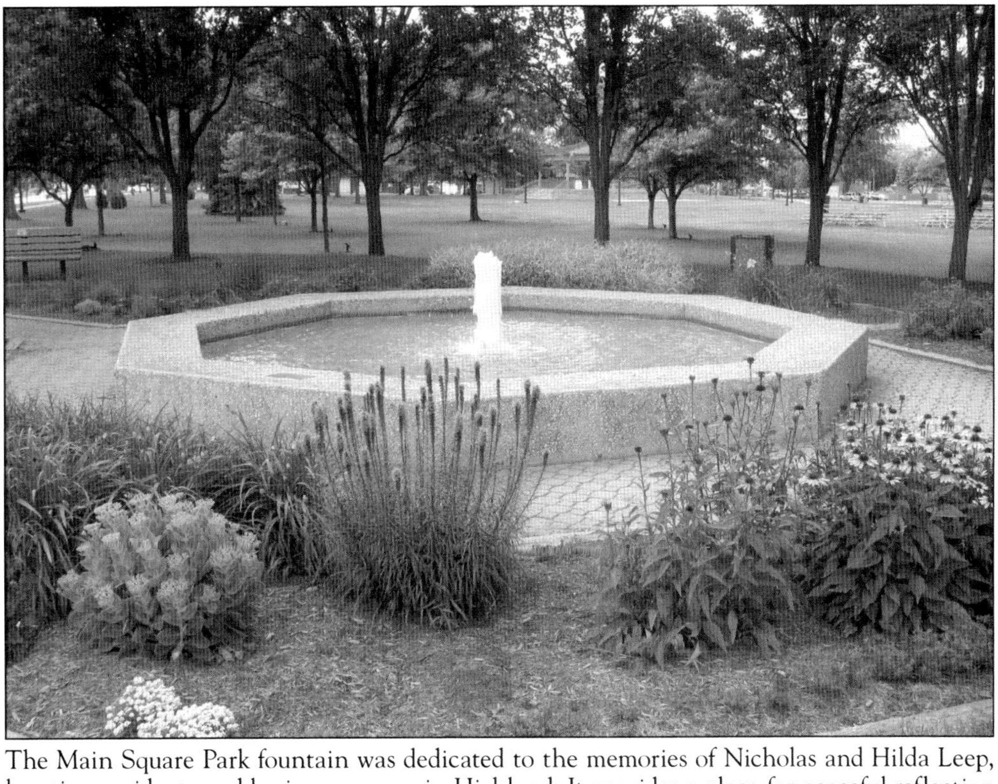

The Main Square Park fountain was dedicated to the memories of Nicholas and Hilda Leep, longtime residents and business owners in Highland. It provides a place for peaceful reflection and is maintained with the help of Leep family donations. (Photograph by Theresa Pecsek.)

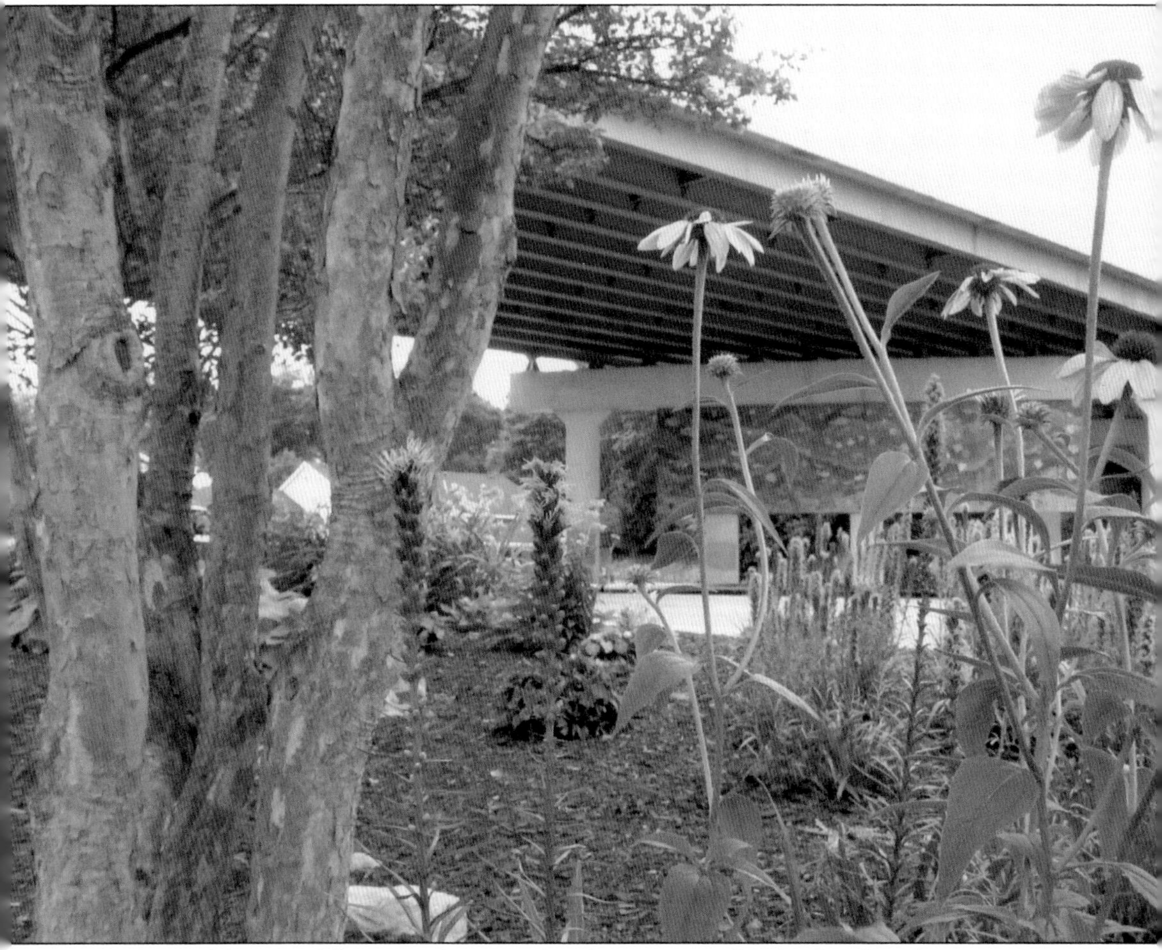

A beautiful array of flowers is shown under the overpass of Ridge Road at the intersection of Kennedy and Jewett Avenues. Underneath the overpass is a town mural called *Water under the Bridge*. This photograph was taken in 2015. At the time of the publication of this book, other murals were being painted downtown. (Photograph by Theresa Pecsek.)

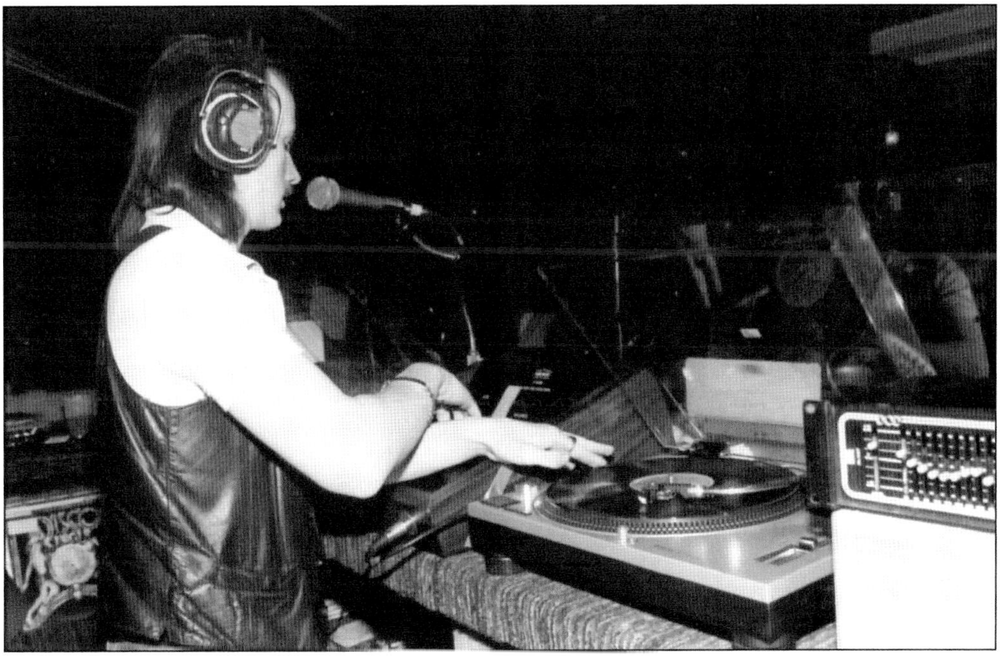

Deejay Tom Lounges is shown working at Club Dimensions during the 1980s. Club Dimensions is now long gone, but it occupied the site of the Ken-Ridge bowling lanes. Lounges still can be heard on Lake Shore public radio. This is now the site of a Vyto's Pharmacy.

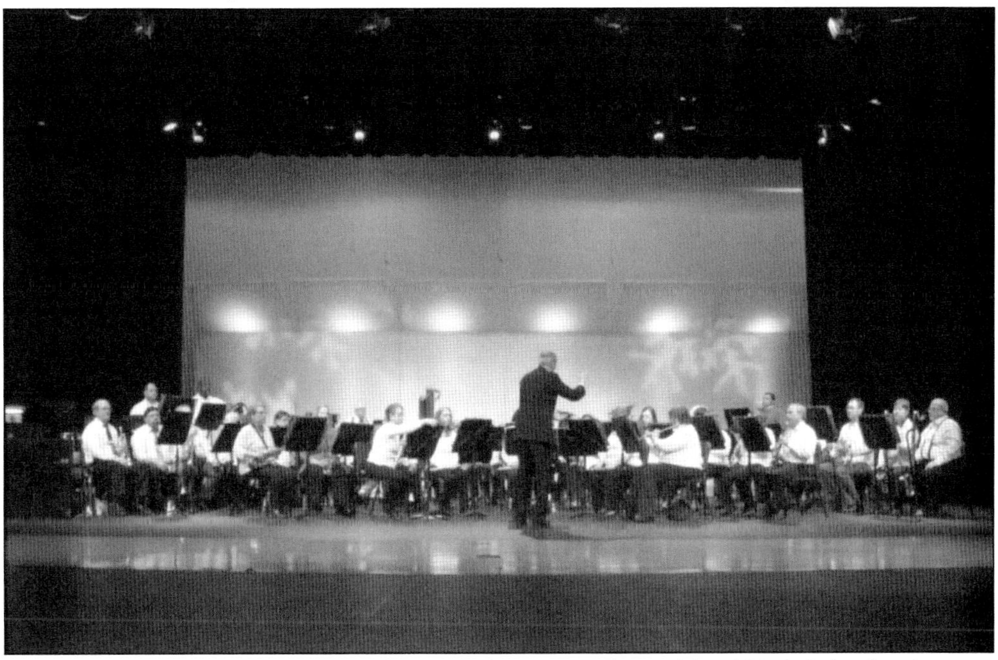

The Highland Community Band is shown performing at the Highland High School auditorium for a Christmas concert on December 18, 2014. The band is made up of volunteer musicians under the direction of conductor Greg Jasek. During warm-weather months, the band performs at the Main Square Park gazebo. At least one concert per year is dedicated to veterans. This band has been in existence since the late 1980s. (Photograph by Theresa Pecsek.)

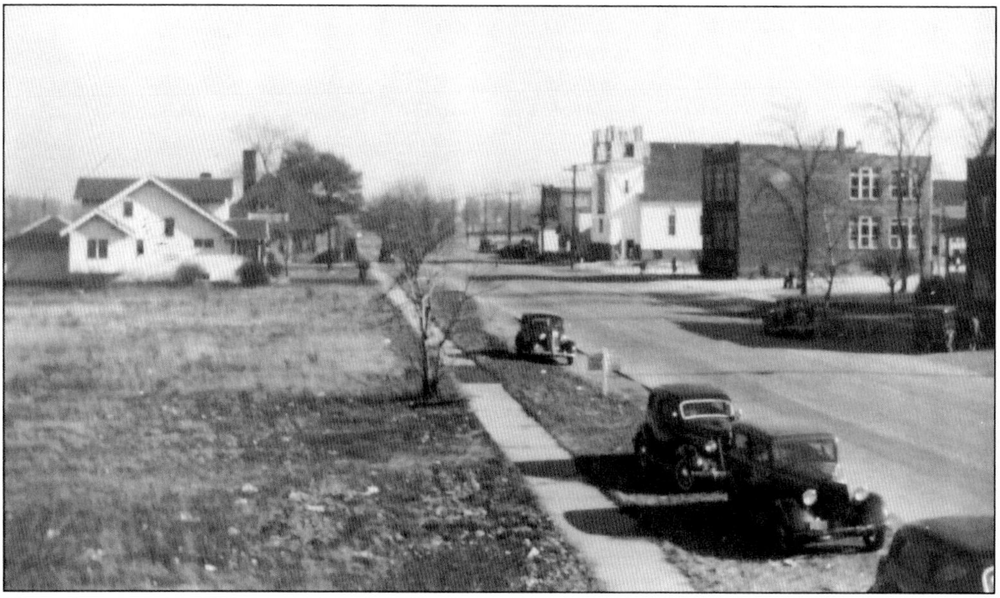

This photograph of Highway Avenue shows some wide-open spaces and cars that may remind readers of earlier times. Highland Christian School is on the right, and the First Christian Reformed Church is behind the school.

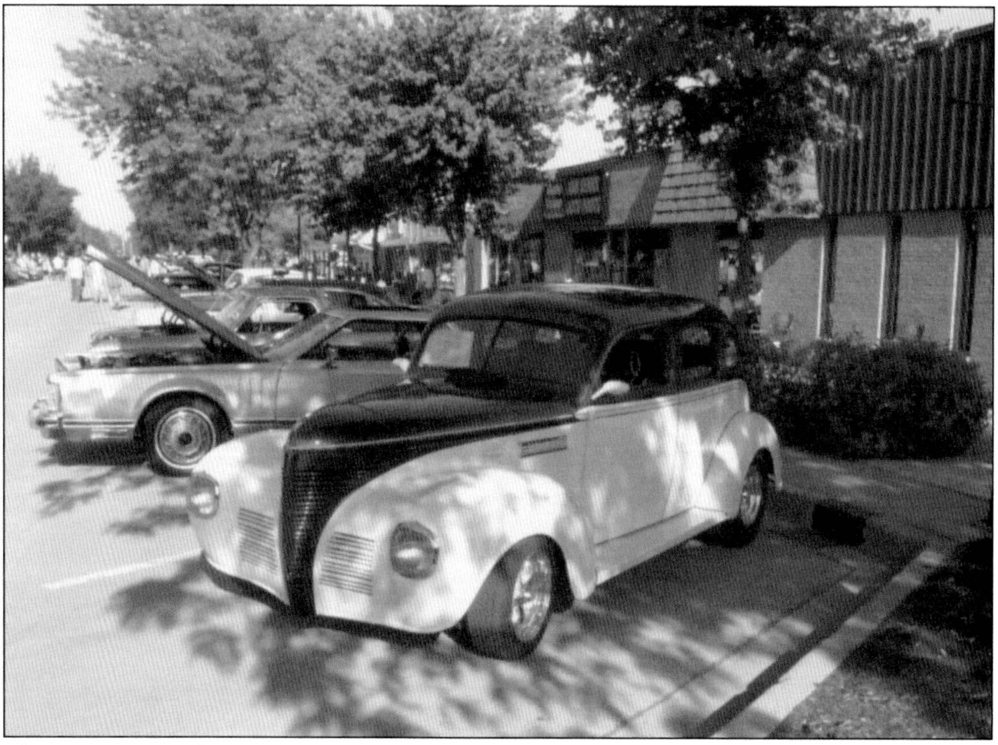

This picture was taken during the Highland Street Car Cruise in the summer of 2014. Anyone who has a unique vehicle can show off their automobile. The purpose is to bring people into the business section of town. The downtown area is busy, and these older vehicles look to be in great shape—even better than the ones in the previous photograph. (Photograph by Theresa Pecsek.)

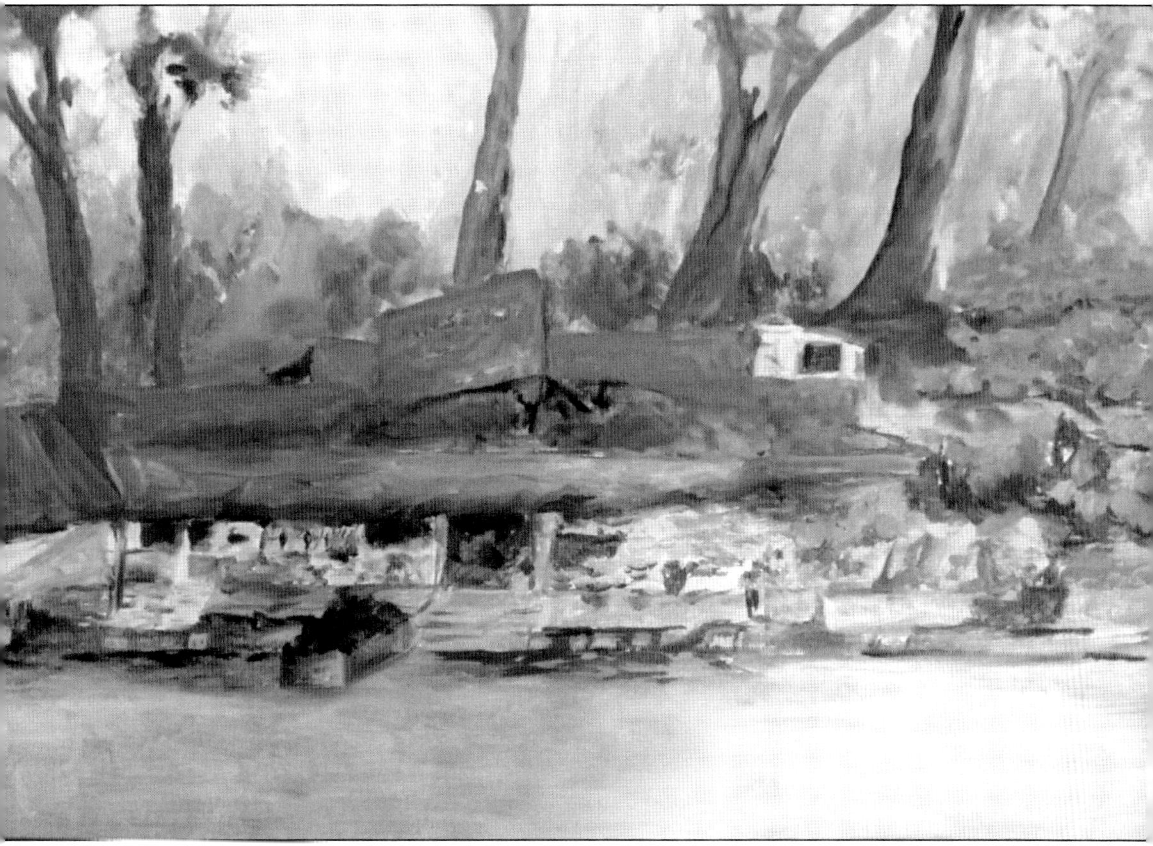

This is local artist Mary Szendrey's rendition of Jansen's Fruit Market on Ridge Road in Highland. Szendrey lost sight in one eye later in life, but she continued to paint until she died in 2004. She also created a rendition of Mary Ann's Produce; she donated both pictures to the Highland Historical Society.

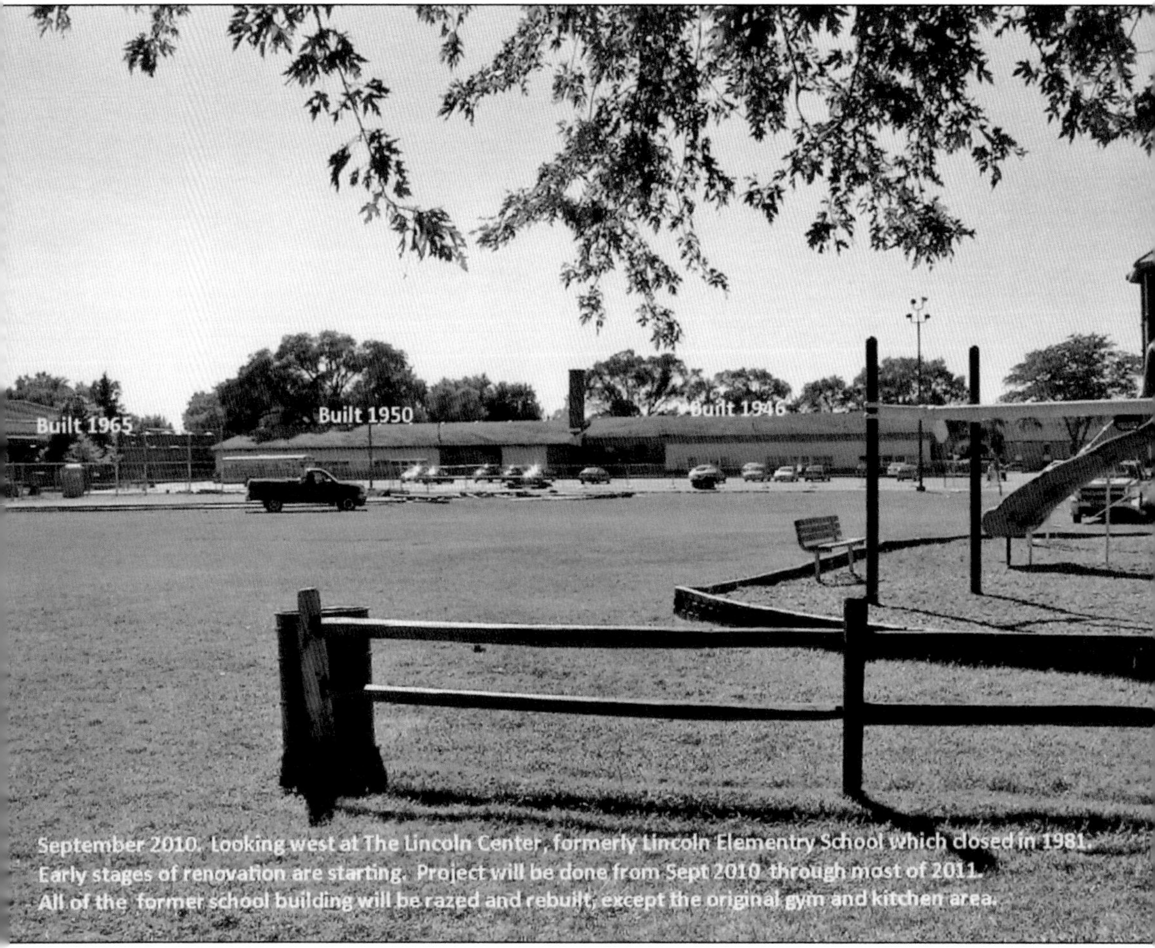

This is the old site of the Lincoln Community Center. A small historical summary of the site is near the bottom of the photograph. Lincoln Elementary School opened in 1946 and was replaced by the Lincoln Community Center. The school closed in 1981.

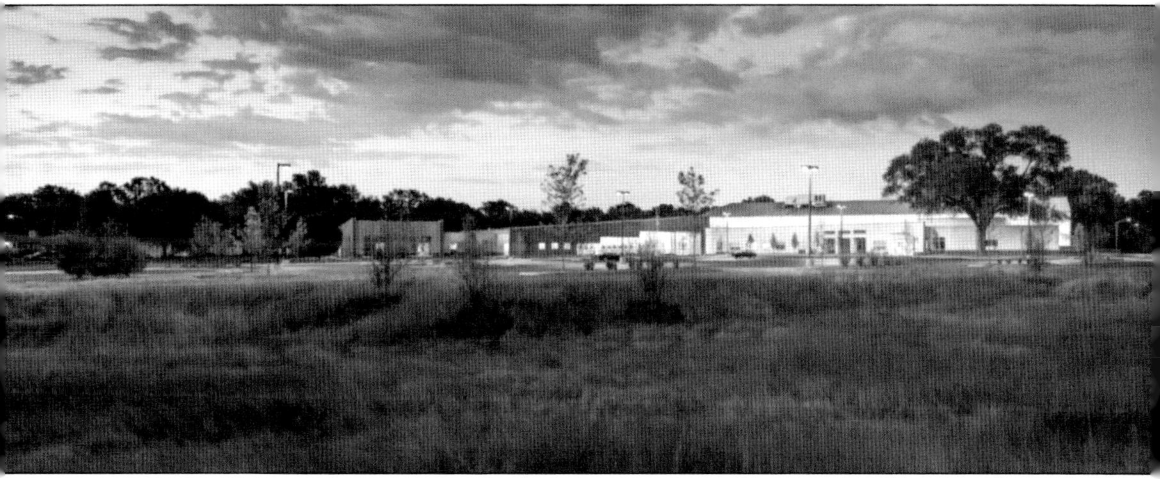

The Lincoln Community Center is shown as it appears today. The center is multipurpose and houses a fitness center, a daycare facility, a room for the Highland Historical Society, and various spaces for meetings, classes, and other activities. The center was dedicated on February 12, 2012. (Highland Parks and Recreation Department.)

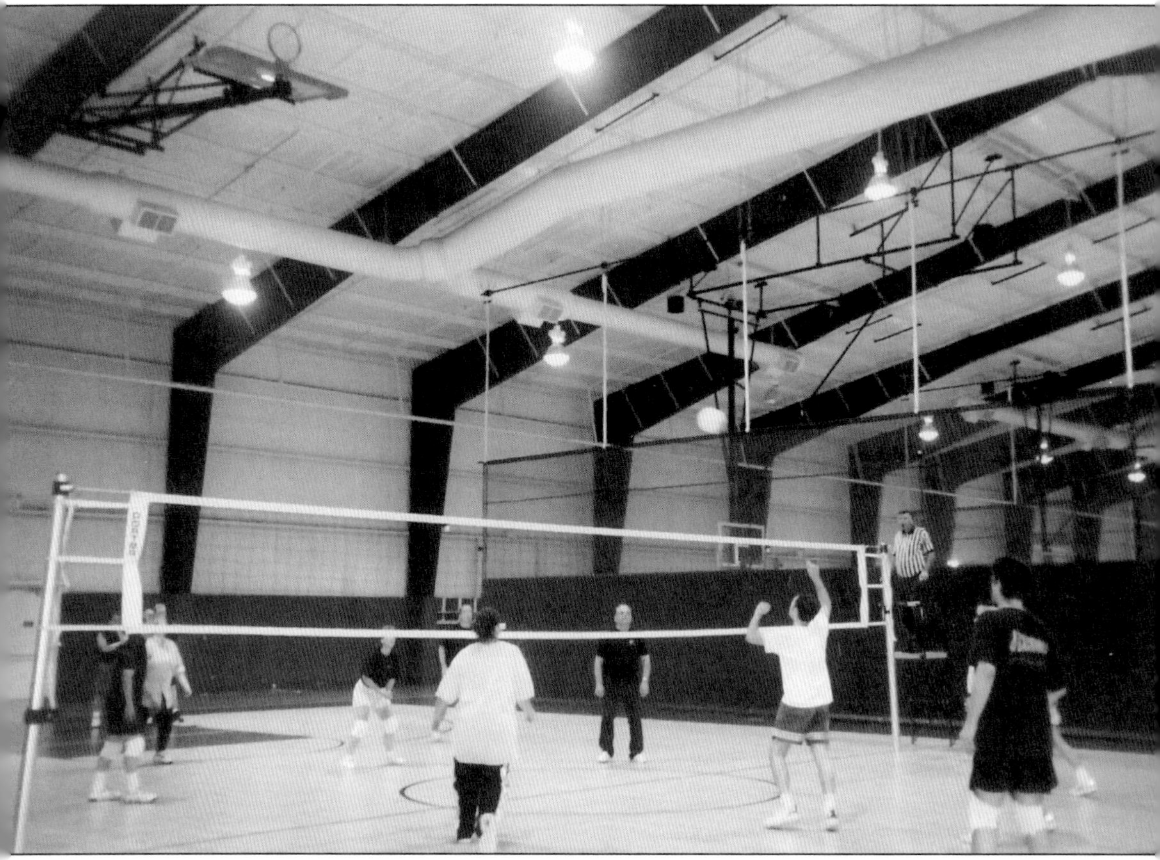

This is the inside of the Lincoln Community Center that opened in 2011. This facility replaced an older building that once housed Lincoln Elementary School. The gym has a track that surrounds the floor that many use for walking. The space is also utilized for large events other than those involving sports and exercising. The original school gym was converted into a banquet facility.

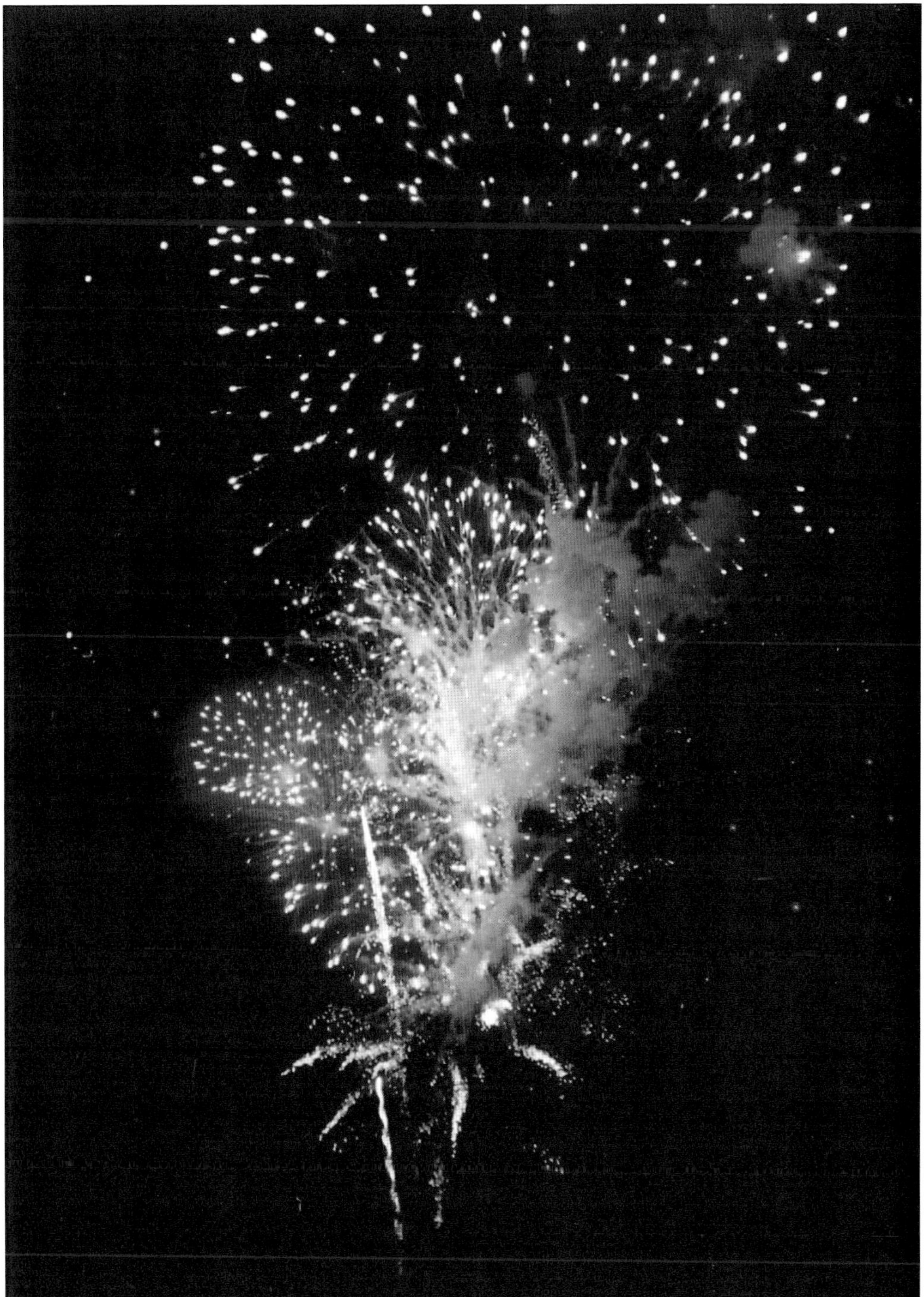

Every year, the Highland Parks Department hires an outside firm to shoot off fireworks to light up the sky during two shows—one on the Fourth of July and the other at midnight on New Year's Day. The fireworks for the New Year's show are at Main Square Park, and the Fourth of July show is at Homestead Park.